BLACKBURN
BUCCANEER

BLACKBURN
BUCCANEER

Kev Darling

The Crowood Press

First published in 2006 by
The Crowood Press Ltd
Ramsbury, Marlborough
Wiltshire SN8 2HR

www.crowood.com

British Library Cataloguing-in-Publication Data
A catalogue record for this book is available from the British Library.

ISBN 1 86126 871 8
EAN 978 1 86126 871 6

Designed and typeset by Focus Publishing, Sevenoaks, Kent

Printed and bound in Great Britain by CPI Bath

Contents

List of Abbreviations

A&AEE	Aircraft and Armament Experimental Establishment	LGB	Laser-Guided Bomb
AB	Air Base	MC	Medium Case
AC	Alternating Current	MDC	Miniature Detonating Cord
ADC	Air Data Computer	MLS	Minimum Launch Speed
ADS	Air Data System	MoA	Ministry of Aviation
AFB	Air Force Base	MoD	Ministry of Defence
AHU	Aircraft Handling Unit	MRCA	Must Refurbish Canberra Again
ASR	Air Staff Requirement	MRG	Maximum Rate Gyro
BAC	British Aircraft Corporation	MU	Maintenance Unit
BAe	British Aerospace	NACA	National Advisory Committee on Aeronautics
BDRT	Battle Damage Repair Training	NAS	Naval Air Station
BLC	Boundary Layer Control	NASU	Naval Aircraft Support Unit
C(A)	Controller (Air)	NBC	Nuclear, Biological and Chemical
CASCU	Combined Acceleration and Speed Control Unit	NDT	Non-Destructive Testing
CBLS	Carrier Bomb Light Stores	OCU	Operational Conversion Unit
CFB	Canadian Forces Base	P&EE	Proof and Experimental Establishment
CSDU	Constant-Speed Drive Unit	PFCU	Powered Flying Control Unit
CWP	Centralised Warning Panel	POL	Petrol, Oil and Lubricants
DARA	Defence Aviation Repair Agency	PRU	Photographic Reconnaissance Unit
DC	Direct Current	QRA	Quick Reaction Alert
DC(TRU)	DC Transformer Rectifier Unit	RAAF	Royal Australian Air Force
ECM	Electronic Countermeasures	RAE	Royal Aircraft Establishment
FAA	Fleet Air Arm	RAFG	Royal Air Force Germany
GP	General Purpose	RFA	Royal Fleet Auxiliary
HAS	Hardened Aircraft Shelter	RNAY	Royal Naval Air Yard
HE	High Explosive	RWR	Radar Warning Receiver
HF	High Frequency	SAAF	South African Air Force
HP	High-Pressure	SAR	Search And Rescue
HSA	Hawker Siddeley Aircraft	SSB	Single Side Bond
IAF	Iraqi Air Force	SWAPO	South West Africa People's Organization
IAS	Indicated Air Speed	TACAN	Tactical Air Navigation System
IFIS	Integrated Flight Instrument System	TAC HQ	Tactical Headquarters
IGV	Inlet Guide Vane	TFW	Tactical Fighter Wing
INS	Inertial Navigation System	UHF	Ultra-High Frequency
JPT	Jet Pipe Temperature	USAF	United States Air Force
LABS	Low-Altitude Bombing System	USN	United States Navy
LOX	Liquid Oxygen	USMC	United States Marine Corps

Introduction and Acknowledgements

When the contract to develop and manufacture the Buccaneer naval strike aircraft was given to Blackburn, most observers were quite surprised as the company had been at its peak during the inter-war period, since when De Havilland, Fairey and Hawker had come to dominate the market for carrier-borne aircraft. Post-war, Blackburn had tried to provide the Fleet Air Arm with a strike fighter in the same class as the Douglas Skyraider, the Blackburn Firebrand. Unlike its American counterpart, however, the Firebrand was something of a failure and quickly disappeared from the scene.

When Blackburn began to design the Buccaneer, their greatest problem was sourcing a jet engine that could both provide sufficient power *and* fit into the airframe. The DH Gyron Junior engine was chosen but, while it was capable of powering the Buccaneer, the margins were tight and the engine showed a tendency to fail at awkward moments. This meant that the first production run was limited. It was the appearance of the Rolls-Royce Spey engine that really saved the design, as this slightly larger engine gave more thrust and was far more reliable. Both versions served with the Fleet Air Arm although the Gyron-powered Buccaneer S.1 was quickly relegated to the training role when the Spey-powered S.2 became available.

Although it was obvious that Blackburn, and later Hawker Siddeley, had a winner on their hands, overseas sales were hampered by the complete lack of knowledge and professionalism exhibited by British officials. The end result was that only one overseas contract was completed, with South Africa; even this was surrounded by controversy as it coincided with increasing distaste for South Africa policy of apartheid that nearly scuppered the deal. However, part of the contract was the Simonstown Agreement that allowed the Royal Navy into South African harbours, so the deal went through. In South African service the Buccaneers were flown hard during the 'border wars', the aircraft being eventually grounded when keeping them airworthy became economically unviable.

Politics also affected the Buccaneer, at least indirectly. During the early 1960s the BAC TSR2 was developed as the replacement aircraft for the Canberra. However, this excellent aircraft was cancelled and its intended replacement, the General Dynamics F-111 swing-wing attack aircraft, soon fell to the Treasury axe as well. The Canberra replacement was then split between the McDonnell F-4 Phantom and the Buccaneer, which dismayed the Royal Air Force somewhat. The Phantoms delivered to the RAF powered by Spey engines similar to those in the Buccaneer – proved to be the slowest and most fuel-hungry versions of that aircraft ever constructed. The Buccaneer was not initially accepted by the RAF, although this changed as time wore on and RAF crews pushed their new mounts to their ultimate limits.

All this excitement came to a shuddering halt when the inner wing structure failed on a Buccaneer manoeuvring at low level across the Nevada desert in early 1980. The entire fleet was grounded while in-depth investigations were carried out. Initially it was expected that older aircraft acquired second-hand from the Fleet Air Arm would be the ones to have suffered the most, though it turned out that some of the newer machines were also badly affected. The aircraft committed to NATO were the priority, so four aircraft for the strike QRA were quickly cleared. For the remainder it was decided, where possible, to combine two aircraft to create one machine for further service. The main engineering work consisted of removing the inner wing sections from one aircraft and grafting them onto another with a greater remaining fatigue life. Not all the Buccaneers needed a replacement inner wing transplant, some just needing the cracks blending out. Many happy hours were spent at St Athan grinding out each crack through access holes in the external skins, using dental drills, burrs and a grinding paste.

Eventually the remaining Buccaneers returned to service, although by this time the Panavia Tornado was beginning to replace that part of the RAF designed in the 1950s. The result was the disappearance of the RAFG-based Buccaneer squadrons, but the RAF was reluctant to dispense with the remaining Buccaneers, so the remaining aircraft were concentrated at Lossiemouth where their role changed from nuclear strike to anti-shipping operations. The Martel missile was replaced by the much improved Sea Eagle which was based on its predecessor. Allied to the weapons upgrade was an improvement in the Buccaneer's avionics under the ASR 1012 programme. Ironically, when the Buccaneer finally saw combat with the RAF during the Gulf War, it was back in the bomber role.

Having been let go by the RAF, the final few Buccaneers remained in use with trials organizations, although they too finally retired in 1994. Fortunately for enthusiasts, a couple of Buccaneers found their way to South Africa where they continue to fly as part of the Thunder City fleet – long may they continue to do so! Just as this manuscript was being completed it was announced that XX885/G-HHAA, operated by Hawker Hunter Aviation, has been given provisional approval to fly.

As with any such undertaking, a book of this kind requires the help of others, therefore I would like to thank Trevor Smith, Martyn Chorlton, the staff at BAES Heritage and the Blackburn Archive, plus all of those at Crowood who have turned my efforts into the book you now hold.

Kev Darling
Wales, 2005

CHAPTER ONE

Naval Warfare – the Evolution of the Aircraft at Sea

Jets Join the Fleet Air Arm

At the end of the Second World War in 1945, the Fleet Air Arm had a strength six large 'Fleet' aircraft carriers, HMS *Implacable*, *Indefatigable*, *Indomitable*, *Illustrious*, *Formidable* and *Victorious*, and five 'Light Fleet' carriers, HMS *Glory*, *Ocean*, *Theseus*, *Triumph* and *Warrior*. Front-line aircraft strength stood at 1,300 machines with a further 1,000 allocated for training and secondary support duties. Manning the Fleet Air Arm were 70,000 officers and ratings. The main Fleet carriers saw little use after the war, being laid up in reserve before scrapping while the more modern Light Fleet carriers carried the flag for the Fleet Air Arm; these, too, were placed in reserve after service in the Korean War and the Suez operation. The withdrawal of the majority of the wartime carriers left the Royal Navy with HMS *Victorious* and six ships completed during the 1950s: two more Fleet carriers, HMS *Eagle* and *Ark Royal*, supplemented by the smaller HMS *Albion*, *Bulwark*, *Centaur* and *Hermes*.

Two very important changes were applied to aircraft carriers in the post-war era. The first was the angled flight deck, invented by Captain D. R. F. Cambell DSC RN. This was first applied to HMS *Centaur*, and allowed aircraft to abort a landing and 'go around' even if aircraft were parked at the front of the carrier deck. The second innovation was the mirror landing aid, developed by Commander H.C.N. Goodhart RN, which helped the pilot maintain the correct approach angle: this more efficient form of control was necessary as the approach speed of naval aircraft

had increased from the 60mph (100km/h) of the biplane Fairey Flycatcher to the 140mph (230km/h) of the Sea Venom.

The appearance of jet aircraft in the FAA inventory also changed the method of approach used by naval pilots. Previously, aircraft had used a steep curving approach to keep the carrier in view throughout; however, jet aircraft – visibility from which was not so obstructed by a forward-mounted engine – were far happier undertaking a flatter approach. This method of landing allowed for a constant speed approach and removed the need for flare out and cutting of the engine until the landing was safely completed. A further aid developed to help the pilot was the audio airspeed indicator, which was heard in the pilot's earphones. This allowed the pilot to concentrate upon the mirror landing aid without being distracted by the need to scan the instrument panel.

The first jet aircraft to enter service with the Fleet Air Arm was the Supermarine Attacker, which joined 800 Squadron in August 1951. Four years later all the FAA's front-line units were equipped with jet aircraft, apart from those involved in such duties as airborne early warning. By this time the role of the aircraft carrier had changed. Gone were the days of heavyweight air strikes; the FAA now found itself supporting troops engaged in localized wars, although the advent of air-dropped nuclear weapons added another capability to the fleet. The first aircraft capable of carrying such a weapon was the Supermarine Scimitar, which entered service with its experimental unit at Ford in August 1957. Following on from the Scimitar came the subject of this book, the Blackburn Buccaneer, which entered service in 1962.

That same year, authorization was given for the construction of a new 'super carrier', CVA-01, which was similar in size and concept to those under development for the United States Navy. This bright vision for the aircraft carrier's future came to a shuddering halt in February 1966 when the Labour government cancelled CVA-01 on cost grounds. Henceforth, the RAF was to shoulder the burden of air defence, strike, reconnaissance and airborne early warning. The Government also proposed that the anti-submarine protection of naval and merchant vessels could be carried out using helicopters and missile systems. These ideas were followed up by the 1968 Defence White Paper, which stated that the entire carrier force was to be withdrawn once Britain had completed its withdrawals from Malaysia, Singapore and the Persian Gulf. This turned the policy of handing over various defence requirements to the RAF completely on its head, by removing many of its overseas bases.

Fortunately from the Royal Navy's point of view, the election of the Conservatives to power in 1970 meant that a modified version of the Labour plan could be implemented. Although CVA-01 was not resurrected, the Supplementary Statement on Defence that October did grant a reprieve. This involved retaining the newly refitted *Ark Royal* with its Phantoms and Buccaneers throughout much of the 1970s, while *Eagle* – which had not been modified to operate Phantoms and so was still using the older Sea Vixen fighter – was retired from service in 1972. The era of the big, fixed-wing aircraft carrier finally ended in December 1978 when *Ark Royal* was retired.

Blackburn

While Fairey and Hawker are the best-known British builders of naval aircraft there are others, one of which was the Blackburn Aeroplane and Motor

Unlike other manufacturers, Robert Blackburn started his manufacturing career building monoplanes, this being the Mercury. Though elevators and rudder sections were fitted, roll control was still achieved using wing warping, which made turning difficult. The Blackburn Archive

The Blackburn Kangaroo was originally built as a long-range bomber for service during the First World War, but as they appeared on the scene late, only twenty were constructed. After the war's end the surviving aircraft were used for freight and joy-riding flights. The Blackburn Archive

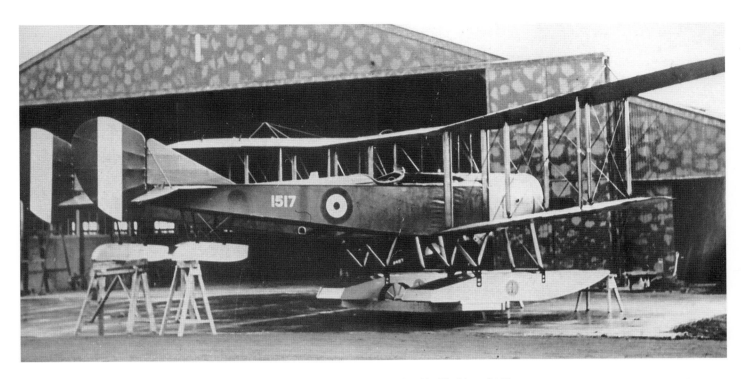

Blackburn also built floatplanes for the RNAS; this was the Blackburn TB.2 torpedo bomber. The Blackburn Archive

Company. Blackburn was based at Brough in East Yorkshire, though it also had an office at Amberley House, Norfolk Street, The Strand, London. The company was formed by civil engineer Robert Blackburn in 1914, building its first factory at Brough in 1916. A name change to Blackburn Aircraft Co Ltd took place in 1939. The company absorbed General Aircraft in 1949, the whole being absorbed itself into Hawker Siddeley in 1960.

Blackburn prepared the first designs in 1909, these being the single-seat monoplane No.1 and the two-seat Mercury. Initially Blackburn Aircraft survived by subcontracting and building BE2Cs and Sopwith Baby fighters. To provide the facilities needed for this work, new factories were built at Olympia near Leeds and at Sherburn-in-Elmet. One of the first Blackburn aircraft produced for the flying services was the RT1 Kangaroo, which was originally built as a long-range bomber. Twenty were built, and they spent their short period of war service flying anti-submarine patrols over the North Sea.

In the immediate post-war period Blackburn, like other aircraft companies, was hit by a sudden shortage of work. However, perseverance and persistence paid off, and the company survived by undertaking any available work. The first

aircraft built after the war was the T1 Swift, from which the T2 Dart was developed. Designed from the outset as a torpedo aircraft, the Dart first flew in 1921 and entered service in 1923. A total of 117 was built, and the Dart stayed in service until 1933.

Following on from the fairly elegant Dart came the Blackburn Blackburn, which was one of the ugliest aircraft ever built. This particular machine was used for fleet spotter duties and entered service in 1929, the final examples retiring in 1933.

When Blackburn produced the T5

One of the ugliest aircraft ever built was the Blackburn Blackburn, which was used by the Fleet Air Arm as a spotter aircraft. The need to include a charting and spotting table within the fuselage resulted in this ungainly-looking machine. The Blackburn Archive

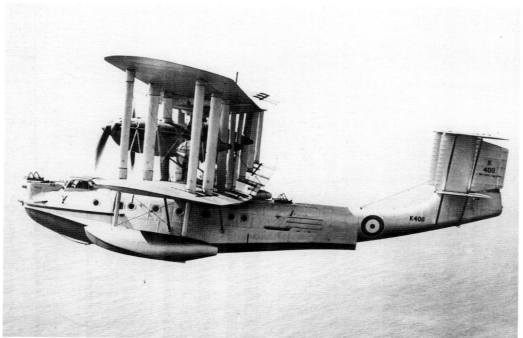

ABOVE: **Blackburn's most successful inter-war aircraft was the Ripon/Baffin series of biplanes for the FAA. Most of the Baffins – including those in this photo – were converted Ripons.** The Blackburn Archive

LEFT: **The inter-war period was the era of the biplane flying boat. These were all magnificent and stately machines, as illustrated by this Blackburn Perth.** The Blackburn Archive

RIGHT: **Blackburn's first monoplane for the FAA was the Skua dive bomber. Unfortunately, by the time the war started in 1939 the design was already obsolescent.** The Blackburn Archive

BELOW: **The Blackburn Roc turret fighter was a final attempt to extend the life of the Skua design. It was even less successful as its land-based equivalent, the Boulton Paul Defiant, and was relegated to secondary duties not long after the war started.** The Blackburn Archive

Robert Blackburn and the Blackburn Aircraft Company

Robert Blackburn was born on 26 March 1885, the son of George Blackburn who was the works manager of a Leeds engineering company. Robert showed early promise as a schoolboy, and went on to graduate from Leeds University with an honours degree in engineering. Further studies in France brought the 22-year-old into contact with that country's fledgling aviation industry, and his weekends were spent at Le Mans, watching Wilbur Wright fly his pioneering biplane. This early exposure to the delights of aviation stimulated Blackburn's imagination to such an extent that while still in France he completed designs for his first monoplane. Determined to show that his aeronautical ambition was genuine, he returned to Leeds and persuaded his less than enthusiastic father to back his plans for building aircraft.

Blackburn's first monoplane proved to be a failure when he tried to fly it from a beach in north-east England during 1909–10. Using a wicker chair purloined from his father's garden as the pilot's seat, he made several attempts to fly the under-powered plane from the sands between Marske and Saltburn. Although the aircraft made a few ungainly hops from the beach, even Robert Blackburn later referred to these attempts as no more than sand-scratching. His experiments came to an abrupt end in May 1910 when, attempting a turn, he crashed the aircraft.

Blackburn's determination to succeed in the emergent field of aeronautics was soon shown by designs for a much better machine, which was constructed during 1910–11. In order to fly the new monoplane, he transported it to the Yorkshire coast where the long, firm sands of Filey Bay were ideal for taking off and landing. Blackburn was able to rent a hanger at Filey aerodrome – which had opened in July 1910 – and an adjoining bungalow for a weekly rent of 10 shillings per building. From the hanger at the top of the cliffs, departing aircraft were winched down a concrete slipway to the beach below to be tested.

Although he had attempted to pilot the first monoplane himself, Blackburn now left the flying to others and concentrated his energies on the construction side of the business in Leeds. A pilot called Benfield Hucks took to the air in Blackburn's second monoplane at Filey on 8 March 1911 and promptly crashed it from a height of thirty feet while trying to undertake a turn. However, the machine was repaired and became one of the instructional aircraft that Blackburn used to start a flying school at Filey. This venture prospered for a short period under instructors like Hucks, who despite his initial crash became a skilled pilot, able to stay in the air for three hours at a time – quite an achievement in those pioneering days. Filey sands were also used to test Blackburn's next design, a two-seater monoplane named the Mercury. This was exhibited at the Olympia Aero Show in London in 1911, and several versions of the Mercury were built over the next two years.

However, the dangers involved in handling these early aircraft were well illustrated when the second of Blackburn's instructing test pilots, Hubert Oxley, took off from Filey beach in the fourth Mercury monoplane on 6 December 1911. A student pilot called Robert Weiss, the son of a well-to-do wool trading family from Dewsbury, was also aboard under instruction. Whether by accident or by pilot error, the machine went

into a steep dive and crashed onto the beach. Oxley was thrown from the plane and died of a broken neck while Weiss died less than an hour later from his injuries.

The flying school at Filey was short-lived, moving to Hendon in September 1912, but Blackburn's business in Leeds prospered with orders from the Royal Flying Corps and the Royal Naval Air Service. The outbreak of the First World War in August 1914 and the consequent government orders for over 100 biplanes meant that the Blackburn Aeroplane and Motor Company Co. Ltd was able to expand rapidly. The company took possession of a disused roller-skating rink in Roundhay Road, Leeds, and this became the centre of the Blackburn aircraft building operation. A machine shop was built at the new factory to turn out the small, standard parts needed by aircraft manufacturers such as nuts, bolts and other standard fittings. This was highly successful and helped keep the company in business in the lean years following the end of the war in 1918.

By 1914 Robert Blackburn had developed an interest in aeroplanes that could take off and land on water, and the Type L seaplane was the first such aircraft to be built at his new factory. One of his staff, Mark Swann, was dispatched in 1916 to find a suitable location for a seaplane testing facility. Swann examined several sites but recommended the village of Brough, on the north bank of the Humber, as the best one available, especially as it was adjacent to the Hull–Leeds railway line and as there was land available to build an aerodrome with access to the Humber for launching marine aircraft. Brough lay at a bend in the river, giving it the advantage that float-planes and flying boats could take off in any wind direction or state of the tide. However, experience showed the base not to be as ideal as had been hoped: the Humber tides restricted the times of day when seaplane could be tested, while the Humber river's own brand of sea mist, known as a fret, could make landings at the Brough aerodrome close to impossible.

Though Brough had been intended to be a seaplane testing base, between 1928 and 1932 much of the work of the Blackburn Aeroplane Company was transferred there from Leeds. This was to cause acute problems for the 1,000 Leeds employees, who were forced to commute daily by train until they could relocate to homes that were closer. Members of the Blackburn family themselves moved to Brough to be closer to the new centre of operations. The focus on Brough led to its expansion, especially during the rearmament years of the late 1930s. By now Blackburn's were well established as specialists in naval aircraft, designing, constructing and producing aircraft like the Swift, the Shark and the Skua that kept the Blackburn works fully employed until the outbreak of the Second World War in September 1939. A Blackburn Skua was the first British aircraft to shoot down an enemy aircraft in World War Two, a Skua from HMS *Ark Royal* shooting down a Dornier flying boat off Heligoland on 25 September 1939.

During the war years the Brough factory and other Blackburn plants at Dumbarton, Leeds and Sherburn-in-Elmet turned out a range of aircraft types, including the Swordfish (under sub-contract) and the Firebrand for the Fleet Air Arm, as well as repairing damaged American aircraft. The end of the war saw a decline in the company's contracts, so Brough was forced to undertake non-aviation work to continue in business. In 1949 Blackburn merged with the General Aircraft Company, based in Middlesex, this bringing with it an upturn in business. That same year the new Universal Freighter Aircraft, better known as the Beverley, took to the skies. For twelve years the Beverley heavy freighter was the Royal Air Force's primary load mover in support of operations all over the world.

Robert Blackburn's remarkable contribution to the history of aviation was marked in 1950 when, at the age of sixty-five, he was made Honorary Fellow of the Royal Aeronautical Society. However, after controlling the fortunes of the company for over forty years, health problems forced him to take a less active role. He retired to Devon, but continued as chairman of the company. In this role he was well aware of an exciting new naval aircraft project that the company had embarked on: the Buccaneer jet-powered, low-level strike aircraft for the Royal Navy. The project was top secret, but Robert Blackburn made guarded references to it at the Company's Annual General Meeting in August 1955, shortly before his death.

In his lifetime Robert Blackburn had seen his aircraft business grow from a tiny undertaking involving himself and two mechanics to a group of companies with over 5,000 employees. A career which had begun with designs inspired by the Wright Brothers and French aviation pioneers ended with jet aircraft like the Buccaneer, at the cutting edge of both aeronautical and technological innovation.

When General Aircraft was absorbed by Blackburn they brought with them the Universal Freighter, better known as the Beverley C.1. When seen flying at night the aircraft was likened to an ocean liner in the sky. BBA Collection

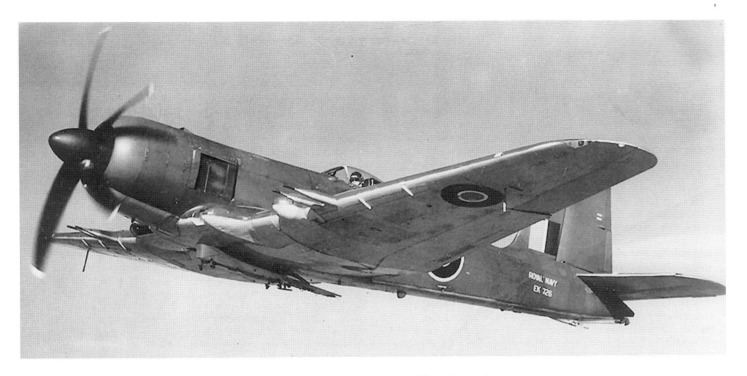

Approximately the size of a Douglas A-1 Skyraider the Firebrand was nowhere near as capable as its American counterpart. Its replacement in the ranks of the FAA was the Westland Wyvern. The Blackburn Archive

Ripon it returned to a more elegant design for its torpedo aircraft. A total of ninety-six of these torpedo bombers was built for the Fleet Air Arm. Its increased radius of action meant that an extra position was needed for an observer who was carried for navigation duties. The Ripon was finally retired in 1934.

The machine that followed the Ripon was the Baffin, which differed from its predecessor in having an air-cooled radial engine instead of a liquid-cooled in-line engine. The Baffin entered FAA service in 1934, although only twenty-nine true Baffins were constructed – the rest were converted Ripons. The Ripon, both original and converted was withdrawn from service in 1936.

The next aircraft built by Blackburn was the Shark, a contemporary of the Fairey Swordfish. Developed from the private-venture B6, the Shark entered service in 1935. Its service life was relatively short, as it was replaced by the Swordfish in 1938.

The Shark was the last biplane built by Blackburn for the Fleet Air Arm, as development had now switched over to monoplanes. The Blackburn Skua was the first operational monoplane purchased by the FAA and the first British aircraft designed from the outset as a dive bomber. A total of 190 Skuas was ordered, the first entering service with 800 Squadron in 1938. The Skua remained in front-line use until 1941, being relegated to second-line duties after this date.

Following the Skua into FAA service was the Roc, which was the first aircraft in naval service to be fitted with a gun turret. While based on the Skua, the Roc was intended to be the naval equivalent of the Boulton Paul Defiant turret fighter then in Royal Air Force service. A total of 136 Rocs was ordered, the first entering service with 806 Squadron in February 1940. As the concept of the turret fighter was unsound, the Roc's front-line service was measured in months.

Blackburn continued designing new aircraft, coming up with the Firebrand in 1942. A short production run of ten Firebrand I airframes was delivered for flight trials, followed by twelve of the slightly improved Firebrand II. For the Firebrand III there was a change of engine to the Bristol Centaurus, which was to be used in production Firebrands. The first production version was the Firebrand IV, which entered FAA service in 1945 as a torpedo-carrying fighter. No. 813 Squadron received the Firebrand in September 1945, and took part in the June 1946 Victory Flypast over London. The final version of the Firebrand was the Mark V, which entered service in 1947. The changes between the Marks IV and V were mainly centred around the flight controls, those fitted to the final sub-variant, the Mark VA, having powered ailerons. The Firebrand was replaced in FAA service by the turboprop-powered Westland Wyvern in 1953.

CHAPTER TWO

Building the Fleet Air Arm's Big Iron

Convinced, as were many other navies in the early post-war years, that the aircraft carrier and its strike wing were the replacement for the battleship, the Royal Navy embraced the concept with as much gusto as post-war circumstances would allow. Aircraft proved to be a problem at first, as the Fleet Air Arm was forced to either buy, sell or scrap the American aircraft that had been supplied under Lend Lease. Although the American aircraft were offered at a vastly reduced price, the cost of extended spares support meant they were not really much of a bargain. Therefore the Fleet Air Arm turned to British aircraft manufacturers to meet its airpower requirements.

Having worked their way through a variety of straight-winged jet fighters and attack aircraft during the early to mid-1950s, the Fleet Air Arm finally moved into the swept-wing era with the Supermarine Scimitar, which entered service in 1957. Although the Scimitar was capable of supersonic flight in a shallow dive and could carry a reasonable weapon load, it was hampered by a lack of

range and a tendency to leak fuel, which made it quite a dangerous aircraft to fly on occasion.

The Growing Threat

Compounding the Scimitar's shortcomings was a vast improvement in the Warsaw Pact forces, especially those of the Soviet surface fleet. Having undergone some growing pains during the Second World War, the Soviet Navy had eventually begun to receive a series of capable cruiser-sized vessels from the state shipbuilding yards. The appearance in the 1950s of the highly capable *Sverdlov* class cruisers gave serious cause for concern. Seventeen ships of this class were launched between 1951 and 1960; they were armed with a full range of conventional weaponry including twelve 5.9in guns in triple turrets, twelve dual-purpose 3.9in guns in twin turrets and two quintuple torpedo tubes. Defensive weaponry included guided missiles and 32 37mm anti-aircraft guns. These well-armed ships

had a maximum speed of 34kt and a cruise range of 5,000nm at 20kt. As the Cold War intensified they were followed by ever-more capable missile-armed destroyers and cruisers, which posed an even greater threat to merchant shipping.

Previously the Admiralty would have pushed for similar-sized vessels to counter the threat, but the lack of cash available for defence spending meant that another solution had to be sought. The answer was suggested by Admiral A. S. Bolt of the Naval Air Warfare Division of the Naval Staff. His solution was to use carrier-based strike aircraft – whose armament could include nuclear bombs – to attack Soviet ships. The aircraft had to be able to fly at high speed and low level to avoid detection by the Soviet Navy's radar detection systems, which were increasing in capability year on year. The reason given for the use of a nuclear weapon was that such an attack would not require pinpoint accuracy, thus giving the aircraft's crew a better chance of survival.

To reinforce the Admirals' beliefs, the School of Naval Air Warfare was briefed

From 1945 the Soviet Navy began to receive the *Sverdlov*-class heavy cruiser, which immediately threatened sea-borne trade between Britain and other countries and which was the spur for NA.39 development. NATO

A *Kashin*-class destroyer, typical of the powerful, missile-armed ships that faced the Royal Navy during the 1960s and 1970s. NATO

to train pilots in delivering weapons with the greatest accuracy possible. The philosophy behind this training initially came to fruition during the Korean war, where FAA pilots carried out their attacks with great precision. Supported by his deputy, Captain F. M. A. Torrens-Spence DSO DFC AFC RN, the Admiral drafted a detailed staff specification which the Admiralty issued as Requirement NA.39 in June 1952. The specification called for a two-seat bomber aircraft capable of flying at Mach 0.85 at a height of 200ft (60m). Range was to be at least 400 miles and weaponry, including a nuclear store, had to be carried internally. Folding wings were specified so the aircraft could fit within the confines on the Royal Navy's aircraft carriers. From any point of view this was a very advanced prospect.

It was during the planning phase that the Admiralty accepted the advice from RAE Farnborough that building an aircraft capable of low-level supersonic speeds was beyond the capabilities of the

British aviation industry at that time. Further advice stated that new techniques of manufacture and construction would be needed, as this kind of flying would consume the fatigue life of a more conventional airframe very quickly. This desire of the Royal Navy to undertake its aircraft strikes at low level was in great contrast to the Royal Air Force, whose philosophy was to fly at high altitude to avoid interception.

Specification M.148T

Naval Staff Requirement NA.39 was presented to the British aircraft industry in August 1952 under the aegis of the Ministry of Aviation. On 27 March 1953 the more defined Specification M.148T was delivered to the various British aircraft manufacturers. This called for a two-seat aircraft powered by two jet engines that could fly as low as 200ft at a speed exceeding 550kt with a range exceeding 400

miles or more; at higher altitudes this had to translate to more than 800 miles. The given maximum take-off weight was set at 40,000lb (18,000kg) although this could be increased to 45,000lb (20,000kg) should the occasion demand it. Disposable load was set at 10,000lb (4,500kg) thus the standard maximum weight for landing was 30,000lb (13,500kg) although there was an overload capability built in up to a maximum of 35,000lb (16,000kg). The size of the aircraft was governed by the size of existing aircraft carrier deck elevators: therefore with various components, including the wings, folded, the length should not exceed 51ft (15.5m) with a width of 20ft (6m).

Originally the specification requested that the aircraft be capable of carrying the Fairey Project 7 air-launched, nuclear-tipped anti-shipping missile that rejoiced in the code name *Green Cheese*. Once the design of the carrier aircraft had been fixed it was discovered that the resulting NA.39 could not carry the weapon which was eventually cancelled in 1956. This left the *Red Beard* freefall nuclear bomb as the NA.39's primary weapon, this being supported in other roles by twenty-four air-to-surface rockets, two 2,000lb GP bombs, four 1,000lb GP bombs or four *Red Angel* weapons. Although it was primarily to be a strike aircraft, the NA.39 was also to be capable of acting as a in-flight refuelling tanker and a reconnaissance platform. It was to be ready for service use in 1960.

The Contenders

The companies presented with this requirement were Armstrong Whitworth, Blackburn, Fairey, Short Bros and Westland, who received their invitations to tender in March 1953 with submissions to be presented within six months. Other companies expressed an interest including Percival Aircraft, which requested permission to build a semi-complete concept to illustrate their ideas. Although not amongst the front-runners, Percival was given permission to produce a shadow design that could be used to investigate the possible use of jet efflux in improving the take-off performance of the winning design.

During September 1954 all the original companies submitted their design proposals and accompanying models; they were joined at the last minute by Hawker who,

carrier lift.

Although Armstrong Whitworth fully investigated boundary air blowing (*see* page 22) to improve landing behaviour, it had already been noted that such a system gave little or no benefit during take-off, so the design featured a deflection system that could divert the engine exhaust downwards by at least 45 degrees. Once airborne, the deflectors would be returned to the normal position.

Designated the AW.168, the design appeared to be capable of undertaking the full range of the Admiralty's requirements, and the company constructed a full-sized wooden mock-up which featured folding wings and a detailed nose section. Should the proposal and mock-up meet the specifications, Armstrong Whitworth proposed that two prototypes be constructed. These were to be basically stripped airframes with minimal systems, for aerodynamic trials work only. After these flying test airframes, it was intended to produce a handful of fully equipped airframes to clear the various systems prior to series production beginning.

The design submitted by Fairey Aviation owed much to that organization's FD.2 delta research aircraft. The Fairey aircraft was powered by a pair of Gyron Juniors, these being housed in the fuselage with the intakes in the flared wing leading edges and exhausting to the rear of the fuselage. To give clearance for the engine mountings, the fuselage was a slab-sided affair, which allowed the engines to be carried high on the fuselage. The bomb bay was in the lower section of the fuselage, the bomb doors retracting inwards and a pusher system being used to place weapons into the airflow. To help control the aircraft during take-off and landing, the wings featured high-speed compressed air blowing over the double slotted flaps. This latter point was noted as being insufficiently developed by the Admiralty assessor. Though the flaps were a weak point, the airframe was determined to be immensely strong and able to house sufficient fuel in the fuselage and wing tanks to give a basic range of 1,660 miles, or 2,130 miles with external wing tanks.

Fairey proposed that basic airframes with minimal systems be built to test the aerodynamics, with production commencing some five years later. Unfortunately for Fairey their conservative approach to their proposal's performance and the problem with flap development saw it slip out of the

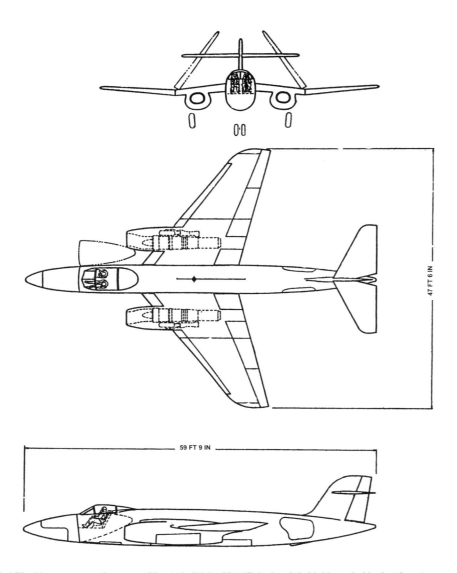

Had Blackburn not won the competition to build the M.148T design, it is highly probable that Armstrong Whitworth's AW.168 would have been chosen. BBA Collection

traditionally specializing in fighter aircraft rather than bombers, had originally shied away from the project. Their inclusion had been as the result of a direct approach by the Admiralty to Sydney Camm, Hawker's Chief Designer. Their proposal resembled a four-engined Douglas A-4 Skyhawk: Hawker's preferred engine supplier, Rolls-Royce, had nothing available at the time powerful enough for fewer than four to suffice. Designated the Hawker P.1108, the design was to carry the *Green Cheese* guided bomb in a recess under the fuselage.

Armstrong Whitworth's proposal was a swept-wing design whose engines, a pair of De Havilland Gyron Juniors, were to be housed in underwing nacelles. Although

mounting the engines closer to the fuselage would have reduced the airframe drag coefficient, the use of podded engines allowed for the carriage of bomb-bay fuel tanks and the *Green Cheese* weapon. The undercarriage main units were housed in the outboard faces of engine nacelles. This gave good deck handling and asymmetric single-engined stability, as the use of the wings to house the undercarriage bays would have pushed the engine mounts further outboard. As the aircraft had been designed from the outset to have the shortest wingspan possible, mounting the engines in pods resulted in the use of only one wing fold joint per wing, keeping the design within the dimensions of an aircraft

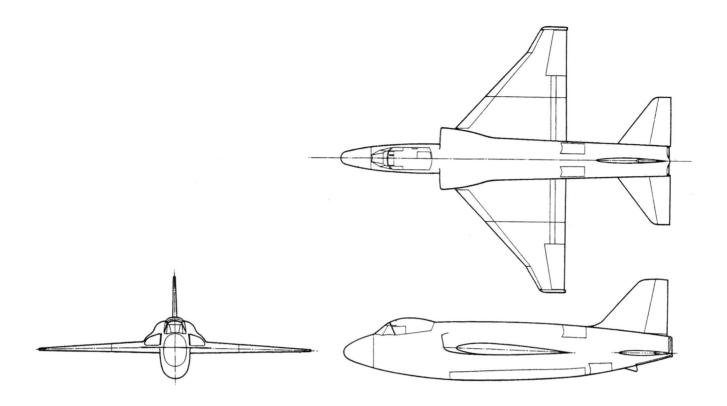

Fairey Aviation presented this rather tubby design for Specification M.148T. BBA Collection

competition.

Short Bros, under Chief Designer David Keith-Lucas, proposed the PD.13. This featured a pivoted wing design, also known as the 'isoclinic' wing, which had been developed by Professor Geoffrey Hill of Westland. The theory behind this proposal was that swept wings have a tendency to twist under load, thus reducing lift. In a tight turn the wing tip's lift reduces, which in turn places greater loads on the remainder of the wing's structure. This then induces an aeroelastic effect that attempts to pull the wing tips towards each other. Countering this could be achieved by moving the wing torsion box aft so that the wing's torsional and flexural axes coincided, thus reducing the twisting movement considerably. Although this was a novel approach to the problem of airflow behaviour, the complexity of such an arrangement counted against the design.

However, Shorts believed in their concept so at their own expense they constructed the SB.1, a third-scale proof-of-concept aircraft. Flying on 14 July 1951 from Aldergrove piloted by Chief Test

Shorts built the SB4 aircraft to test their flight control system, which used the outer sections of the wings as the control surfaces as shown on this view of G-1-14-1. BBA Collection

Pilot Tom Brooke-Smith, the unpowered SB.1 behaved as planned. Manufactured mainly from wood, the aircraft was a low-cost product whose sole purpose was to carry the wing. This assembly had a span of 38ft (11.6m) with a leading edge sweep of 42.5 degrees, while the trailing edge sweep started at zero degrees before tapering out to 30 degrees at mid-span. The outer third sections of each wing were pivoted to act as elevators or ailerons as needed. In a similar manner to other prototype aircraft developed by Shorts, the aircraft was finished in a black and silver scheme with yellow bands, being 'B' registered as G-14-1.

Having made two successful ground launches, Shorts decided to use one of their Sturgeon TT.2 target tugs to tow the SB.1 to altitude. The SB.1 was towed behind the Sturgeon to an altitude of 10,000ft (3,000m), although some turbulence was encountered from the tow aircraft. On the second flight the tow cable was extended, which caused even greater turbulence and led the pilot, Tom Brooke-Smith, to cut the tow cable and land the glider. The resultant crash landing caused him severe injuries, although the damage

to the SB.1 was slight.

Determined to prove the concept, Shorts built a new fuselage into which were mounted a pair of Turboméca Palas turbojets rated at 350lb (160kg) thrust, this being designated the SB.4 Sherpa. Test flying was undertaken from both Aldergrove and Sydenham, during which the underpowered SB.4 managed a top speed of 250mph (400km/h) at an altitude of 5,000ft (1,500m). After an appearance at the 1954 SBAC Farnborough air display, the SB.4 was passed on to the College of Aeronautics at Cranfield for further flight trials, as the various Ministries had become privy to cheaper and easier methods of achieving control in high-speed flight. The SB.4 remained in use until 1964.

Given all the trials work undertaken by Shorts it came as no surprise to find that the PD.13 was a tailless design whose outer wing sections rotated to provide control. The engines were intended to be a pair of Rolls-Royce RA.19s with exhaust deflection for better low-speed control. As before, *Green Cheese* was intended as the primary weapon. Weighing in at just over the 40,000lb (18,000kg) mark, the first machine was intended to fly some thirty

months after the contract was signed, with production aircraft entering service four years later.

Better known in recent years for its helicopters, Westland had originally made its name through the design and manufacture of unusual and innovative designs such as the Lysander army co-operation aircraft and the twin-engined Whirlwind fighter. Westland had already provided the Fleet Air Arm with the turboprop-powered Wyvern strike fighter, and offered for NA.39 a most unusual aircraft that resembled the Chance Vought Cutlass.

The Westland proposal was a swept-wing, twin-finned design powered by a pair of Gyron Junior engines. The rear end was protected by a tail bumper, which was also to be used to hold the rear fuselage down during carrier take-offs, thus raising the nose to give a better presentation of the wing leading edge to the airflow. As with all the NA.39 designs it had folding wings, though thanks to its stumpy stature no other sections needed this capability. To further assist in launching the aircraft, jet deflection of the engine exhausts was incorporated, although this required movement of the actual engines for both take-off and landing. Westland projected first flight of a prototype within twenty-seven months of the contract being signed, while production machines would be in service within four years.

The Decision

To make a final decision concerning the manufacturer of the M.148T, the Ministry of Supply conducted in-depth investigations of each company's manufacturing capabilities. On 18 November 1954 the assessment of the company was completed, following which the Tender Design Conference was undertaken at the Ministry of Supply on 3 December: this was the crunch meeting at which the winner was chosen.

The first to go were Hawker and Westland. Hawker had not submitted a formal design proposal and in any case was heavily involved in fighter production. Westland were rejected because their proposal was lacking in detail; they had also admitted that, though they were heading towards becoming Britain's primary helicopter manufacturer, the M.148T was really beyond their ability.

Remaining on the table were the

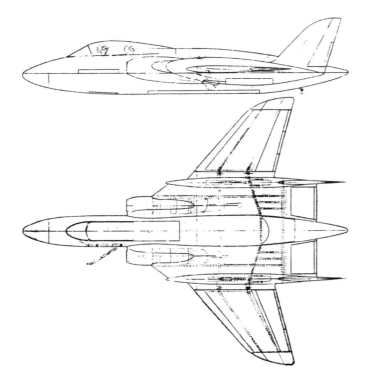

Bearing a striking resemblance to the Vought Cutlass was the proposal from Westlands, although this design relied on jet deflection to assist the take off process. BBA Collection

proposals from Armstrong Whitworth, Blackburn, Fairey and Short Bros. Fairey were quickly eliminated even though they had a reasonable background in building aircraft for the FAA as it was felt that their small design team was already fully stretched with the Gannet programme and could not handle the M.148T programme as well. Also, their design was deemed to be below the specification as issued.

Short Bros were quite lightly loaded for government contracts and their PD.13 was certainly strongly favoured. In the end, however, it was considered to be too advanced for the technology available at the time. Even if the capability to develop the technology had been available, the lack of operational success up to that point of tailless aircraft counted strongly against the company's proposal.

The two final contenders, Armstrong Whitworth and Blackburn, had both delivered strong proposals that had been thoroughly investigated by scientists at the Royal Aeronautical Establishment at Farnborough. Armstrong Whitworth, with a long background in the design and development of military equipment, was originally the favoured designer from the RAE point of view. Another factor in Armstrong Whitworth's favour was their proposed timescale for delivery in 1960. What counted against Armstrong Whitworth was the limitations of their design which, although well within the specification, left no room for further development. They were also seen as a good subcontractor, but not a front line-manufacturer.

Blackburn was the favourite as their Beverley transport programme for the Royal Air Force was coming to a close and as development work on their M.148T design was well advanced. They also had won a good reputation while building aircraft for the Royal Navy. On the other hand, Blackburn's submission meant that their first deliveries would not be ready until 1961 and that significant amounts of money would have to be invested in the development or purchase of new machine tools. Also giving a slight concern was the ability of the company to bring to fruition the aircraft's boundary layer control system (of which more later).

The final decision rested with the Naval Staff who in the end were more impressed with the B.103 as it, on paper at least, gave indications of better performance, ease of

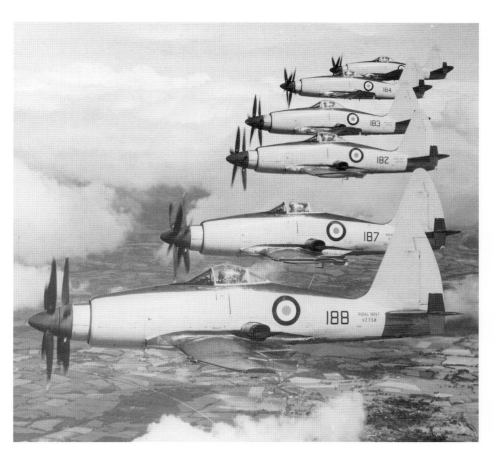

Although touted as a torpedo bomber, the turboprop-powered Westland Wyvern was in reality a strike aircraft. Here an echelon of the S.4 version pose for the camera. BBA Collection

maintenance and the potential for further development. While Blackburn was given the unofficial confirmation that they would win the contract, no final decision was made. The official answer was for both Armstrong Whitworth and Blackburn to undertake further wind tunnel work, after which they were to collate the data and present their proposals.

For Blackburn this meant that in February 1955 they were given the go-ahead by the MoS to begin initial design work. The final design appreciation conference, held a few weeks later, finally confirmed that Blackburn was the favoured manufacturer, the Naval Staff determining that the company displayed sound technical knowledge and the right amount of production capability. In July 1955 a letter of intent was sent to Blackburn confirming that a batch of twenty pre-production development aircraft was to be manufactured, the first being slated to fly in April 1958. For the other contenders the only result was a

letter of rejection.

The B.103 Starts to Take Shape

Blackburn's Chief of Future Projects was Roy Boot later to be known as 'Mr Buccaneer'. Boot became the Chief Designer in 1966 having been the Assistant from 1962 to that date. His team now turned their attention to the naval strike aircraft, their design being internally designated the B.103. Beginning in 1952, the initial layout was followed by the construction of a low-speed wind tunnel model, just to see if the initial premise was feasible. The starting point was a twin-engined aircraft to be powered by a pair of Armstrong Siddeley Sapphire AS.Sa.7 jets, rated at 11,000lb (49kN) each.

Unlike land-based aircraft, those operating aboard a carrier are constrained by the size of the elevator between flight deck and

Developed as an all weather fighter, the Gloster Javelin encountered a few problems with its 'T' tailplane, which could stall if 'blanked' by the mainplane during a turn. BBA Collection

hangar, and by the height of the hangar itself. To keep the B.103 within these limits the design office drew upon the experience gained from the Blackburn YB.2 – better known as the HP.88 – which had been built to test the unusual wing layout of the Handley Page Victor. Blackburn had built a simplified, scaled-down version of the Victor wing and fitted it to the Supermarine 510 fuselage, the resultant aircraft, VX330, being a very unorthodox design. The first flight of this test bed took place on 21 June 1951. The wing design and shape was known as a 'compound' design Blackburn were impressed enough by the concept to use it in a number of schemes for various naval fighters.

During the B.103 research phase two angles of wing sweep were settled upon, that of the inner leading edge being sharper than the outer section; this feature had appeared on the YB.2. The wing's trailing edge was straight while the thickness:chord ratio decreased from the root to the tip. Initially the design required leading edge slats on the outer wing sections, though due to their weight and complexity boundary layer blowing was adopted early on. The location of the tailplane also gave rise for concern. Blackburn having settled upon a 'T' tail layout, worrying reports began to surface concerning the behaviour of a similar assembly that was

fitted to the Gloster Javelin. After wind tunnel testing of the Blackburn layout it was discovered that the reduced sweepback of this assembly was less prone to stalling than that of the Javelin.

In order to reduce the complexity of the wing the span was restricted to 45ft (14m), which gave a wing area of 650sq ft (60.4sq m) and a single fold point. In order to improve the low-speed handling of the wing, a method had to be found to increase its low-speed lift. Trials using a modified Nene-powered Gloster Meteor engaged in jet lift trials seemed to offer a solution, so Blackburn investigated the possibility of deflecting the Sapphire engines' exhaust by up to 60 degrees to reduce the aircraft's approach speed by up to 25kt. To complicate matters, the deflection would probably be inoperable during take-off and there would be handling problems should an asymmetric approach be needed after an engine failure.

Boundary Layer Control

While the company maintained the deflector system in the design, Brough were less than keen on the idea. To make it work the engines had to be as close to the centreline and as far forward as possible. Placing the engines in this position meant that the

structure would be stronger as the wing and jet pipe layout were encompassed by circular spar sections; the bomb bay primary structure was cranked and curved, which also increased structural strength. In this configuration the airframe weighed in at 42,000lb (19,000kg), which was high for a carrier aircraft in comparison to any of its predecessors. To reduce the aircraft's all up weight Blackburn was directed by the Ministry of Supply towards a new engine under development in 1954. Promised to have a thrust of 7,500lb (33.4kN), the new engine was also projected to be lighter than the Sapphire.

Although a lighter engine appealed to Blackburn, the problem of increasing low-speed wing lift was still troubling the designers. Coming to their rescue, however, was Dr John Attinello, working for the National Advisory Committee on Aeronautics and the Naval Bureau of Aeronautics in the USA. He postulated that bleeding high-pressure air from the engines and blowing it over the wings' upper surfaces and flight control surfaces would prevent an aerodynamic phenomenon known as 'airflow separation'; this would create extra lift at lower speeds. The result of his work, which became known as Boundary Layer Control (BLC), eventually surfaced in the Lockheed F-104 Starfighter, an aircraft that really benefited from such a system.

While boundary layer control seemed like a new idea it had in fact been test flown in 1936. The aircraft involved was the Miles M.8 Peregrine, a twin-engined aircraft capable of carrying between six and eight persons. Initial orders for the Peregrine had been cancelled in favour of Magister trainers for the Royal Air Force and only two machines were built: a prototype and a special research machine constructed for the Royal Aircraft Establishment. The special test aircraft, known as the BLC Peregrine, was powered by two Menasco Buccaneer engines and featured metal sheeting on the wing and tail surfaces. The upper wing skin had small perforations in the skin in the section that covered the gap between the two spars. Unlike other types of boundary layer control aircraft, the BLC Peregrine drew air into the wings, the suction being provided by a 10hp Ford engine mounted in the cabin. Although most BLC systems relied on blowing air through slots, the work done using the BLC Peregrine contributed greatly to aviation's understanding of assisted airflow over flight surfaces.

The idea looked good on paper and two scientists were asked to investigate, Dr John Williams of the National Physical Laboratory and Lewis Boddington, Director of Naval Aircraft Research and Development at the Ministry of Supply. They confirmed that the data was correct and that Blackburn should continue development of the B.103 design. The first aircraft to utilize a BLC system in service was the Supermarine Scimitar, which entered service with the FAA in 1958.

With this in mind the Brough team led by Barry Laight redesigned the wing leading edge to incorporate boundary wing blowing which, it was estimated, would reduce take-off and landing speeds by up to 25kt. To gain the greatest advantage from this system the boundary blowing slits were extended almost to the wing tips. Testing using models was undertaken during 1954, which indicated that a dramatic increase in lift would be available, almost double that of a conventional wing without leading edge slots. Such were the promised benefits of this system that the idea of jet deflection was quickly abandoned. The increase in lift also meant that the design team could concentrate on reducing the size of the wing for the B.103. Two benefits of a smaller wing would be a reduction in size of the aircraft, making it easier for carrier storage, and the already-known benefits of a small wing in the high-speed, low-level flight regime.

The slots were located along the leading edge of the wing and in front the ailerons and flaps, which created an effect known as 'supercirculation'. All this was in anticipation of using the ailerons as part of the flap system because the actual flap surfaces were small in area, covering no more than 45 per cent of the trailing edge instead of the more normal 65 per cent on other aircraft. Initially the flaps were going to be split over both wing sections, but the decision to incorporate aileron droop meant that the flaps would occupy the fixed inner section of the wing only, while the ailerons occupied much of the remaining trailing edge. It should be noted that in droop mode aileron movement for roll control still remained possible, although its range was restricted.

One extra benefit gained from the installation of boundary layer blowing was that the Naval Staff requirement for full anti-icing was met by the blowing system,

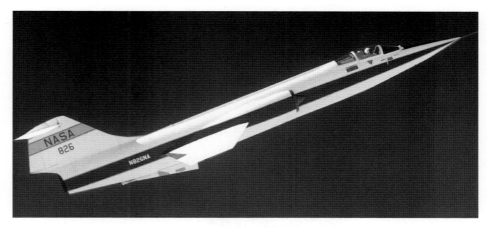

Boundary layer control was deemed necessary for the Fleet Air Arm's forthcoming strike aircraft. One of the earliest exponents of BLC was the Lockheed F-104 Starfighter. Courtesy NASA

so the original idea of installing a fairly crude electrical system was quickly deleted. While the use of engine bleed air might seem a fairly easy idea to implement, it did carry with it some penalties. These included adding shut-off valves to the bleed system and regulator valves to restrict the pressure of the air flowing through bleed air slots during operation.

In order that further weight reduction could be achieved the tailplane span was made smaller and a BLC system added to the leading edge. This was a miniature version of the system incorporated into the wings, complete with the same series of control valves. The other factor that required tailplane blowing was the use of

aileron droop, which increased the pitching moment of the aircraft. As increasing the size of the tailplane to counter the pitching was not a possibility, boundary layer blowing coupled with the use of tailplane flaps that were integrated with the wing flaps and the aileron drop system was the answer, especially as this system would counter the tendency to tailplane stalling as the speed decreased and the load increased. The pipework and slot areas for the BLC system were made from an alloy that was capable of resisting high temperatures, as the normal materials used in aircraft construction were not able to cope.

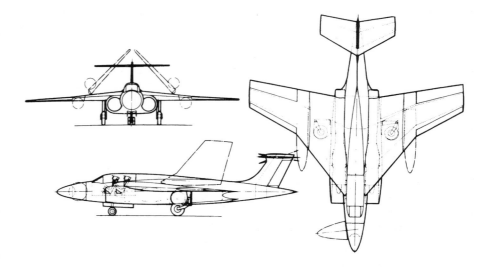

This first effort from Blackburn shows that the design team already had some of the essential elements in place such as the 'T' tail and the engine intakes. BBA Collection

Engine Problems

To further prove the boundary blowing system Blackburn constructed a one-fifth scale wing complete with a representative wing blowing system. Power was supplied by a Palouste air starter trolley that had enough output pressure to blow air across the wing upper surface with positive results. Some doubts were raised during these trials concerning the accuracy of the data collected, so RAE Farnborough was charged with confirming the figures: this they did, but they also commented that such a system would reduce the available engine thrust. To counter this Blackburn began investigating the possibility of replacing the original engine, the Sapphire, which could produce more than enough thrust, but which was rather too heavy for the design. Furthermore, it was calculated that with area ruling only 14,000lb (62.3kN) of thrust would be needed for each launch and a cruise speed of Mach 0.85 at sea level.

A saviour appeared in the shape of Rolls-Royce seemed to appear on the horizon in December 1953. They proposed a lighter engine with an output of 7,500lb (33.4kN). This news allowed Brough to redesign the airframe for the new power plant, but just as the new drawings were completed Rolls-Royce decided not to proceed with this engine. With its two first

choices not available, Blackburn turned to the De Havilland Engine Division and their Gyron engine. The original Gyron project had been a big, 20,000lb (89kN) thrust engine; this had first been scaled down slightly for the forthcoming Hawker P.1154 supersonic fighter and then for another fourteen projects – in the event, however, only one flew, in the Short Sperrin experimental bomber.

Although the full-sized Gyron engine was far too large for the B.103, design a scaled-down version known as the Gyron Junior was in development, this being a two-fifth size version of the original with an added compressor stage and two rows of variable stators. It was originally rated at 8,000lb (35.6kN), but it was decided to derate the engine to 7,000lb (31.1kN), which would allow the engine to run at a lower temperature while improving fuel consumption and fatigue life. The chosen version for the Blackburn aircraft was the Project Study 43 version, which gave the B.103 an increase of 35 per cent in range.

Further investigation revealed that operation of the blowing system would reduce the available engine thrust to 6,000lb (26.7kN). This in turn would reduce the aircraft's performance and impinge upon the overall safety margin of the design. This deficiency and its consequences having been grasped, it was proposed to restore the original engine

performance, although this was originally held at 6,500lb (28.9kN) with wing blowing in operation. A later version of the Gyron Junior incorporated turbine blade cooling, which allowed the full 7,000lb with wing blowing to be restored. While Blackburn concentrated on developing the airframe, the De Havilland Engine Division successfully bench-ran a Gyron Junior; this was followed by test flying in a Canberra with a rudimentary blowing system, which exceeded expectations.

While De Havilland laboured to develop the Gyron Junior for the B.103, Blackburn was approached by Bristol Engines, who proposed their under-development BE.33 for the same purpose. Rated at 11,400lb (50.7kN), the proposed engine would have been slightly heavier, the trade-offs being a better projected set of fuel consumption figures and plenty of high-pressure air to power the boundary air bleed system while retaining an abundance of thrust for the engines. Initially Blackburn was thrilled at the prospect of having an alternative engine for the B.103 and were well advanced in redesigning the relevant parts of the structure when Bristol Engines cancelled the entire project.

Preparation for Production

With the power plant issue now settled, Blackburn began to refer to the design as the NA.39 as per the original Naval Requirement designation. It was a time for great rejoicing as the Managing Director, Robert Blackburn, happily informed both employees and shareholders of the order – unfortunately, within twelve months Robert Blackburn was dead, being replaced by Eric Turner.

The decision to manufacture twenty development aircraft had followed on from the experience of the Hawker Hunter and Supermarine Swift programmes. The latter had proven almost disastrous as the Ministry of Supply had previously ordered small batches of prototypes, an idea that had been fine in the piston-engined era, but was totally inadequate for more modern programmes. The other reason given for such a large development batch was the need to thoroughly investigate all of the intended systems for the production NA.39: the loss of a single aircraft in a small batch could delay or stop development flying completely.

Blackburn intended that the aircraft

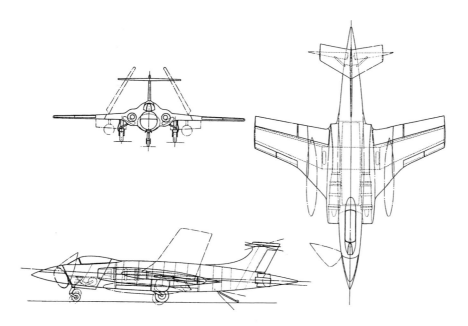

Edging closer to the final design, this is the proposal that was entered as part of the NA.39 portfolio. Comparisons with production arrangements will reveal that little would alter. BBA Collection

would be initially built in batches of three. The first three were used for basic aerodynamic flying; the second machine was equipped with extensive instrumentation to measure flutter and airframe stressing. A further six were allocated to development flying while another five went to the Aircraft and Armament Experimental Establishment at Boscombe Down for system clearance trials. The final six aircraft were to be delivered to the Fleet Air Arm for service trials.

As Blackburn geared up to begin production of the development aircraft they assumed control of the entire programme; thus they liaised direct with the manufacturers of the equipment with which the aircraft was to be fitted, which meant that the NA.39 was one of the first prototype 'weapons system' concepts undertaken in Britain. Reflecting this change was a doubling in technical staff in three years from 1952, when N.E. Rowe became Technical Director. Barry Laight joined Blackburn as Chief Designer in 1953, while Bert Smith joined in 1954 as head of the aerodynamic team. Roy Boot became deputy head of aerodynamics while the project designer for the entire project was Harold Brumby. This was also the time when the computer started to come to prominence as both analogue and digital computers began to appear. This jump in technology and the need to thoroughly test all aspects of the design meant that the number of staff employed by Blackburn tripled in size to cope with the workload.

Machine Tool Shortages

Advances were made not just in the aircraft's electronics: the airframe was also subject to much development as the environment in which the NA.39 was expected to operate was fairly hostile and a strongly built airframe was needed to counter the buffeting and load reversals that could be experienced at low level. Therefore the aircraft's structure featured integrally machined spars, ribs, frames and skins, these being machined from solid ingots. The only problem with such a process was that no suitable machinery was available in Britain to machine components from the solid; Blackburn was left with no option but to travel to the United States in order to acquire a milling machine, as the Americans had been using

While highly detailed drawings can show how the designers visualise their aircraft, a good mock-up like this not only makes their ideas solid, but allows systems engineers to move components around, should it be needed. The Blackburn Archive

such equipment since 1948. Much to Blackburn's chagrin the trip was fruitless as no such machine could be made available for at least three years. Whether this was a genuine delay or an American ploy to delay the NA.39 and sell the Royal Navy US-made aircraft has never been established.

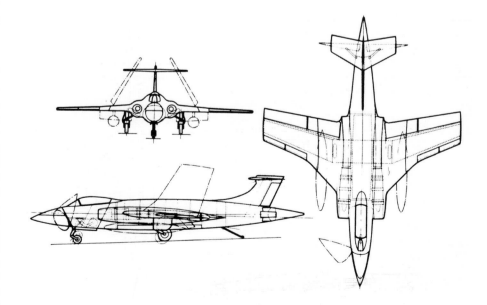

Although a certain amount of nipping and tucking had been applied to the M.148T layout, it was the application of area ruling that created the final Buccaneer layout. Here is the NA.39 before any form of aerodynamic tweaking had taken place. BBA Collection

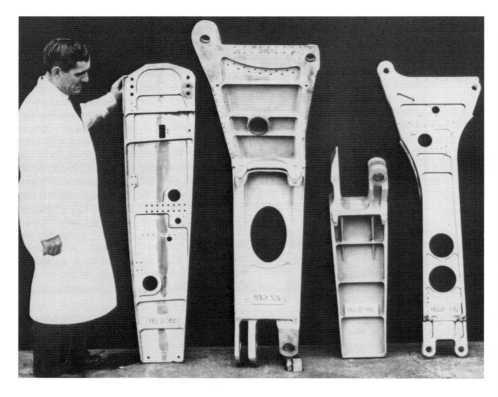

The Buccaneer's solid design is demonstrated by this view of parts of the inner wing assembly spars and frames. The Blackburn Archive

The Buccaneer/NA.39 centre section spars and frames. Note the ring spars, through which passed the engine and the jet pipe. The Blackburn Archive

As the NA.39 contract was one of the most important for both the manufacturer and the Fleet Air Arm, the answer was for Blackburn to design and build their own milling machine, which was ready for operational use within twelve months. As the first milling machine was a success Blackburn quickly commissioned three similar machines, which turned out Buccaneer components for the next twenty years. One other machine essential for the manufacture of the NA.39 was a skin-stretch press, which was also not available in Britain. In this case the Ministry of Supply was able to purchase a Hufford one from the United States. These difficulties led to the Ministry of Technology, formed in 1964, beginning a development programme to ensure that such a situation concerning machine tools, or the lack thereof, would never occur in Britain again.

To support the presentation of solid alloy ingots to these massive machines, Blackburn devoted a great deal of time and effort to creating the necessary infrastructure. A great deal of time was invested in ensuring that each component was free from imperfections, as the airframe was designed to endure a regime of high stress loading at low level. Should imperfections have remained in any part of the structure, they would have been a source of weakness that could lead to a catastrophic failure. The answer was to avoid small radii and any sharp changes of shape and section, all of which stood the NA.39 in good stead throughout its long and illustrious career. Prior to assembly each component was thoroughly inspected and any imperfections were carefully polished out.

Radar and Weapons

While there were a few hitches in creating the machinery and its support needs, and some of the system layouts had not been settled, the design process at Brough was proceeding smoothly. The main systems that needed concluding were the radar and the method of carriage for the weapons load. Initially the radar was to consist of two separate scanners, one focused on long-range scanning and the other for the final run to the target. As this made for a complicated system, Ferranti was ask to create a single unit for both tasks. This eventually emerged as the *Blue Parrot* radar system, with a single scanner.

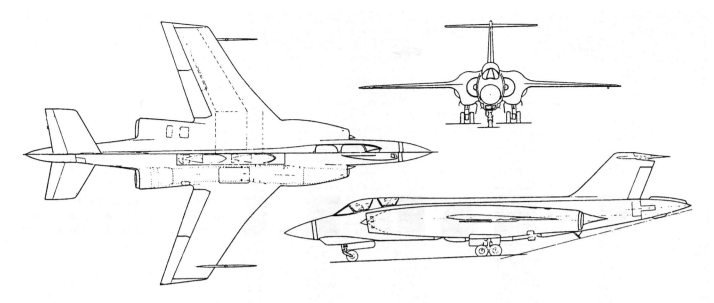

Blackburn and later Hawker Siddeley expended much time and effort suggesting improved versions of the Buccaneer to both the Royal Navy and the RAF, this being the 2**, which featured reheated Spey engines, increased fuel and weapon loads and a bogie undercarriage to carry it all. BBA Collection

When the NA.39 specification was formulated the primary nuclear weapons were intended to be the *Green Cheese* guided bomb and the *Red Beard* free-fall weapon, which was referred to in the initial documentation as a 'Target Marker Bomb' to conceal its true nature. The size of the NA.39 bomb bay and the method of delivery was dictated by these two weapons. Each required a different method of delivery: *Red Beard* had simply to be dropped into free fall while *Green Cheese* needed to be positioned outside the aircraft before the moment of release, for target acquisition. Matters were complicated by the need to carry conventional weapons as an alternative to the nuclear bombs, the loads being two mounting points for a pair of 2,000lb bombs and four mountings for 1,000lb bombs carried fore and aft, while the nuclear weapons required a centre carriage point.

A conventional bomb bay could not be contemplated: such a layout in an aircraft that was travelling at high speed and low level was impractical as the aerodynamics of moving a pair of bomb doors into the open position would cause excessive turbulence. As *Green Cheese* needed lowering into the airflow for target acquisition, the inclusion of a pair of bomb doors and a trapeze extension beam also brought with it an unacceptable weight penalty.

The answer was to develop a rotating bomb door on the inside face of which would be the mountings for the various intended loads. In both the open and closed positions there would be very little turbulence or aerodynamic interference, and the bomb door being hydraulically driven kept the rotation speed down to mere seconds. Another option that was briefly investigated was inward-sliding doors that moved up the bomb bay walls, these being coupled to a lowering roof; however, this was quickly abandoned as complicated and impractical. The rotating bomb door which was eventually adopted had already been proven successfully in the Martin B-57, a derivative of the English Electric Canberra, and in the McDonnell F-101 Voodoo. The principle had to be refined by Blackburn as the door had to be lowered slightly into the airflow using a rack and pinion drive. Fortunately for all, *Green Cheese* was cancelled and a simple hinge pin arrangement was mounted at each end of the door.

The bomb door having been fixed, the next stage was to test the concept in the wind tunnel as some concerns had been raised about the handling of the aircraft during its rotation and in the fully open position. Fortunately no obvious problems were encountered and the possibility of turbulence during rotation was solved by driving the door round at high speed.

Area Ruling

The initial design for the NA.39 showed an aircraft with a fuselage of a fairly steady shape. Wind tunnel testing revealed that airflow across various parts of the airframe was quite turbulent, so the newly emergent concept of 'area rule' was applied to the airframe. Developed by Richard Whitcomb of NACA, area ruling created a smooth streamlining affect across the entire airframe by keeping cross-sectional area constant, this normally being represented as a gentle falling and rising curve on a graph. The application of area ruling always applied a bulged 'coke bottle' shape to the fuselage, which was not easy with the B.103. Certain parts of the fuselage could not be altered, especially around the weapons bay, so the bulge was applied to the rear fuselage, giving more room for extra equipment while the pinch was applied to the forward fuselage. As area ruling was applied, the wings had their trailing edge sweep changed from 10 to 20 degrees, which increased the area of the fuselage close by the trailing edge and helped emphasize the fuselage shape change.

One unexpected benefit was a reduction in the amount of engine thrust needed to maintain maximum cruising speed, which in turn reduced overall fuel consumption. To fully test the new configuration the

NA.39 was fully wind tunnel tested in the facilities at RAE Bedford, these tests being followed by further trials at Blackburn's own facility at Brough, which had been opened in 1958 by the First Sea Lord, Earl Mountbatten.

Air Brakes

Sitting at the rear of the airframe was another Blackburn innovation, the clamshell air brakes. Used for speed control during approach, these massive structures were also required to control the aircraft during a dive. The reasons for placing the air brakes at the rear of the fuselage were twofold: effectiveness and location. One was dependent upon the other as the normal locations for air brakes, such as the wings or as petals on the rear fuselage, were not suitable in this case: the panels in these areas were not large enough to be effective if used as air brakes. The answer created by Blackburn was to split the rear fuselage and design two clamshell air brakes of great structural strength; these were driven by hydraulic jacks using draglinks and a cross-head assembly.

One of the first concerns raised about this installation by the Admiralty was the possibility of trim changes when the air brakes were opened. This concern was justified, as during the initial test flights there were significant trim changes that took some time to work out through intensive test flying and airframe tweaking.

The positive side to the NA.39's air brake system was the great control it gave during approach and landing; in fact, the aircraft had to approach and land with the engines at a higher thrust than would otherwise be the norm. This improved the landing 'go-around' capability, as closing the air brakes gave an immediate increase in forward speed – a welcome standby when attempting a carrier approach. Having the engines running at a higher thrust also increased the air pressure being blown through the wing and tailplane boundary layer control, which in turn improved the aircraft's handling. Another benefit gained from the use of this type of air brake was the reduction in the overall length in the fuselage when the air brakes were open and the nose folded back, which ensured that the NA.39 was well within the Admiralty's length requirement.

The Design is Refined

Having sketched out the basics of the NA.39 the aerodynamics team was faced with the task of creating the actual aircraft. The first area to be refined was the wing, which featured a leading edge with two sweep angles while the section of the wing changed constantly from root to tip, to give a near-constant critical Mach number spanwise; the wing sweep ensured that any wing stall occurred at the root first. This form of wing had one disadvantage: at low speeds as it required extra lift. Under other conditions and on a larger aircraft the answer would have been to use leading edge slats, but as weight control was paramount boundary layer control was chosen for the NA.39.

The wings being centrally mounted, locating the tailplane along the same plane was a non-starter due to the potential for aerodynamic conflicts. The answer was to mount the tailplane on top of the fin to create a 'T' tail, even though there had been problems with other aircraft using this configuration. These troubles included stalling, aerodynamic 'flutter' and structural failure. Countering this included preventing wing tip stalling that could cause a heavy inboard downwash and induce a stable stall, while preventing flutter was a burgeoning art form and required much wind tunnel time with models being flown in the transonic speed range.

The inclusion of the boundary layer control system and other air supply systems also had a considerable effect on the aircraft. At least 2 per cent of the total engine air output is ducted to various parts of the airframe, being mixed in some cases with ram air for cooling. A further 10 per cent of the engine's output was directed towards the bleed air system, of which 75 per cent was directed along the wing ducts to vent over the flaps and ailerons while a further 15 per cent was vented over the wing from the leading edge slots. The remaining percentage was directed to the tailplane.

With the all the various details concerning the production of the NA.39 settled, manufacture of the first pre production airframe, XK486, could begin. The centre fuselage section was built within three months, being removed from its construction jigs on 6 July 1957. This machine was

After the S.1 came the Buccaneer S.2, this being the version seen here. The large wooden frame mounted in the engine bay was to assist in the placement of the engine nacelle panels. The Blackburn Archive

The first NA.39 heads south on the back of a lorry for its first flight. Watched by passers-by, the heavily shrouded airframe carefully negotiates the streets. The Blackburn Archive

quickly followed by the second prototype, which featured thicker wing skins and would be dedicated to exhaustive flutter and airframe resonance trials in order to closely represent the production standard aircraft. Initial ground running trials were carried out on XK486, resplendent in blue grey above with white underneath in early March 1958.

As Brough airfield was far too small and open for the NA.39's initial test flight, it was decided to break the airframe into movable components and transport it by road to RAE Thurleigh, near Bedford. As the Cold War was at its height, each section was carefully shrouded in heavy duty tarpaulins for the trip south, keeping the NA.39 free from prying eyes. Further confusion techniques included applying different-sized roundels and other markings to each of the test aircraft, to ensure that no obvious fixed point could be determined. However, various parts of the aircraft had already been displayed, including aerials and the Martin Baker ejection seats, all of whose dimensions were well known: thus *Flight* magazine was able to create a series of drawings that were only out by a few inches dimensionally.

First Flight

Having arrived at Thurleigh the NA.39 components were quickly reassembled, this being followed by a full range of airframe system functional tests and engine runs. For the following three weeks XK486 underwent taxi tests at various speeds up and down Thurleigh's runway.

The crew selected to fly the NA.39 were ex-Fleet Air Arm pilot Derek Whitehead and observer Bernard Watson, who had arrived at Blackburn from Boscombe Down in January 1958. Both crew were aboard XK486 on 13 April 1958 when the brakes overheated and caught fire. The NA.39 was steered off the runway, but the starboard main wheel burst, causing

On the production line Buccaneer S.1s are coming close to completion. Of note are the wing fold doors on the upper wing and the spine, which is waiting for its covering panels. The Blackburn Archive

The Hunting H.126

Following on from the NA.39 development programme, the Ministry of Aviation decided to carry out further investigations into blown flaps and ailerons. The concept applied to this aircraft had first been investigated by the National Gas Turbine Establishment at Pyestock during 1952, although the means to create a practical test bed were not available at that time so it took the appearance of the Blackburn NA.39 to stimulate further research.

Specification ER.189D was issued for the construction of an aircraft for such a purpose. Designed by Hunting Aircraft of Luton, part of the British Aircraft Corporation, the H.126 was a single-seat aircraft powered by a Bristol Siddeley Orpheus turbojet. As it was a pure research aircraft it was of necessity fairly basic, so no pressurization system was installed; a full oxygen system and an ejection seat were, however, fitted.

The system installed in the H.126 blew over a conventional wing using a series of fishtail vents that issued the heated air drawn from the engine over the flaps and ailerons. In this case the air was drawn from the jet pipe, instead of tappings from the engine as in the Buccaneer.

The H.126 made its first flight on 26 March 1963 from RAE Bedford piloted by Mr S.B. Oliver from Huntings. Getting the airframe to this point required much development work as there were large changes in trim due to the amount of gas being vented over the wing. To help counter this, the control column and rudder pedals were not only connected to conventional flight controls but also to a series of nozzles fitted at the wing tips and the tail, all being controlled by an auto-stabilizer. The tailplane was a variable incidence unit, hinged around the rear spar and driven by a hydraulic PFCU connected to the front spar. The engine intake was a simple pitot type, the engine itself being fitted with an air starting system. The efflux from the Orpheus was fed into a master chamber, which in turn distributed air to the nozzles, the wing blowing

mechanism and the bifurcated jet pipes. Unlike the Buccaneer, much of the H.126 was constructed of light alloys, with certain parts being heavily insulated against heat.

The wings were of conventional construction, although their mounting points were designed to allow the dihedral angles to be selected as 4 or 8 degrees on the ground. Mounted on the trailing edge, the flaps and ailerons were multi-hinged, each being fitted with control jacks housed in fairings under the wings. The fin and tailplane were similar in construction to the wings, and the fin had an anti-spin parachute at its tip.

The fixed undercarriage consisted of single main wheels and a twin nose wheel assembly, all three having shock absorbers installed. Driving the hydraulics were two independent systems, each of which was capable of providing the aircraft's requirements should the other fail. Supporting the primary systems was an emergency accumulator, while a second accumulator provided braking power. Electrical requirements were taken care of by an engine-driven generator supported by a standby battery.

When XN714 made its maiden flight it required no more than 80kt and 60yd (55m) to become airborne with the flaps set at the 'zero' setting. The entire flight lasted eighteen minutes, being recorded and shepherded by a Meteor chase aircraft. After landing the pilot expressed his delight with the handling of the H.126. Hunting used the aircraft for six months before handing it over to the Royal Aircraft Establishment. The H.126 undertook over 100 test flights between 1963 and 1967 with Hunting and the RAE before departing to NASA in the United States in 1969 for flight trials. Upon completion of the trials the aircraft returned to Britain in May 1970, being placed in storage. XN714 was finally struck off charge in September 1972, eventually being sent to the Cosford Aerospace Museum for display. While the H.126 took the idea of boundary layer control and jet flaps even further than the system applied to the Buccaneer, the complexity of such a system precluded its further development.

The Hunting H.126 was constructed to develop the BLC concept further. Although successful, the complexity of this system plus later advances in wing design meant that the H.126 was no more than an interesting diversion. BBA Collection

One of the benefits revealed by the H.126 was that of a reduced take off run: when the BLC was operating, this was measured in tens of yards rather than the normal hundreds. BBA Collection

NA.39 XK486 with the original nose radome fitted to the aircraft. A look at the airbrakes shows that Blackburn was struggling to determine the shape, location and size of the airbrake strakes. BBA Collection

extensive damage to the inner wing structure. Repairs were finally completed by 29 April and taxi trials were resumed. All was well, and the maiden flight was set for the following day.

On 30 April Whitehead and Watson climbed aboard XK486, started engines and taxied out to the runway threshold. Power was applied and the aircraft took off. During this flight an altitude of 17,000ft (5,000m) was reached, the entire sortie lasting forty-two minutes. This was a fine effort, especially given the complexities of developing such a design, as it had taken just thirty-three months from contract placement to first flight. The crew report was also positive, as both were convinced that the Blackburn NA.39 would more than fulfil its specification.

Subcontractors	
Electro-Hydraulics Ltd	hydraulic system control
Avica Ltd	BLC components
Girling Ltd	low-friction dampers
Ferranti	standby gyro system and TR.150 transformer rectifier unit
Ward Brooke Ltd	electrical connections
Cadmium Nickel Batteries	onboard batteries
English Electric	constant-frequency electrical generating system
Goodyear	tyres, wheels, brakes and anti-skid systems
Elliots	gauges
Dowty	main and nose undercarriage legs, nose wheel steering, turbo alternator, fuel systems, gear boxes and hydraulic pumps
Whiteley Electrical Radio Ltd	control knobs, CWC Equipment, sealed switches
Ericsson Ltd	sealed relays
Diamond H Controls	relays
McMurdo Instruments	electrical components
Cannon Electrics	electrical components
JN Summers	electrical components
V Vinten Ltd	camera equipment
Teddington Aircraft Control	flight control system parts
Teleflex Products Ltd	flight control system parts

CHAPTER THREE

Pirate of the Skies – The Buccaneer Begins Flight Testing

Having survived its destructive wheel burst and a successful first test flight, NA.39 XK486 returned north from RAE Thurleigh to the Blackburn airfield at Holme-on-Spalding Moor some eighteen miles from Brough. Blackburn had taken over the airfield in 1958 as the runway and other facilities at Brough were not extensive enough to support XK486 and the remainder of the test fleet. It had begun life as a Bomber Command base and so was equipped with a runway long enough, at 6,000ft (1,800m) to accommodate a modern jet aircraft. The airfield had become a bit tatty since its closure, so the runway was made good, the perimeter track was resurfaced, a handful of buildings were refurbished for use as offices and labo-

ratories and a 'J' Type hangar was prepared to house the aircraft. As the programme expanded later on, two further hangers were repaired to house chase aircraft and test equipment.

One of the first uses to which the hangar was put was canopy jettison trials using XK486 and a representative canopy. To initiate the test, string was attached to an ejection seat and was pulled from a safe distance by the trials team. As this was the first prototype there was some concern for the safety of the aircraft, so the airframe was surrounded by catch nets to prevent the heavy canopy from striking the airframe. Once this test had been completed the type was cleared to fly faster than 350kt for the first time.

The pilots assigned to the development programme were ably managed by Holme-on-Spalding-Moor's Flight Test Manager, J. T. Stamper. Derek Whitehead was the senior pilot, the others being G. R. I. 'Sailor' Parker, J. G. 'Bobby' Burns, R. J. Chandler, D. Lockspeiser and Lt Cdr E. R. Anson RN, who left the flight test programme in 1961 to join the Buccaneer Intensive Flying Trials Unit at Lossiemouth.

The second aircraft, XK487, was towed by road from Brough to 'the Moor', as Holme-on-Spalding-Moor was known locally. Arriving in an almost complete condition, XK487 made its maiden flight on 27 August 1958. As the role of XK487 was to be aerodynamic handling testing,

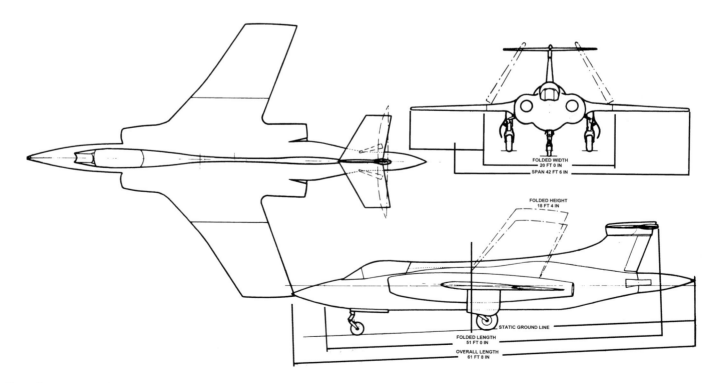

General arrangement of the NA.39 prototype and development batch aircraft. BBA Collection

With everything out and down, the first NA.39 passes the crowd at Farnborough. By this time, near-definitive airbrake strakes were fitted, just the lower sections requiring installation. BBA Collection

Photographed early in the flight test programme, XK486 still sports one of the early airbrake strake layouts. It also lacks vortex generators on the outer wing panels and the extended wing tips. BBA Collection

The first in-flight refuelling probe developed for the Buccaneer was a neat affair that folded into the nose. Unfortunately, the probe caused airflow problems with the starboard engine. The Blackburn Archive

XK490, which featured a fully operating bomb door and pylons, while the last of this batch, XK491, was fitted with a retractable in-flight refuelling probe, the full production AC electrical system, auto stabilizer, autopilot and a radar altimeter system.

Land-Based Catapult and Arrestor Trials

The arrival of XK489 at the Moor saw the installation of two types of arrestor gear for landing trials and to prevent an overrun in the event of a brake failure. One system used the nylon pack principle, which was effective in operation but took a long time to reset, while the other was of the water compression type. Manufactured by John Curran Ltd of Cardiff, this system used pistons mounted in water-filled tubes that acted as dampers to slow down the extension of the cable. The arrestor cable itself was held some 4.5in (11cm) clear of the runway by circular rubber supports: low enough to let the aircraft wheels roll easily over the cable, yet high enough to allow the cable to catch the aircraft's arrestor hook. Such was the effectiveness of this system that one aircraft that had suffered an inadvertent hook deployment engaged the cable and failed to proceed far down the runway, even though the engines were at full power. The NA.39 being a naval aircraft, the airfield was equipped with a mirror landing aid; unlike those fitted to aircraft carriers, though, it required

its structure was of a more robust nature and the airframe was extensively fitted with strain gauges and flutter exciters – also known as 'bonkers' – mounted on the wing tips. During these early flights only a small amount of flutter was discovered and this was cured by installing balance weights on the tip of each tailplane.

The next task was to create a transonic speed table to assist in the calibration of the airspeed indicator and the Machmeter. Getting the readings required that the test aircraft enter a dive from high altitude, pulling out when certain strain gauge read-

ings were observed. So that these readings could be as accurate as possible, each flight had to be undertaken in the calmest conditions possible: therefore flying took place just after sunrise or just prior to sunset.

XK487 was followed into the skies by XK488, which made its maiden flight on 31 October, and by XK489 on 31 January 1959. In contrast to the earlier machines, XK489 was fully navalized with the folding nose, folding wings and arrestor hook destined for the production version. Next came

Sailing at height above the clouds, XK486 sports an instrumentation boom on the nose and an anti-spin parachute housing on the airbrakes. Note the absence of the fairing between the fin and tailplane that was added to the production machines. BBA Collection

Pictured at Farnborough, XK486 sports the definitive airbrake strakes, as fitted to the production version. Clearly shown here is the distinctive rear fuselage applied to improve the type's aerodynamics. By this time the name Buccaneer had been applied to the NA.39. BBA Collection

manual adjustment for each set of practice approaches.

As the Moor is located in a fairly desolate area there was plenty of free airspace in which to carry out the NA.39 flight trials. As each aircraft took off to undertake a test flight it would be accompanied by a chase aircraft: either a Meteor NF.12 or a Hunter F.4, depending on photographic observation requirements. Running in parallel with the live flight tests were extensive wind tunnel trials being undertaken at the NASA Langley Research facility in Virginia. The use of these facilities for flutter trials was partly funded by the American Mutual Weapons Development Programme, which provided aid for the development of weapons by friendly nations. Further US funding to the tune of $13 million helped in the provision of data recording and analysis, and flight instrumentation. Such aid to a British company created an adverse reaction in the American Senate,

---

Pirates on the Moor

When Blackburn took over the redundant bomber airfield at Holme-on-Spalding-Moor in 1958 to test-fly the NA.39/Buccaneer, they inherited a classic three-runway airfield laid out in a triangle, a control tower that was modernized with the latest communications equipment and a pair of hangers that housed the Buccaneer test fleet. As accommodation at 'the Moor', as the airfield was generally known, was initially restricted, the test pilots were located in an office in the bottom floor of the control tower. On the roof of the control tower was a balcony area facing the gap between the tower and the hangers, between which the test flight crews were wont to fly at very low level to impress visitors with the capabilities of their aircraft.

The hangers were home to the fleet of trials Buccaneers whose support personnel were provided by Blackburn and the Fleet Air Arm. The aircraft were towed by road from Brough to the Moor, a distance of some 18 miles (30km). This was made possible by the type's folding wings: most other aircraft would have had to be moved in pieces and reassembled before flying.

Flight operations were controlled by J.T. Stamper whose responsibilities covered the development of the aircraft, its engine and ground equipment, plus the embodiment of modifications that emanated from Brough. Carrying out the actual flight testing was the responsibility of a chief test pilot, D. J. Whitehead, five other pilots, G. R. I. Parker, J. G. Burns, Lt Cdr E. R. Anson RN, D. Lockspeiser and R. J. Chandler and eight test observers, E. J. Solman, M. R. Bailey, G. R. C. Copeman, T. D. Dunn, J. B. Pearson, T. Jackson, E. J. D. Nightingale and N. Graham.

To make the airfield more representative of both an aircraft carrier and the forthcoming standard naval airfield. the main 6,000ft (1,800m) runway had two arrestor systems installed, one based on the water-squeeze system and one of the nylon pack type. A mirror landing system was also added to the airfield to aid in the Buccaneer's development. This was not an automatic unit as installed on aircraft carriers, but had to be set up manually; however, the system was designed for practise use only and was not aligned to the arrestor gear.

The air traffic control system installed at the Moor was based on the Cossor 21 radar, which incorporated talk-down equipment most useful to the senior controller, H.N. Smith, and his assistants. This radar gave the controllers the range and azimuth of an approaching aircraft, though not its elevation. A UHF homer was installed, although the pilots preferred to use the 'topographical homer': the canal that stretched from the Humber almost to the airfield!

Test flying of the Buccaneer development fleet was normally carried out towards the north or north-east of the airfield, while low-level flying was carried out over the designated low flying zones in Lincolnshire. Flying at altitude in the vicinity of the Moor required some careful manoeuvring and clearances as airway Green Two was located to the south and stretched between 3,000 and 11,000ft (900–3,350m). To the north-east, test crews had to be aware of RAF Leconfield and its swarms of Hunters and Javelins, while to the south-west and RAF Finningley the occupiers of the airspace were Vulcans flying let-down patterns.

When the crews were involved in flight testing, data was collected both on the aircrews' kneepads and by equipment located in the control tower. At the end of each flight both crew members had to write extensive reports incorporating both data and observations, which in many cases took longer than the actual test flights. Supporting many of these flights was a Hunter F.4 chase plane, which acted as an external observer aircraft. The data for each flight was recorded on standard Hussenot trace recorders that recorded the normal flight parameters upon magnetic tape. This was found to be most useful during oscillation testing, which required the use of 'bonkers' to create the flutter response. In-depth testing for flutter was needed as the NA.39's behaviour at high and low speeds was well known, but the part of the flight envelope in between gave cause for concern as any problems with the controls at low level and high speed could result in the loss of the aircraft. Fortunately the Buccaneer went on to prove its worth, while Holme-on-Spalding-Moor would see all of the type launch into the sky.

ABOVE: **XK489 and XK488 en route to Farnborough on 4 September 1960. The nearer aircraft, XK489, has been fitted with the definitive nose radome while XK488 sports the original version.** BBA Collection

LEFT: **NA.39 XK489 was also engaged in the development of the airbrake strakes for the Buccaneer. By the time this photograph was taken, some of the airflow problems affecting the tailplane fin interface had been addressed by the installation of a bullet to the rear of the tailplane.** BBA Collection

where the development by the British of the VC10 competitor to Boeing's 707 was considered unfair.

While Holme-on-Spalding-Moor was suitable for normal operations, XK489 was flown to RAE Bedford on 1 June 1959 to test the arrestor and catapult launch equipment. The launch trials placed a force of 5g on both the aircraft and crew under normal circumstances, but part of the trials period involved determining the NA.39's Minimum Launch Speed – the minimum speed at which an aircraft could be launched and climb safely away. The force exerted was between 2.5– 3g, this

varying with wind speed. During these launches acceleration rates as low as 0.5kt/sec were achieved however this was by way of an experiment not a definite lower minima in the pilots notes.

Some of these launches were quite close to the aircraft's safety limits as the NA.39 sometimes dropped back onto the runway, leaving the pilot with the choice of taking the crash barrier further down the runway or opening the throttles and taking off. As damage to a rather precious airframe could result from the former, the crews opted for the latter course. One catapult launch saw the NA.39 hit the ground quite heavily,

bounce into the air to clear the barrier and slowly climb away. At the conclusion of the flight the airframe was given a full inspection and no damage was found, which showed the strength of the aircraft's construction.

It was during these trials that the hands-off launch technique was developed, as it had been found that pilots had a natural tendency to over-control their aircraft just after catapult launch. This was normally found to be a pull back on the control column, which in turn led to excessive pitch-up. To counter this, trials were carried out to find a setting point for the tailplane, which was trimmed to a determined position depending on weight and wind speed. In this condition the NA.39 could be launched hands-off, although in practice the pilots had a tendency to keep one hand circled lightly around the control column.

Further alterations to the aircraft's flight control system centred on the ailerons in droop mode, where evidence of adverse yaw became apparent. Countering this meant reducing the droop angle slightly, while the gearing from control column to aileron was made slightly coarser: this improved the behaviour of the Buccaneer during landing.

Whilst undertaking these flights XK489 came close to crashing during an approach to Bedford. While being flown by 'Sailor' Parker, the NA.39 began to experience tailplane control restrictions that required great skill from the pilot to counteract. Eventually a safe landing was effected, the subsequent investigation showed that the potting compound insulation around a restrictor had failed, which in turn had caused a differential lock to engage.

As there were problems with the fin and tailplane interface, some test sorties were flown with both surfaces heavily tufted in order to map the airflow paths. The Blackburn Archive

Carrier Trials and Air Shows

After the controlled violence of throwing the airframe down the Bedford runway, XK489 was flown out to the aircraft carrier HMS *Victorious* over the period 25–29 May 1959 to undertake 'touch and go' landings. After these flight trials, XK489 was flown to Paris air show in June. A return to flight trials under the care of C Flight of the A&AEE (which was charged with testing naval aircraft) at Boscombe Down involved preparing the aircraft for full deck landing trials aboard HMS *Victorious*. On 19 January 1960 the aircraft carried out its trials aboard the carrier, which was cruising in the English Channel.

A modified flight control system was then installed by Blackburn, after which the NA.39 returned to Boscombe Down. Further modifications to the flight controls were undertaken during May 1960, following which C Flight took the aircraft out to the aircraft carrier HMS *Centaur* in July for further touch and go landings. The NA.39 appeared at the Farnborough air show during September 1960, where it was demonstrated to the West German defence minister, Franz-Josef Strauss, as the West German Navy

Deck testing of the NA.39 was undertaken in all weathers, as this view of XK523 aiming for the deck of *Victorious* shows. The Blackburn Archive

was in the market for a maritime strike aircraft for use in the Baltic region. The test flights, although impressive, failed to secure an order, which eventually went to the Lockheed F-104G Starfighter – ostensibly to reduce spares requirements, as the same type was on order for the Luftwaffe.

Although the Germans did not order the production NA.39, the Fleet Air Arm kept faith with its new aircraft, allowing it to land aboard HMS *Ark Royal* for trials, although XK489 was based at Hal Far, Malta, for the duration. Next came stalling and handling trials at A&AEE back in the UK. The aircraft's time as a trials vehicle ended in December 1963 when it was returned to the Moor for disposal, being officially struck off charge on 22 September 1964. Stripped of all useful items, the remains were transported to the Proof and Experimental Establishment at Shoeburyness in January 1965. By now the aircraft had achieved some 270 flying hours.

Flight Testing Continues

It was during the first eighteen months of the flight trials that much effort was expended on completely harmonizing the flight controls. The first area of concern involved the air brakes and the possible trim changes when they were deployed. Having put various models through extensive wind tunnel testing, the Blackburn design team was convinced that the results were not accurate enough. During this phase it was also discovered that although no trim change normally occurred upon their deployment, excess loading was being placed upon the tailplane and its mountings. To determine the extent of this loading, strain gauges were installed in those aircraft involved in various aspects of the flight test schedule. Eventually the flight trials and constant tweaks resulted in a set of correctly shaped strakes being installed on all of the extant prototypes and production machines.

Having dealt with the air brakes and aileron droop, the flight crews turned their attention to yaw auto-stability. This, too, required numerous flight trials to determine the correct gearing ratios. Once these trials were completed duplicate systems were installed on all extant aircraft. Roll auto-stability also required extensive testing, the result of which was slightly altered gear ratios. However, the complicated aileron set-up generated excessive system friction, which required

much testing on ground rigs and the NA.39 fleet. Curing it required the fitment of mass balance weights onto the ailerons as well as re-jigging the control runs out to the wing PFCUs. It was also at this stage that the aileron gear change system was installed which cured these problems. This fitment was coupled to a limiting system connected to the control column, which countered the excessive roll control available during low-speed handling; this was set at two thirds of the full range.

During flight above 520kt, some slight longitudinal snaking and tailplane vibration had been experienced on XK489 and XK490; this required investigation. The cause was traced to shock-induced airflow separation at the tailplane/fin juncture. Curing this required the installation of a large bullet fairing that extended fore and aft of the tailplane/fin junction.

These early flight trials also revealed that the NA.39 had a tendency to 'bounce' on landing which lifted the aircraft over the arrestor wires. This kind of behaviour was obviously unacceptable in a carrier-based aircraft, so changes were made to the main undercarriage rebound ratios and the deployment time of the arrestor hook was speeded up. Troubles were also experienced with the tail skid, which exhibited a tendency to strike the catapult shuttle during launch. Curing this required that the catapult shuttle be modified, as was the tail skid shock absorber strut's compression ratio.

Also worrying for a life at sea was the tendency of the electrical relays to corrode, leaving the aircraft open to numerous potential in-flight faults – some were minor while others could result in the loss of the aircraft. Yet again much time and effort was expended on dealing with this problem, the end result being the provision of better-quality relays and improved sealing and protection. Such was the importance attached to this problem that two years were devoted to its solution, instead of the intended eight months.

Another long-winded process involved clearing the autopilot. Initially the system was operable as built, but the initial built-in tolerances were too close to the acceptable limits. An extended flight trials programme was put in hand to find areas of autopilot operation that could be relaxed, reducing the need to alter any of the gearing already determined for the remainder

Seen from underneath XK489 has its airbrakes partially extended; also visible is a Doppler aerial under the rear fuselage. BBA Collection

XK490 lines up on the Farnborough runway. Note the dropped flaps and the ailerons in the drooped position for take-off. Under normal operating conditions – as here – the tail skid was in the 'down' position, although in an emergency its services can be dispensed with to conserve hydraulic power. BBA Collection

of the flight control system. Even though many of the trials aircraft were involved in these flights, the fact that it was a long drawn-out affair resulted in parts of this programme going backwards as aircraft were diverted away to other tasks before resuming autopilot trials flying.

This disturbance to the programme threw up some complications, the first of which was troubles with the height-lock switch, which had initially operated without any problems. After a period of tinkering and diversion, one of the flight test aircraft resumed autopilot testing only to find that the height lock would not engage correctly. It was initially determined that the cause lay with the transducer being sensitive to the 'g' forces imposed upon it during high-speed, low-level flight and so causing the lock to disconnect.

This conclusion was later found to be incorrect, the fault being eventually traced to the static side of the pitot head where pressure alterations were not as smooth as needed. Known as 'static errors', these generated an instability within the transducer, causing it to fail; the cure required no more than a minor tweak to the setting angle of the pitot head. While this was sufficient to allow flying to continue, it was recognized that an improved pitot head was required and one was fitted at the earliest opportunity. Programme diversions and the curing of the height-lock problem finally extended this phase of testing from the planned thirty months to fifty-four months.

The retractable refuelling probe was also causing problems. While a neat installation, its location was such that very little room was available in the nose for a decent-sized probe. Located on the starboard side of the nose, its extension into the airflow and its closeness to the fuselage generated a bow wave effect that not only created drogue instability for the tanker, but also caused engine problems including compressor stalling. The final culmination of these problems saw XK491 diverting to Elvington with the drogue still attached to the probe tip, the former having broken off the Valiant tanker's extended fuel line. The first attempt at a cure was to make the probe longer, but flight trials revealed that even this modification still caused problems with the engine compressor. The eventual cure was to delete the retractable installation and fit a larger, permanent probe offset slightly to starboard, just in front of the windscreen.

Escape from the NA.39 was also put under intense scrutiny. As both crew were housed under a single-piece canopy, it was decided that the escape sequence needed to be as close as possible for both crew members. Initially the canopy was blown clear by a single cartridge, but this took too long to clear the aircraft, especially given the low-level regime the aircraft was expected to operate in; also hindering a quick departure was the 200lb (90kg) weight of the canopy. After much development the single cartridge was replaced by a system of multiple cartridges, which fired quickly in sequence to blow the canopy clear. Both versions generated gasses that unlocked the canopy guide rails and pushed the assembly into the airflow using rams. Under certain circumstances, this method of clearing the canopy caused an unacceptable delay to the crew escaping as a time delay unit was used to sequence the ejection.

While the ejection trials were continuing, further investigations centred around the wind blast on the rear cockpit when the canopy had been jettisoned, which was deemed unacceptable especially at speeds above 270kt. Wind tunnel tests were confirmed later during canopy-off flight trials and then during the loss of XK486 (*see* below), when the observer had waited until the NA.39 had slowed down sufficiently to escape as the turbulence around the rear cockpit had been violent. To improve the crew's escape chances at low level and to protect the observer it was decided to alter the method of ejection. Modified canopies with slightly thinner perspex were installed, to allow the crew to fire straight through. Such an alteration also meant strengthening the ejection seats to absorb the impact of striking the canopy; even so, a blast protection shield was fitted in front of the observer's position. Trials to prove that these changes were fully viable were conducted using a high-speed rocket sledge at the China Lake test centre in the United States.

Although the normal ejection system had been resolved, much effort was expended on improving the underwater escape system. It was obvious that a

Buccaneer S.1 XK527 was one of the first fourteen aircraft ordered for the Royal Navy. This particular aircraft spent its entire life in the trials role before retiring in 1985, after its final role as a ground training airframe. Eventually much of the airframe was scrapped, although the nose was preserved and is currently located in North Wales. BBA Collection

manual system would not suffice, so a fully automatic system was developed. This used a sensing orifice in the fuselage which, when blocked by water, would initiate the discharge of a clutch of high pressure air bottles. These in turn operated the ejection seat guns, followed by the crew separating from their seats whilst their life jackets inflated. Testing of this system took place at Glen Fruin and in the diving tank at HMS *Vernon*.

While XK489 was undertaking some of the more naval-orientated trials the first prototype, XK486, was at Boscombe Down with A&AEE's C Flight for handling trials. During this period the NA.39 was displayed at the September 1958 Farnborough Show, after which it was returned to Blackburn for maintenance. A return to Boscombe Down followed in October for aerodynamic trials, although these only lasted a fortnight, after which XK486 returned to Blackburn for autopilot and general handling flights. During April 1959 the aircraft was again with the A&AEE for boundary layer control trials, during which it was damaged and obliged to make a forced landing at Elvington. The cause was found to be a restriction in the flight control circuit – caused, it was suspected, by a hydraulic leak in the aileron control circuit – which caused the differential lock to engage. During the

remainder of 1959 the aircraft was used as and when required by crews from A&AEE, and was also free for display at the Farnborough show.

In June 1960 when XK486 began fuel jettison trials, but after just four days the aircraft crashed after an artificial horizon failure in cloud, which disoriented the pilot. Both crew, G.R.I. Parker and D. Nightingale, ejected safely and the aircraft crashed at Low Hunsley, near the Moor. The airframe was officially written off on 11 July 1961. As a result of this crash the remaining aircraft and the production machines were fitted with a standby artificial horizon.

The Second Prototype

The second airframe, XK487, having made its maiden flight on 27 August 1958, was retained by Blackburn for initial flight trials. Resplendent in a dark blue and white colour scheme, the aircraft was sent to the A&AEE in March 1959 for Controller Airworthiness release trials. The aircraft alternated between C(A) trials and general aerodynamic trials with C Flight AAEE before returning to the Moor for modifications in June 1960. During flight trials with Blackburn a weld in one of the jet pipes failed, which caused

heat damage to the aircraft's structure. Such was the extent of the damage that repairs took until January 1963 to complete, although there was a short delay while the aircraft was modified with a TSR2 radome for trials work. XK487 remained with Blackburn for aerodynamic flight trials to clear the new radome for use, and on 8 May 1963 was dispatched to Ferranti Avionics at Turnhouse where it was employed on Buccaneer and TSR2 radar development.

Flight trials occupied XK487 without incident until 8 May 1965 when the crew encountered an undercarriage retraction problem. The Ferranti Chief Test Pilot, L. J. S. Houston, landed safely and the damage was quickly repaired on site by a team from the manufacturers; XK487 resumed its trials career within days. Hawker Siddeley Aircraft took over the operation of the aircraft in April 1966, HSA having absorbed Blackburn in 1960. By this time XK487 wore an overall white finish and was employed in high-speed flight trials in an effort to improve the type's stability. The aircraft was grounded at RAE Farnborough on 14 December 1966 for ground trials. These continued until 17 May 1967 when the stripped airframe was struck off charge; it was placed on the dump as a fire training aid in July 1968, as which it only survived for two months.

The Third Prototype

One of the few aircraft from this batch to survive was the third, XK488, which made its maiden flight on 31 October 1958. This particular machine was allocated for engine trials, moving from Blackburn in January 1959 to RAE Bedford on C(A) charge. After initial assessment by RAE, XK488 was passed onto De Havilland Engines at Hatfield for Gyron Junior flight trials, arriving in April. 1959 was a busy year for this aircraft as it departed Hatfield for Bedford in June before returning to Blackburn three months later.

The flight test department at Holme-on-Spalding Moor held onto XK488 until April 1960 when DH Engines regained use of the machine; during this period the aircraft was displayed at the 1960 SBAC Farnborough air show. It disgraced itself on 24 July 1961 when, after an aborted take-off, the NA.39 overran the Hatfield runway and ploughed through glasshouses, scattering glass and plants in all directions. The crew D. Lockspeiser and R.A. Buxton, were uninjured. Repairs were carried out by a team from Hawker Siddeley and the aircraft resumed test flying with Bristol Siddeley Engines, later Rolls-Royce, at Filton from May 1965. After use as a structural test specimen and engine installation trials, XK488 was retired in February 1966, having flown some 374 flying hours.

Unlike the other aircraft from this batch, XK488 was retained for display purposes. It was taken by road to the Fleet Air Arm Museum at Yeovilton where it was placed on display, *sans* engines, from July 1967. XK488 is currently stored at the FAAM storage facility at Cobham Hall, where it arrived in November 2001 for refurbishment.

XK490

While much of the development glory went to XK489, some the more important groundwork for weapons development was undertaken by XK490; this was the first NA.39 to feature a rotating bomb door and weapons hard points under the wing. The first flight of this aircraft was undertaken on 23 March 1959 and it joined C Flight at A&AEE in May. At Boscombe Down XK490 was used for short take-off and catapult launching trials, although its sojourn there was short as the aircraft was

bailed back to Blackburn for display at the Paris air show.

In July XK490 returned to A&AEE, who took it to the FAA base at Hal Far, Malta, for air conditioning and 'hot and high' trials before returning to Britain for the SBAC Farnborough show in September. These flight trials revealed that the existing air conditioning system was less than adequate, so a more powerful cold air unit was developed while the equipment in the radio bay was given individual cooling rather than just generally cooling the bay as previously. This reduced the number of hot spots in the radio bay that had been causing localized overheating. Having been looked at by all and sundry, XK490 was returned to C Flight A&AEE for further airfield-based catapult trials prior to carrier trials, although these ceased the following month as the NA.39 was required for initial weapons trials at Boscombe Down.

It was intended that XK490 would be dispatched to America for low-level flight trials, prior to which a full range of flight trials was undertaken including a low-speed handling test. During this test the engines were fully throttled back, reducing the functionality of the boundary layer control. This resulted in the aircraft stalling at an altitude of 10,000ft (3,000m), going into an immediate uncontrollable spin. Although evidence showed that the pilot had tried to recover the aircraft the crew were left with no other option but to eject. Unfortunately at this point the aircraft was inverted and both ejection seats were operating outside their parameters, which resulted in the loss of the crew, test pilot W.H. Alford from the US Office of Naval Research Flying and J.G. Joyce from Blackburn. The aircraft crashed at Ashurst in Hampshire. At the time of its loss XK490 had flown seventy-six hours. The accident was later determined to have happened because the pilot had attempted a manoeuvre outside the aircraft's cleared flight envelope, which caused the aircraft to go out of control.

XK491

The sixth and final machine from this batch, XK491, made its maiden flight on 25 May 1959. This aircraft featured further systems intended for the production version including a retractable refuelling

probe, a full AC electrical system, an autopilot and other avionics involving the flight control system. After initial Blackburn flight trials XK491 was transferred to RAE Bedford where it undertook tanker approaches plus dry probe/drogue trials with a Canberra operated by Flight Refuelling Ltd that was specially equipped with a flight refuelling pack in the bomb bay. After maintenance at the Moor XK491 was returned to Bedford to assess the behaviour of the auto-stabilizer. Further flight refuelling trials were undertaken using a Valiant tanker on 29 October 1959, during which the tanker's drogue broke off, remaining on the end of the probe. Fortunately the crew retained control of the aircraft, making a safe emergency landing at Elvington.

Flight trials resumed after the aircraft had been inspected, XK491 returning to Boscombe Down in February 1962 to investigate autopilot runaway – this was completed within a month. Further development flying was carried out with Blackburn at Holme-on-Spalding-Moor, this being followed three months later by a major inspection. Further autopilot trials resumed in June 1963 at Boscombe Down, these being completed in February 1964. The aircraft was officially struck off charge on 17 September after completing 280 flying hours, being stripped for usable spares soon afterwards. The remains were moved by road to P&EE at Shoeburyness for use in gun-firing trials, which continued until July 1969 when the remains were sold for scrap. The nose avoided all this violence, being moved to Brough for development work in 1976.

The Second Batch

The contract for the second batch of fourteen aircraft had been confirmed in June 1955, all being allocated initially to development flying. The first aircraft, XK523, featured full avionics and navigation systems, the airframe being allocated first to radio trials. It first flew on 29 July 1959 and was being used for manufacturer's trials when, on 3 September, both main wheels burst on landing. The resultant damage was minor as XK523 was delivered to Boscombe Down five days later, where acceptance flying and deck landing trials were undertaken. For the remainder of 1959 the NA.39 alternated between the manufacturers and the various trials organizations, all of whom investigated various aspects of the aircraft's systems.

In January the venue changed to the aircraft carrier HMS *Victorious*, which was cruising in the English Channel. During this phase a full range of arrested landings and catapult launches was undertaken. These trials only lasted a week, after which XK523 was flown to C Flight at A&AEE for a full range of weapons trials, including the dropping of inert bombs. Not only was the rotating bomb door given a full work-out, but the underwing pylons were also tested for correct bomb departure.

One of the first weapons to be cleared during these trials was the enigmatically named 'Target Marker Bomb', which in fact was a dummy *Red Beard* nuclear weapon. This was now the primary weapon for the Buccaneer as the *Green Cheese* guided weapon had been cancelled. The first test weapon arrived at the Moor in December 1960, being kept under armed guard until being required for use. Temperature control and flight trials were the first tests carried out on this weapon; not surprisingly, the large 2,000lb (900kg) bomb created a large amount of turbulence that was cured by the fitting of a special fairing. The weapons system having been cleared, further flights were undertaken to ensure that the radio systems would not interfere with the weapons systems. Further flight trials took the aircraft and the TMB to the ranges at West Freugh, where level release trials were undertaken at speeds between 250–580kt. Having completed the level drops the next task was to undertake toss bombing flights, these including the long toss completed at 540kt with a release angle of 30 degrees and the over-the-shoulder release at an angle of 105 degrees.

After weapons release trials the stresses of deck landing upon the bomb had to be confirmed. As *Red Beard* was a first gener-ation bomb it was vulnerable to accidental detonation due to accidental impact. This made use of this weapon with the Supermarine Scimitar, which mounted it on an underwing pylon, very dangerous so carrier landings in this condition were forbidden. However, the carriage of the bomb in a bomb bay reduced the chances of accidental detonation, allowing the Buccaneer to land on an aircraft carrier with the bomb on board.

Throughout the latter part of 1961 XK523 divided its time between Blackburn and the A&AEE, being used in various trials mainly concentrated upon deck landing performance both on land and sea. In February 1962 the aircraft was transferred to West Freugh, Scotland, for live bomb dropping over the range there. This continued until July when the NA.39 returned to Blackburn to undergo a complete overhaul that was completed in January 1963. After initial flight trials XK523 resumed its regime of bomb bay door weapons trials these being followed by trips to A&AEE with a side diversion to West Freugh for further bomb dropping in July.

It was during this sequence of flights that problems were encountered with a bomb mounted on the rotating door. In this condition severe buffeting was encoun-tered, caused by airflow turbulence between the weapon and the door mount-ing. After much trial and error a series of bomb door fairings was developed that cured this problem. Multiple weapon releases of smaller stores also caused prob-lems as after release the individual bombs pitched and jostled for position, causing inconsistent strike patterns. Alterations to the bomb carrier mounting angles and to the release intervals overcame this fault. Overall, the weapons release trials occu-pied XK523 and other aircraft from the development fleet for sixty-six months instead of the forty-three months allo-cated.

A change from dispensing bombs began in February 1963 when XK523 joined A&AEE for trials of the autopilot, avion-ics, navigation systems, radio and handling, and in-depth testing of the brake units. XK523 returned to Blackburn in May 1963 for a refit although the aircraft's flight time after this maintenance was short as it was grounded in August. After slightly more than 215 hours of flight time, XK523 was dismantled for use as a source of spares for XK525. Having given up its useful spares the remains of XK523 were delivered to P&EE at Shoeburyness for use as a target.

The second aircraft of this batch, XK524, undertook its maiden flight on 4 April 1960 and was delivered to Farnborough for catapult and arrestor gear testing. For eight months up to June 1961 the aircraft was with the manufacturers for upgrading to a standard close to that intended for the production machines. The following month the NA.39 was at Bedford for minimum launching speed evaluation, this being completed in October 1961. These flights were termi-nated prematurely when an engine-driven hydraulic pump failed, causing shards of metal to scatter throughout the hydraulic system. The result was an aircraft on the ground while the hydraulic system was stripped and flushed clean.

Flight refuelling, for which a dummy probe was installed, was the next role for XK524, the tanker aircraft being Scimitars and Sea Vixens. Arrestor equipment was used for some of landings to evaluate the shock resistance of the radar system and its scanner, avionics being especially vulnera-ble to such shocks. XK524 was one of this batch fitted with strain gauging equip-ment, which was brought into play in December 1962. During these flights general handling was investigated, flutter trials were carried out and handling with external stores was undertaken, all results being recorded for further evaluation. Having completed this aspect of the devel-opment programme, XK524 flew to Boscombe Down in December 1963 where further refuelling probe trials were under-taken, although they were limited to dry probe contacts only. It was during these flights that the radome was damaged by the drogue of a Valiant tanker; fortunately the damage was fairly superficial, though the opportunity was taken to return the aircraft to Blackburn where a full refit was undertaken and Bullpup missile carriage and control equipment was installed.

Bullpup trials were undertaken at West Freugh and RAE Bedford during the early part of 1964, the aircraft returning to the manufacturers in August. At the Moor XK524 undertook high-lift trials, which ended abruptly on 13 May 1965. The aircraft was flying with extended-chord ailerons and with its flaps down. In this condition the NA.39 was flying straight and level under increasing acceleration, during which the nose-down attitude increased, the pilot applying increasing back pressure on the control column to no avail. Eventually the tailplane stalled, causing the pilot to lose control, at which point the crew, P. Millett and J. Harris, ejected safely. The aircraft crashed near Land of Nod in the Moor airfield circuit, being formally written off on 8 October 1965.

The third aircraft in this batch, XK525, made its first flight on 15 July 1960 and was delivered to RAE Bedford in September for catapult and arrestor trials. The Controller (Aircraft) took XK525 on charge on 7 October, initially for dummy drop tank trials. A return to Blackburn followed as the aircraft was required for development flying, this being completed in May 1961 when A&AEE acquired XK525 for pilot conversion flying. This lasted until 29 June when XK525 was transferred to West Freugh for weapons trials that lasted until 30 March 1962 when the aircraft had to make an emergency landing after partial hydraulic system failure.

After repairs the aircraft resumed weapon release trials, which continued unabated until 7 February 1964 when XK525 suffered complete failure of the undercarriage hydraulic system. Fortunately for both crew and aircraft a safe belly landing was, made although repairs took until June to complete. It was during this period that wing tip cameras were mounted in special fairings to record future bomb-dropping trials. A return to flying at Boscombe Down began on 2 June, this stopping on 10 August when, after a low-altitude bombing run that required a sharp pull-up, the aircraft's canopy was forced open. The damage required extensive repairs, which kept the aircraft on the ground until September 1964.

XK525 was a very unlucky aircraft as on 23 November 1964, while undergoing handling trials with a full load of underwing stores, it suffered an instrument failure. During the resulting heavy landing the port main wheel tyre burst on landing. After repairs and the installation of production-standard weapons delivery systems, XK525 resumed flying with both Farnborough and West Freugh in April 1964. A transfer to Boscombe Down followed in December 1971 for general handling duties, these continuing until March 1973 when the aircraft was withdrawn from use. Spares recovery followed before the remains were moved to West Freugh for ground trials. Once these were completed another use was found for XK525 – being a target at P&EE Shoeburyness.

One of the most heavily modified NA.39s was XK526, which first flew on 29 August 1960 and was handed over to C(A) control in December. Three days before its first flight the name Buccaneer had been allocated to the type after a company competition – those that failed to make the grade included ARNA ('Another Royal Navy Aircraft'), although other unofficial ones stuck, such

as 'Banana' and 'Brick'. After initial test flying the aircraft was used for instrumentation trials after modification before joining A&AEE in February 1961. The Boscombe Down team took XK526 to Gibraltar for overseas engineering evaluation and trials of the air conditioning. These ended in April when the aircraft returned to Blackburn to be prepared for tropical trials in June 1961, the aircraft being moved by ship to Tengah, Singapore. These trials were completed successfully in September and XK526 returned to Britain soon afterwards.

Further flight trials occupied XK526 until November 1962 after which it returned to the manufacturers for conversion to Buccaneer S.2 standard. The original Gyron Junior engines were replaced by a pair of Rolls-Royce RB.168 Spey engines and the earlier DC electrical system was replaced by an AC system. Initial engine runs in its new guise were undertaken in April 1963 and XK526 made its first flight as an S.2 on 17 May 1963, the crew being D. J. Whitehead and J. Pearson. RAE Bedford acquired the aircraft once initial flight trials were completed XK526 was returned for further evaluation flying. Low-speed handling and

XK526 on an early test flight at low level, resplendent in a white anti-flash finish. This aircraft was converted to the first Buccaneer S.2 prototype during 1962–3. BBA Collection

minimum launching speeds were evaluated between July and September 1964, after which the aircraft was returned to Blackburn for air intake turbulence trials, these continuing until March 1965. Having completed the intake trials, XK526 was allocated to flutter tests during which the flaps were damaged, although the crew were able to make a safe landing.

With the minor flap damage repaired, XK526 resumed flying and joined A&AEE for night familiarization flying in August 1966. Having introduced new crew members to the NA.39, XK526 was returned to the manufacturers during November 1966 for modifications including a modified bomb door. Handling trials for this new equipment began the following month and continued until the aircraft was grounded in September 1967 after a bird strike.

The repairs took longer than expected and XK526 did not fly again in earnest until 12 June 1972 when it was flown to Marshalls of Cambridge, later Marshalls Aerospace, for preparation for the aircraft's new role as the avionics test vehicle for the forthcoming MRCA (Multi-Role Combat Aircraft), later to become the Panavia Tornado. These modifications were quite extensive and the aircraft did not fly again until 15 January 1976. Having completed initial flight trials, XK526 was first flown by crews

from RAE before moving to the Royal Radar Establishment at Pershore, which undertook extensive trials of the MRCA's avionics and projected sideways-looking airborne radar system. After further test flying at RAE Bedford, XK526 was withdrawn from use in March 1980. It was sent to RAF Honington, ostensibly for battle damage repair usage, but this decision was changed and XK526 became the station's gate guard in February 1983, a duty it performs to this day.

Following on from XK526 came XK527, which made its maiden flight on 12 October 1960. After a short period of company test flying the aircraft was dispatched to the FAA base at Hal Far, Malta, arriving on 2 November. Landing and catapult trials aboard HMS *Ark Royal* in the Mediterranean were carried out over the following three weeks, after which the NA.39 was sent to Boscombe Down. General handling occupied XK527 until April 1962 when the airframe was dismantled into its major components and moved by road to Brough for conversion into the second Buccaneer S.2 prototype.

XK527 undertook its maiden flight in its new guise on 19 August 1963 and was retained by the manufacturers for trials flying until dispatched to Boscombe Down in May 1964. The team from Boscombe Down took the aircraft to RAF Idris for

tropical trials prior to the granting of a C(A) release. Upon its return to Britain, the use of XK527 was shared by A&AEE and the manufacturers before it passed to Rolls-Royce at their base at Hucknall for engine trials that included measuring the effects of crosswinds upon the later versions intakes. These being completed satisfactorily, XK527 was shipped to the US Navy base at Pensacola in July 1965 for further tropical trials. This jaunt in the sunshine was completed a month later, A&AEE bringing the aircraft home for further test flying.

A move to Hawker Siddeley at Brough occurred in October 1966 where XK527 was prepared for use as the Martel missile trials aircraft. This modification was completed by November 1967, the aircraft being moved by road to Driffield to undertake its first flight in this guise. Having completed its manufacturers test flying, XK527 was dispatched to Boscombe Down in August 1968 for Martel test flying. Over the following seven years XK527 was used for various aspects of Buccaneer flight trials before arriving at RAE Bedford in April 1975 for arrestor gear trials. These were completed in September, when the airframe was returned to the manufacturers for radio altimeter trials and *Pave Spike* targeting pod trials. Having thoroughly investigated the functionality of *Pave Spike*, XK527 was then modified for the

XK527 seen soon after conversion into the second prototype S.2. This aircraft was used for much of the S.2 development programme before retiring from flying in 1982. BBA Collection

carriage of laser-guided bombs, this role lasting until August 1982. Originally the airframe was retained at Brough as a ground systems trainer before being reduced to spare parts; the majority was scrapped except for the nose, which now resides with a private owner in North Wales.

One of the more unlucky aircraft from this second batch was XK528, which made its maiden flight on 21 November 1960. It first went to Boscombe Down for C(A) trials, these continuing until May 1961 when XK528 returned to the manufacturers for modifications, which included the fitment of the *Blue Pencil* ECM system. A return to A&AEE followed in July 1961 so that C(A) release trials could continue. During these flights doubts were expressed about the efficiency of the radio bay cooling system and XK528 was returned to Brough so that an improved system could be installed. Four months later the NA.39 had returned to flying with A&AEE who put the aircraft through thorough engineering and avionic trials, followed by a flight to RAF Idris for further tropical testing. Having completed these flights successfully, the aircraft went to Brough for maintenance, returning to Boscombe Down in August 1962 for further avionics and armament trials.

Bomb dropping trials began at West Freugh in May 1963, although they ceased after twelve days when a weapons release ejector unit misfired causing damage to the airframe. Repairs kept XK528 on the ground until August 1964, the aircraft resuming its weapons trials at West Freugh almost immediately. Further modification work was undertaken at the manufacturers from October 1964 until June 1965, by which time the aircraft was bedecked with Day-Glo stripes on the fin and wing tips. After test flying with RAE Farnborough the aircraft flew to Boscombe Down for further bomb dropping trials. It was during one of these flights, while undertaking a simulated LABS (Low-Altitude Bombing System) attack that XK528 broke up and exploded over the Luce Bay bombing range. The crew, Flt Lt W. C. Mackinson and Flt Lt C. M. Pridmore, were killed. The airframe was declared a write off on 30 June 1966.

The seventh machine in this batch, XK529, undertook its maiden flight on 2 January 1961, moving to Boscombe Down a week later. After ten days of familiarization flying it was transferred to RAE Bedford for deck landing trials, during which the arrestor hook mountings were damaged; this required repairs by Blackburn that kept the aircraft grounded for five days.

In August 1961 XK529 joined HMS *Hermes*. During catapult launching trials on 31 August the boundary layer control system failed on take-off, causing the aircraft to assume a severe nose-up attitude. In this condition XK529 was unflyable: it stalled and crashed into the sea just ahead of the aircraft carrier, killing the crew, Lt Cdr O. Brown [RN] and T. D. Dunn. The aircraft was struck off charge that same day.

The final machine of the development batch was XK536, which first flew on 6 December 1961. It moved to RAE Bedford in March 1962 for land-based catapult trials. During one of these launches the starboard tyre failed just prior to take-off, the resultant failure of the hub injuring some of the personnel attending the aircraft. After repairs XK536 moved to Boscombe Down in May 1962 to undertake a short work-up prior to carrier trials aboard HMS *Hermes*, these starting on 16 May. A return to Blackburn followed, the aircraft being prepared for armament trials; during this period fully functional underwing 250gal fuel tanks were installed for testing. In December 1962 XK536 returned to Boscombe Down for preparation for further aircraft carrier flight trials aboard HMS *Ark Royal* in the English Channel.

Having successfully completed these trials the aircraft returned to Blackburn for maintenance before resuming its test career with A&AEE in May 1963. This phase included handling of the aircraft with external loads both from land and sea, a task inherited from XK529. The aircraft carrier used for these trials was HMS *Victorious* and it was during one of these flights that the starboard undercarriage leg failed to fully retract, necessitating an emergency diversion to dry land. Repairs completed, XK536 resumed its flight trials aboard the *Victorious*. With these completed the aircraft was employed at RAE Bedford for bomb bay fuel tank testing, and trials with the air-portable starting pod.

After completing the trials programme XK536 joined the Fleet Air Arm's 736 Squadron at Lossiemouth in November 1965. In naval hands the aircraft seemed prone to accidents. On 14 December there was a runaway problem with the tailplane actuator, this being followed by collapse of the port main undercarriage oleo on landing on 8 March 1966. A hydraulic systems failure on 20 September resulted in the aircraft landing on the emergency systems. In October of that same year XK536 had to make another emergency landing at night after the port engine failed. Although the problem was supposedly rectified, the same engine caused another emergency three weeks later on 3 November. The port engine having been replaced, it was the turn of the starboard engine to misbehave, the generator failing just eight days later, which again required a precautionary landing.

The generator problem having been sorted out, XK536 embarrassed itself again on 25 November when the primary hydraulic systems failed, requiring yet another precautionary landing with control from the emergency systems. Further hydraulic problems afflicted the aircraft nineteen days before Christmas, and this time the crew elected to use the airfield's arrestor gear to stop the aircraft, as the available braking power was limited.

The following six months passed without much of significance, but in June 1967 the inlet guide vanes on the starboard engine malfunctioned, which caused erratic power output. As the aircraft was fully fuelled the crew were faced with the tedious task of flying round the circuit, juggling with the starboard throttle, while excess fuel was dumped. With the starboard engine fault repaired XK536 took to the skies again, but an emergency return to base was needed on 3 July 1967 after a wing fold warning light came on during a shallow dive over the Tain range; the problem was traced to a maladjusted microswitch.

The starboard engine again caused problems on 12 December 1967 when the starboard intake fairing came adrift, which required that the engine be shut down as a precautionary measure. After repairs the aircraft resumed its trials flying with 736 Squadron, though this came to an end in January 1968 when A&AEE reclaimed it. In August XK536 returned to Lossiemouth for further trails flying, which continued until it was struck off charge on 28 November 1969. Eventually the remains were divided between the P&EE's Shoeburyness and Pendine ranges, where it was used for target practice.

XK531 at Lossiemouth. It wears the 680/LM coding of 700Z Squadron, the Intensive Flight Trials Unit for the Buccaneer. By this time many of production aircraft were sporting dark sea grey upper surfaces. BBA Collection

The IFTU

The last pure test vehicle was XK530, which first flew on 15 February 1961 and arrived at Lossiemouth and the nascent Initial Flight Trials Unit (IFTU) on 6 March. At the completion of this visit XK530 was officially taken on charge by the C(A) on 4 April 1961, being used by both Blackburn and RAE Bedford for deck landing trials centring around the vibration proofing of the installed equipment. A temporary halt to proceedings occurred at the beginning of August when the aircraft was grounded for repairs to the arrestor hook mountings. Further delays centred around the engines, which were now at Phase 3 production standard, featuring turbine cooling. Unfortunately a microswitch installed as part of this system, which indicated whether the cooling was engaged or not, had a tendency to deliver false warnings in the cockpit. Originally the microswitch was located in such a position that to replace it an engine had to be removed. As this was impractical in operational service, the decision was taken to relocate the microswitch so that engines could remain in situ when the switch was changed.

Flying resumed on 17 August with the A&AEE taking charge of the NA.39 for landing trials aboard HMS Hermes in the English Channel. Ten days later XK530 was allocated to in-flight refuelling trials, which continued until late March 1962. A return to RAE Bedford followed so that the crew and aircraft could prepare for

further trials aboard HMS Hermes. Between 17–22 May 1962 XK530 was aboard HMS Hermes for deck handling, landing and catapult trials, after which the aircraft returned to Blackburn for modifications to the armament system.

Prior to undertaking Bullpup missile and nuclear weapons trials in September, XK530 was used for Blue Parrot radar vibration absorbency trials. Weapons handling started in earnest in early June 1963, the Bullpup being the first weapon tested. This did not pass without incident as at least one missile fell off during these flights. Eventually these trials were completed, XK530 flying north to the weapons range at West Freugh for trials with the 2,000lb MC bomb, these drop trials continuing until April 1964 when the NA.39 returned to the manufacturers. Hawker Siddeley, in conjunction with RAE and A&AEE, continued to use the aircraft for weapons development trials until August 1971.

RAE Farnborough was the aircraft's next venue, where the engines and other useful components were removed to provide support for XK525. The remains were transferred by road to RAE Bedford for use as a dummy load for catapult launches and crash barrier trials. Having survived these violent machinations, XK530 was put up for disposal and purchased by the Nene Valley Aviation Society. However, this organization failed to collect it, leaving the airframe open to burning during an exercise that finally finished it off.

The remaining five aircraft from this

development batch each spent at least a part of their working lives with the Fleet Air Arm. The first of these machines, XK531, made its first flight on 7 May 1961 and moved to Boscombe Down on 27 June for familiarization flying prior to joining the IFTU, coded 680/LM. The IFTU became 700Z Squadron at the beginning of August. By the end of the month the aircraft was in trouble as the port undercarriage began leaking hydraulic fluid, resulting in a precautionary landing. Having been repaired, XK531 was in trouble again in the middle of October and had to make another precautionary landing. A similar set of circumstances overtook XK531 on 2 November, requiring yet another landing under emergency conditions.

Although one might think that these defects would damage the aircraft's reputation, the flight trials units existed for the express purpose of discovering these faults. Further problems that arose included wing fold and undercarriage warning lights that flickered during flight and under some circumstances indicated that a major hydraulic component had become unlocked. Curing these problems required ground functional tests to ensure that the microswitches made a more positive contact.

In September 1962 XK531 suffered a kind of fault that seemed to plague these early machines: the starboard engine inlet guide vanes jammed in the open position causing a loss of thrust, the end result being an emergency landing on one engine. Another problem that required further investigation was the tendency for the main wheel hubs to disintegrate under sideways loading: in September 1962 XK531's port wheel failed, causing minor damage to the airframe.

Having completed its time with the trials unit, XK531 was transferred to 809 Squadron – also at Lossiemouth – on 15 January 1963, with whom it was initially coded 680/LM, changing to 227/LM in early 1964. Although a few minor niggles afflicted the aircraft while it was being operated by 809 Squadron, none kept the aircraft on the ground for an excessive period. A return to Brough followed in early 1965, this keeping the aircraft grounded until February 1966.

After its overhaul XK531 returned to Lossiemouth and 736 Squadron, with whom it was coded 643/LM. This was a training unit, which role brings its own problems. The first concerned the fairing for a rocket projectile pod that failed to clear the aircraft correctly and struck the wing, causing minor damage. Engines also continued to cause problems: the starboard engine gave a fire warning indication during a flight in August 1966 that required a precautionary landing, this being followed two months later by another precautionary landing when the port engine started vibrating, a possible indication of blade failure. Further problems to beset the aircraft included a nose wheel steering failure, fuel leaks and further starboard engine failures.

After a career training both naval and air force pilots, XK531 was retired at Lossiemouth on 3 October 1967, being moved to Honington for gate guard duties in February 1968. A transfer to British Aerospace at Harwarden followed in 1974 and in December 1984 XK531 was delivered there Chinook helicopter to Winterbourne Gunner and the NBC school.

The next aircraft to join 700Z Squadron was XK532, which made its maiden flight on 31 May 1961 and moved to Lossiemouth in August, coded 681/LM. During its early weeks there it suffered undercarriage retraction problems; this was followed by a port tyre bursting on touchdown in wet conditions that put the aircraft into the grass, making the recovery team's job very difficult. After minor repairs and the required inspections XK532 resumed flying, only to make a premature return to Lossiemouth in February 1962 when a wing fold indicating light flickered. A problem that would afflict the Buccaneer fleet throughout its early life raised its head in November when problems with the tailplane occurred – another precautionary landing was needed.

With repairs effected XK532 resumed flying although its new operator was 809 Squadron, with whom it was coded 228/LM. A transfer to the manufacturers took place in March 1964, XK532 undergoing maintenance and modification prior to joining the RAE at West Freugh for weapons trials in August 1964. These were completed by June 1965, the aircraft returning to Lossiemouth and the training unit, 736 Squadron. During a flight on 9 December 1965 a serious hydraulic failure led to the undercarriage, flaps and the arrestor being lowered by emergency systems, the aircraft making a successful landing. XK532 continued flying with 736 Squadron before retiring in June 1966. After a period as a training aid the airframe ended up as the gate guard at Lossiemouth in 1984; it has since moved onto Inverness Airport in 2003 for preservation.

The least successful of this batch of machines was XK533, which undertook its first flight on 16 June 1961 before joining 700Z Squadron at Lossiemouth in November, with whom it was coded 682/LM. Twelve months later, XK533 was diverted on loan to Boscombe Down returning to navy hands in November 1961. A few days after its return the aircraft suffered a surge in the starboard engine whilst practising formation flying. With the defective engine shut down, the aircraft made a successful precautionary landing at Lossiemouth. In January 1963 XK533 transferred to 809 Squadron, but on 10 October it suffered a double engine flame-out after a fuel feed problem. Although the crew tried every method to relight the engines, the problem with the fuel flow system left them with no option but to eject. The aircraft crashed into the Moray Firth, but both crew escaped safely and were picked fairly quickly by a search and rescue helicopter.

Buccaneer S.1 XK532 was allocated to 700Z Squadron as 681/LM before service with the other units at Lossiemouth. After retirement XK532 became the gate guard at Lossiemouth, although it has since been purchased by the Fresson Trust at Inverness Airport. BBA Collection

After its first flight on 19 August 1961, the first people to see XK534 were the West German Navy, for whom the aircraft would be displayed at Schleswig on 25 August. Although they were impressed by the NA.39, it lost out to the Lockheed F-104G Starfighter in the competition to provide West Germany with a maritime strike aircraft. Having returned to Britain, XK534 was next displayed at the SBAC Farnborough show in September. Another trip to Germany followed on 22 September, the location being Fürstenfeldbrück and the hosts being the Luftwaffe.

The Fleet Air Arm finally acquired the aircraft in November when 700Z Squadron started to operate it, coded 683/LM. The aircraft flew without incident until early February 1962 when the port engine failed, requiring a precautionary return to base. After repairs XK534 resumed flying, though it was grounded again in May 1962 after suffering a loss of control in inverted

flight: having regained a measure of control the crew decided that the safest way to reach the ground without further incident was to make a flapless landing. Investigation and rectification of the control problem kept XK534 on the ground until January 1963 when, after the obligatory shakedown flights, it was delivered to 809 Squadron, also at Lossiemouth, with whom it was coded 230/LM.

Incident-free flying continued until early September 1963 when the aircraft suffered a major hydraulic systems failure – an emergency diversion to Leuchars was the outcome, though repairs were completed within days. A further hydraulic failure afflicted XK534 at the end of August 1964 when the port engine-driven pump failed, necessitating yet another emergency return to base. The port engine in this aircraft must have been jinxed as the compressor then stalled in a turn, although on this occasion a normal approach and landing was possible. After

this the engine was removed for further investigation, being replaced by a serviceable unit. Having spent ten days on the ground XK534 resumed flying on 10 October, only to suffer a nose wheel retraction problem that again required a hasty landing.

Although the port engine had been replaced the installation seemed to have a permanent problem: the fire warning illuminated in January 1965, followed by an inlet guide vane fault in March. The engine troubles of XK534 continued in May 1965 when the port engine suffered power fluctuations: again, this required a diversionary landing. By this time the aircraft was being operated by 736 Squadron in the training role. Two months later XK534 was diving through 25,000ft (7,600m) when the fire warning light illuminated, leading to another single-engine precautionary landing at Lossiemouth. After investigation the aircraft was returned to flying status, only to experience undercarriage retraction problems on take-off which yet again required a premature return to the ground. XK534 with its unreliable port engine installation finally ceased flying in August 1966, being reassigned to ground training duties that it performed until finally struck off charge for scrapping in March 1969.

The last of the aircraft allocated to the IFTU was XK535, which undertook its maiden flight on 23 November 1961. Initially used by the manufacturers, XK535 joined the Fleet Air Arm in January 1962 when it arrived at Lossiemouth for use by 700Z Squadron, with whom it was coded 684/LM. This was another aircraft plagued by engine troubles: the port engine malfunctioned in February, the starboard following in March. After rectification by Blackburn the aircraft resumed flying, only for the main hydraulic systems to fail and therefore a precautionary landing in June 1962. XK535 was selected as the display aircraft for the 1962 SBAC Farnborough show and it was during a pratice flight for this display that the aircraft was lost. During a steep approach prior to a slow flypast XK535 entered an uncontrollable spin that could not be recovered. The observer attempted to eject but the seat was outside its parameters; the pilot failed to eject and both crew were killed. Obviously a write off the NA.39 was cleared from the inventory on 18 August 1962.

The 632/LM coding indicates that XK532 was on the strength of 736 Squadron, the Buccaneer training unit based at Lossiemouth, when this photo was taken. BBA Collection

After service with 700Z and 809 Squadrons, XK532 was flown by 736 Squadron for training duties before being retired in July 1966. BBA Collection

XK533 flying off a snow-covered Scottish coast, wearing the coding of 700Z Squadron. During its time in service the aircraft was loaded out for various trials, including tropical testing at RAF Idris. BBA Collection

XK533 sits on the end of the Lossiemouth runway, waiting to undertake a pairs take-off. The 682/LM coding indicates that the Buccaneer is on the strength of 700Z Squadron. The aircraft was lost on 10 October 1963 after both engines flamed out. Fortunately the crew ejected to safety, while the wreckage was recovered. The cockpit is currently located at East Fortune. BBA Collection

XK534 was the aircraft displayed to the West German Navy in August 1961. By November, XK534 was on the strength of 700Z Squadron as 683/LM, although in this view it sports the 'Buccaneer' name on the air intake for that year's Farnborough air show. BBA Collection

A flying contrast of Buccaneers as representatives of both versions fly in formation for the camera. XN953 represents the earlier mark, while an unidentified prototype S.2 is in the foreground. BBA Collection

Buccaneer S.1 XK535 was initially operated by 700Z Squadron as 684/LM and is seen here in the white anti-flash scheme. It was lost in a fatal crash on 18 August 1962 after just 152 flying hours. BBA Collection

Work on the S.2 Starts

The NA.39 Buccaneer S.1 was finally given its C of A release in July 1961 when the flight trials officially came to an end, although this process had taken 18 months longer than originally planned. The Blackburn team now turned their attention to using some of the development aircraft for the next version, the S.2. The requirement for this version had arisen due to the lack of thrust of the Gyron Junior, which was only just adequate for the task. The NA.39 carrier launch trials at RAE Thurleigh in 1959 had revealed just how marginal was the available thrust in these early aircraft, and now the Gyron Junior was to be replaced.

The replacement chosen was the Rolls-Royce Spey. The major change to the airframe centred around the engine installation, which required a whole new engine bay and intake assembly. Flight trials were completed in 78 launches instead of the expected 100, while some of the carrier qualifications were carried out aboard the aircraft carrier USS *Lexington*.

During this sojourn with the US Navy over 100 launches and flights were made, which was estimated to simulate 115 hours of low-level flying in rough, turbulent weather. Flight trials having been completed, production of the new version could begin quickly. In fact, so confident were the Admiralty that the Spey-powered version of the Buccaneer was the version that would fulfil their long-term strike needs, that the first contract was issued for production to Blackburn on 8 January 1962, before the S.1 had even entered service.

The Buccaneer Joins the Navy

Although the pre-production aircraft had suffered various failures, these machines served their purpose as they helped both the Fleet Air Arm and Blackburn to discover and rectify the aircraft's problems before production aircraft entered service. The first production batch of forty aircraft was ordered in September 1959 under Contract No.KC/2F/05/CB.9(a), the aircraft being serialled XN922 to XN935 and XN948 to XN973.

XN922

The first aircraft from this batch, XN922, made its maiden flight from the Moor on 23 January 1962. It remained at Blackburn under the auspices of the C(A) for trials with the production flight refuelling probe, this occupying the greater part of February – there was a slight interruption when the Buccaneer was displayed to the First Sea Lord, Lord Carrington. Having completed the probe trials, XN922 was transferred to Boscombe Down for engineering and tropical trials. It was during

these trials that the aircraft's operational life ended in tragedy. On 5 July 1962 the crew attempted an unblown take-off with the switches incorrectly set for a blown take-off. Part way down the runway with an asymmetric load of a 1,000lb bomb under one wing, the Buccaneer swung violently off the runway, one of the wings was torn off and the aircraft ran into an office block. Two civilians were killed in the office block, the pilot was injured and the observer killed.

XN923

The second machine, XN923, was delivered to the IFTU, 700Z Flight, part of 700 Squadron, in May 1962, having made its first flight on 11 March. This was the only Buccaneer S.1 allocated to the IFTU: the rest of the Flight's aircraft came from the pre-production batch. Having completed its time with the IFTU XN923 was returned to the Aircraft Handling Unit at Lossiemouth for maintenance work, transferring south to A&AEE in July for

clearance trials aimed at clearing the S.1 for deck landing, and for tropical trials at RAF Idris. Active flight refuelling trials were the next task for XN923, these starting in December 1962, using a Sea Vixen based at Boscombe Down as the tanker aircraft. These were carried out successfully, allowing the Buccaneer to complete the type's deck landing trials aboard HMS *Ark Royal* in the English Channel during February 1963.

While the Buccaneer was frequently seen with specially designed fuel tanks under their wings, these were not permanent fixtures as is often supposed. Flight trials of these tanks were undertaken at RAE Bedford during July, this being followed by further deck landings aboard the aircraft carrier HMS *Victorious*. For the remainder of 1963 and the greater majority of 1964 XN923 alternated between the manufacturers and the various trials organizations. At the former various modifications were undertaken while at the latter clearances were obtained for the external fuel tanks, napalm bomb carriage and the flight refuelling probe.

Buccaneer S.1 XN923 first saw service with 700Z Squadron at Lossiemouth before being transferred to the RAE for trials work. After withdrawal in 1974, the airframe was used for various ground trials before ending up at the Charlwood Collection in Surrey during 1990. BBA Collection

Buccaneer S.1 XN924 of 809 Squadron, with whom it was coded 220/LM, is caught on film as its wings spread to fully open. After serving in the front line the aircraft was later used by 736 Squadron, with whom it remained until withdrawn from use in 1965. BBA Collection

The following year XN923 was at Bedford for rocket-powered ejection seat testing, trials with a longer arrestor hook – this including the 'bounce' test of the hook – and aft centre of gravity trials. Flights with the wing fold door covers removed followed, as these were proving problematical in service. In good, undamaged condition they would move in conjunction with the wing as it folded, but once slightly distorted the doors exhibited a tendency to catch the wing as it folded, causing damage to both. The flight trials were required to determine if there was a detrimental affect upon the aerodynamic behaviour of the Buccaneer from removing the doors. Fortunately no obvious problems were encountered, so both versions of the Buccaneer eventually had their doors removed.

In August 1966 the aircraft was withdrawn from flying, being used at Farnborough for various weapons trials. However the grounding order was later rescinded and XN923 started flying again in September 1969, moving to West Freugh for weapons trials twelve months later. These were completed in June 1973, the aircraft being stored soon after. A transfer to A&AEE took place in May 1974, withdrawal from service occurring upon arrival. After use as a ground trials vehicle the remains of XN923 were purchased by the Charlwood Collection, Surrey, in 1980.

XN924

XN924, the third Buccaneer S.1, undertook its maiden flight on 31 March 1962, being bailed back to the manufacturers so that the aircraft could be displayed at the Hannover show in April. Back in Britain, the Handling Squadron at Boscombe Down became the operators of XN924. On 16 June it suffered a port engine failure that required a return to base for a single-engined landing, fortunately completed without incident. After repair XN924 finally joined the Navy arriving at Lossiemouth for 801 Squadron in August 1962. Its sojourn in Scotland was short as

the Buccaneer was required for flight refuelling trials at A&AEE in October. These were completed five months later, the aircraft returning to Blackburn for modification work. In August 1963 XN924 rejoined the Navy, this time with 809 Squadron.

Front-line service occupied XN924 until March 1965 when the aircraft was transferred to the second-line Buccaneer training unit, 736 Squadron, also based at Lossiemouth. This change of duties came about as the more potent Buccaneer S.2 had entered service thus the Admiralty decided that the earlier version had one more role left that of a training vehicle.

The 220/LM code signifies that XN924 was on the strength of 809 Squadron at Lossiemouth when this photo was taken. During its operational career it also served with 801 and 736 Squadrons. BBA Collection

After training both FAA and RAF aircrew XN924 would finally be retired in July 1965. Withdrawn from flying duties the Buccaneer would become a ground instructional aid remaining in this role until March 1967. No longer required XN924 was put up for tender ending up in an Elgin scrapyard by mid 1971.

XN925

XN924 was joined at Lossiemouth by XN925, which had first flown on 27 April 1962. It joined 801 Squadron, which formed as the first operational Buccaneer unit in July 1962. During its early months of service XN925 was plagued by various serious defects. The first would occur in August when the port engine inlet guide vane malfunctioned. Having fixed this, the squadron's engineers were faced with a malfunctioning starboard engine, which had surged in flight.

Four months later XN925 was in trouble again after the port flying control hydraulic system failed in flight, although the Buccaneer made a safe landing after some careful flying by the pilot. Then in January 1963 the port engine hydraulic pump failed in flight. For reasons best known to the Fleet Air Arm and Blackburn it was decided to transport XN925 to the manufacturers for modification work instead of replacing the defective pump, although the decision may have been forced on both parties if traces of metal shards had been discovered in the system filters. After an eventful road and sea journey the Buccaneer finally arrived at Blackburn, where modifications and rectification work was undertaken.

Flying resumed in January 1964, the Buccaneer flying north to Lossiemouth and joining 809 Squadron in February.

Over the following two years XN925 seemed to have a penchant for hydraulic failures, the first occurring in March 1964 when a seal failed in the port aileron PFCU; had the crew not shut down the PFCU, the rate of venting of the fluid would have drained the entire hydraulic system in minutes. After replacement of the wing PFCU package and the inevitable sequence of functional checks the Buccaneer resumed its flying career, only to suffer the failure of a hydraulic pump in June which caused a fluid surge that in turn damaged other components. A successful landing was made by the crew, the Buccaneer entering the hangar at Lossiemouth for repair.

These completed, XN925 resumed flying only this time the operator was the second-line training unit, 736 Squadron, the aircraft going on inventory on 17 June 1966. However, just thirteen days later the aircraft suffered a major hydraulic leak that required the use of the emergency system to return to base safely. Flying resumed after a short period of rectification, but after just two months XN925 had to make a quick return to earth after yet another hydraulic pump failure. The Buccaneer was successfully repaired and then joined 803 Squadron, the Buccaneer headquarters squadron at Lossiemouth, with whom it flew, apparently without incident, until being grounded in October 1969. After a period in the ground instructional role XN925 was eventually sent to Catterick where it is currently used for special emergency procedures training.

XN926

XN926, the fifth Buccaneer S.1, started its career in a most inauspicious way by suffering an undercarriage collapse whilst awaiting its maiden flight from the Moor on 26 March 1962. It took some time to arrange movement, so XN926 did not return to Brough until 9 April. After investigation of the undercarriage failure and associated repairs, XN926 finally made its maiden flight on 11 May. Having undertaken the required tranche of manufacturer's shakedown flights the Buccaneer was cleared to depart the Moor for Lossiemouth, but soon after take-off inlet guide vane (IGV) failed, requiring the aircraft to make a quick return to base. After further repairs the Buccaneer finally made it to Scotland in June. Pre-issue acceptance checks followed, after which XN926 was delivered to 801 Squadron a few weeks later. XN926 was in trouble again in September after an engine failure caused a premature return to base. Birds were the aircraft's next problem when, during a low level navigation exercise in December 1962, the port engine ingested a bird at low level, this too requiring an emergency return to base, which was completed without further incident.

A transfer to 809 Squadron at Lossiemouth took place in May 1965 after a trip to Blackburn for modifications. One of the aircraft's first tasks was to undertake flight refuelling trials; during these the drogue struck the radome on at least two occasions, both requiring a return to base and minor repairs. Undercarriage problems again beset XN926 when the starboard undercarriage collapsed on landing at Lossiemouth. The ensuing slide saw the Buccaneer travelling across the grass for some considerable distance, the pilot being unable to keep the aircraft on the runway. Fortunately grass causes slightly less damage to airframes than tarmac, so the overall damage was minor and the aircraft was ready for service again on 16 December 1964 after a few days of rectification.

As with other Buccaneer S.1s the next role for XN926 was that of training with 736 Squadron, this beginning in November 1965. With this unit XN926 spent much of its time on weapons delivery duties during which bombs frequently either fell off prematurely or else hung up while the final straw was a flap overstress during a dive-bombing run in January 1966. A further bomb release embarrass-

The first operator of XN928 was 801 Squadron, with whom it was coded 119/R prior to undertaking a deployment aboard the carrier *Ark Royal*. The aircraft ended its days as a target on the Pendine ranges. BBA Collection

XN928 still survives as a nose only, having served with 809 Squadron as 119/R. After a period at St Athan as a training airframe the aircraft was moved to the Wales Air Museum where it remained intact until the museum closed in 1996. Trevor Smith Collection

ment occurred in March 1967 when XN926 was involved in the bombing of the grounded oil tanker *Torrey Canyon*, in an attempt to break up and sink the wreck, which was a danger to shipping. On the first pass the bombs failed to release, though they did release on the aircraft's next pass over the ship. XN926 completed its flying career in May 1968, being passed to Shoeburyness and then the Pendine ranges for use as a target.

XN927

One of the shortest serving Buccaneer S.1s was XN927, which first flew on 30 May 1962. A delivery flight to Lossiemouth took place in July, the aircraft joining 801 Squadron the following month. A transfer to 809 Squadron took place in February 1963 and it was while departing on a flight on 25 March 1964 that a spurious fire warning lit up for the port engine. This indication, plus a visible fuel leak, convinced the crew that a quick return to

base was needed; however, during the approach the aircraft's speed decayed rapidly causing the crew to eject. Although the aircraft was destroyed both crew landed safely.

XN928

In contrast, XN928 had a fairly normal career for a Buccaneer S.1. Having first flown on 2 June 1962 the aircraft was dispatched to Lossiemouth in July, joining its operational unit, 801 Squadron, that same month. That November XN928 suffered minor damage when a tyre burst on landing at Lossiemouth, which required the crew to engage the arrestor wire. After repairs the Buccaneer was transferred to 809 Squadron in February 1963, this unit having been formed the previous month.

Over the following two years XN928 alternated between 801 and 809 Squadrons during which it suffered two serious engine failures, including an explo-

sion during take-off in September 1964. Further extensive damage was caused in February 1965 when the port leg collapsed on landing: such was the violence of undercarriage's failure that the starboard leg collapsed soon afterwards. Repairs, once the airframe had been moved by road, were undertaken at the manufacturers, taking until September to complete.

Having been restored to flying status XN928 returned to Lossiemouth, joining 736 Squadron in November 1965. A temporary diversion to C(A) for further investigation into single engined handling kept the aircraft employed between April and June 1966 before 736 Squadron resumed ownership. During its time as a training aircraft XN928 endured the usual range of defects that seemed to afflict the Buccaneer S.1 fleet. Problems were encountered with the hydraulics while the starboard powerplant seemed especially prone to faults, the first being an IGV failure on take-off, followed on a later date by an engine surge that left the engine running at full power. On both occasions,

Prior to joining the Royal Navy XN929 was displayed at Farnborough in September 1962, where it was displayed with a full range of underwing accessories. BBA Collection

after much throttle juggling, the pilot made a safe landing. Tyre failures were the next defect to plague XN928, this occurring in May and June 1967. XN928 was then damaged after the radome was removed while still pressurized, this causing damage to the radar scanner and the surrounding structure.

Although this Buccaneer seemed to be plagued by various serious defects it did remain in use until February 1970 before retiring. After moves to Belfast and St Athan, XN928 ended up at the Wales Air Museum at Rhoose before being scrapped in February 1996 when the museum was forced to close.

XN929

The eighth production Buccaneer S.1, XN929, undertook its maiden flight on 5 July 1962, appearing at that year's SBAC show at Farnborough. Having completed its time as a display object the Buccaneer was dispatched north to Lossiemouth, joining 801 Squadron in October. Its life was uneventful until 5 August 1963 when a missed landing over all of the arrestor wires on HMS *Victorious* required the pilot to initiate a full power climb out and make another, successful, landing aboard the carrier. A transfer to 736 Squadron took place in December 1966, in support of Buccaneer S.2 squadron work-ups. Three months later XN929 was damaged at low

level after hitting a bird, and this was not the end of the aircraft's woes as it was then damaged by falling heating ducting whilst parked in the hangar. Eventually the aircraft rejoined 736 Squadron, only to be damaged by compressor failure whilst throttling up for take-off. Although originally slated for repair XN929, finally ended up at Honington for ground instructional usage. Eventually only the upper nose section was left, this ending its days on the Cranwell fire dump.

XN930

Another Buccaneer S.1 that ended its days as a fireman's plaything was XN930, which made its maiden flight on 19 July 1962. Instead of being allotted to a flying squadron the aircraft was required for trials of a modified fishtail shuttle launch assembly, and the associated deck handling trials. Most of these were undertaken at RAE Bedford before carrier trials were out aboard HMS *Hermes*. The trials were successfully completed by November, the aircraft flying north to Lossiemouth three months later.

The aircraft's new unit was 801 Squadron, with whom it went to sea aboard HMS *Victorious* for a cruise to the Far East where the carrier was the Far East flagship. When *Victorious* arrived off Singapore the Buccaneer was subjected to a series of 'hot and high' trials in the

company of XN925, the latter eventually ending up as a spares source for XN930. Having completed the high-temperature trials XN930 resumed normal operations from *Victorious*, although these came to a literally shuddering halt after a night flight in June 1964. The central warning panel lights flickered during a landing approach which hastened the aircraft's landing, but on touchdown the Buccaneer ploughed into the cross-deck barrier, causing the nose leg to collapse under the strain. After repairs ashore at Tengah the Buccaneer resumed its flying career aboard *Victorious* in December. When *Victorious* started its voyage home at the end of its commission, XN930 was transferred to 800 Squadron operating from the aircraft carrier HMS *Eagle* in February 1966.

The squadron disbanded in November, but XN930 took a little longer to return to Britain. On 17 July the Buccaneer experienced an uncontrollable port engine surge, which resulted in it being diverted to RAAF Butterworth, Malaysia, where a wheels-up landing was made as the undercarriage would not lower. A repair party was sent to Butterworth, their remit being to get the aircraft back on its undercarriage so it could be shipped home for repair at Sydenham, Belfast where XN930 arrived in September 1966. The extensive nature of the damage meant that the Buccaneer was grounded until March 1968 when Lossiemouth became its new home. Acting as a 'hangar queen', XN930 remained grounded until February 1969 when 736 Squadron became its new operator. The Buccaneer remained in service until withdrawal in January 1971, moving to St Athan not long afterwards for ground training use. By January 1977 the airframe was at Honington for training purposes before finally being sold for scrap in 1991.

XN931

The aircraft that initially sparked an interest in the Buccaneer from the South African Air Force was XN931, which had undertaken its maiden flight on 4 April 1962, being flown for General Viljoen of the South African Air Force (SAAF) six days later. By December XN931 was at Lossiemouth, and it joined 801 Squadron in January 1963. Unlike many other Buccaneers, this aircraft's early career was not marred by too many incidents – just a tyre burst on landing and an engine malfunction in the first twelve months. However this changed when XN931 and other aircraft from 801 Squadron was based at Eastleigh, Kenya from 7 February to 22 February. During a routine flight over the African bush the aircraft experienced severe hydraulic problems that first came to light when the air brakes malfunc-

tioned. The pilot used the hydraulic system's switching ability to supply power to enough of the aircraft's systems for an emergency landing at Embakasi Airport near the capital.

After repair the Buccaneer returned to HMS *Victorious*, which continued its voyage and ended up in the vicinity of the Philippines in early May 1964 for exercises with the US Navy and locally based USAF units. By the end of that month XN931 had disgraced itself when a fluttering IGV in the port engine resulted in a hasty landing at the USAF base, Clark Field. The engine fault was quickly repaired and the Buccaneer resumed flying operations soon afterwards. A hydraulic fault in June required a diversion to the US Navy airbase at Cubi Point in the Philippines. Yet again the hard-pressed maintainers worked their magic, the Buccaneer being cleared to fly a few days later. Having departed the Philippines HMS *Victorious* arrived off Singapore in August 1964. As before some of the carrier's aircraft were operated from a shore base, in this case the RAF airfield at Tengah.

Except for a handful of minor engine and brake problems XN931 performed without serious incident until 15 November 1964. The Buccaneer was flying in formation with four other aircraft

from 801 Squadron when it was affected by wake turbulence that caused it to pitch up uncontrollably: the crew had no other option but to eject. This they did successfully, though suffering minor injuries in the process.

XN932

XN932, which had first flown on 18 September, joined XN931 on the inventory of 801 Squadron. In company with other aircraft from the squadron XN932 embarked on board HMS *Victorious* for its 1964 commission. A land detachment to Kenya began in February, during which XN932 suffered a bird strike to the port engine intake assembly that required a precautionary landing be made. After inspection of the engine and repairs to the intake the Buccaneer resumed flying with the squadron. The detachment rejoined *Victorious* to continue the voyage, which XN932 completed without further incident. Upon returning to Lossiemouth the aircraft moved to 800 Squadron in April 1965, remaining with them until retiring to Lee-on-Solent for ground instructional use in March 1967. It was last reported as derelict in 1970, probably being scrapped soon afterwards.

ABOVE AND LEFT: XN930 (121/V), XN934 (117/R) and XN932 (115/R) 801 Squadron aboard HMS *Ark Royal*. BBA Collection

XN933–XN935

Other aircraft from this part of the production run that joined the inventory of 801 Squadron included XN933, XN934 and XN935 which had made their maiden flights on 2 October, 15 October and 31 October 1962, respectively. Not long after joining HMS *Victorious* the crew flying XN933 reported rudder problems that required a quick return to the carrier. Further troubles afflicted the aircraft in September 1963 when, launching from *Victorious*, the canopy became unlocked and separated from the airframe, hitting the tailplane in passing. To increase the amount of safety equipment available, the aircraft landed at RAAF Butterworth. The repair work occupied the FAA artificers until the beginning of January 1964, although the aircraft's troubles were not over as it had not even undertaken its first post-repair flight before further damage was incurred when, as it was being lowered off jacks, the nose-support jack slipped and damaged the nose. Further repairs kept XN932 in the hangar until early April.

Having finally rejoined 801 Squadron the Buccaneer then suffered a bird strike a low level, which damaged the windscreens. The aircraft then endured a spate of port engine problems, the first occurring in September and requiring a diversion to Changi. The next occasion was aboard the *Victorious* when the port engine caught fire during ground runs at night. The port

engine caused further problems during March 1965, the final straw being severe vibration just before launching from *Victorious*, which caused the launch to be cancelled. As curing this fault was beyond the carrier's resources the aircraft was returned to Britain aboard HMS *Eagle*. Eventually XN933 was offloaded at Belfast where investigation and repairs were carried out.

By the time it was ready to resume flying the S.2 version was coming into service, so XN933 was transferred to 736 Squadron for aircrew training duties. A period as hangar queen from mid-1967 to early 1968 ended when the aircraft was rebuilt, serving with 737 Squadron from April 1968 until its flying career finally ended the following September. From 1970 the airframe was used by Shoeburyness and Pendine for target practice, a task that currently continues.

In contrast to other aircraft assigned to 801 Squadron, XN934 operated from *Victorious* during its commission with little incident, remaining a squadron stalwart until transferring to 736 Squadron, the Buccaneer training unit at Lossiemouth, in October 1965. During its time with 736 Squadron the aircraft endured various hydraulic problems including leaks, and problems with the pumps and the proportioners. Notwithstanding that, XN934 remained in operational service until withdrawal in mid 1968 when the aircraft became a ground instructional aircraft at

Lee-on-Solent. Eventually XN934 moved to Culdrose for use by the School of Aircraft Handling although this role ended in June 1968 when the Buccaneer was moved to the Predannack fire dump in June 1983.

XN935 was another aircraft that suffered very few defects in operational service with 801 Squadron, most being confined to hydraulic system faults, though the crew flying the aircraft in May 1963 did overstress the aircraft after lowering the undercarriage during a climbing turn, and a diversion to Tengah was needed after a hydraulic fault in October 1963. After repair the Buccaneer became part of 801A Flight in company with XN930, both being used for high-temperature trials that were completed by July 1964 when both aircraft rejoined 801 Squadron proper and resumed flying from HMS *Victorious*.

On 19 August 1964 the Buccaneer had departed *Victorious* when it experienced undercarriage retraction problems, the extent of which only became clear when the aircraft attempted to land aboard the carrier. It was later deduced that the undercarriage shortening system had failed, causing a massive hydraulic leak. This in turn resulted in the undercarriage collapsing on landing. As the aircraft had no means of stopping the crew ejected while the stricken Buccaneer slid off the flight deck into the sea, both crew landing unhurt in the water.

After periods spent at sea aboard *Ark Royal* and *Victorious*, XN934 was transferred to 736 Squadron for training duties, being coded 631/LM in the process. Its had been burnt on the Predannack fire dump by 1995. BBA Collection

XN948

XN948 would be the last Buccaneer S.1 delivered outright to 801 Squadron, arriving in March 1963 having first flown on 14 November 1962. Problems with the fuel system not long after arriving at Lossiemouth resulted in a swift return to base, this being followed a few days later by a brake system fault. These were serious enough for the Buccaneer to be returned to Blackburn for deeper investigation in April 1963. Two months later the aircraft rejoined 801 Squadron and embarked with the rest of the unit aboard HMS *Victorious*. Most of the commission was uneventful for XN948, until operations began off the island off Singapore. During a night approach to HMS *Victorious* in October 1963 the port engine inlet guide vanes closed completely, effectively shutting the engine down. The crew elected to undertake a missed approach and divert to the RAF base at Tengah.

Having been repaired XN948 rejoined *Victorious* and behaved itself until just after a catapult launch in January 1964 when the starboard engine surged violently. After dumping fuel to reduce the aircraft's weight, the crew made a successful single-engined landing aboard *Victorious*. Its engine problems dealt with, XN948 resumed flying only to disgrace itself in March when the starboard undercarriage leg collapsed on landing on *Victorious*. Apparently safely ensconced in the hangar, the Buccaneer slipped off its nose-support jack, causing damage to the lower fuselage. After further repairs XN948 resumed carrier flying, although this was further interrupted when the port engine malfunctioned, requiring an emergency diversion to Tengah. Changi was the Buccaneer's next venue after undercarriage problems in September and October 1964, the latter being a nose leg lowering problem.

On 26 November 1964 the Buccaneer had just departed Changi when the starboard engine suffered a catastrophic failure, resulting in a massive fire that in turn caused No.4 fuel tank to rupture. The resultant fuselage fire caused extensive damage to the flying control circuits, which in turn led to an uncontrolled pitch up. The observer successfully ejected but the pilot was killed, while the Buccaneer crashed into the sea.

XN948 was originally issued to 801 Squadron for service aboard HMS *Ark Royal*, after which the aircraft was transferred with its unit aboard *Victorious* as 119/V. BBA Collection

XN949

When 809 Squadron reformed at Lossiemouth on 15 January 1963 one of the first Buccaneer S.1s to arrive on the inventory was XN949, which had undertaken its maiden flight on 8 December 1962. Ten days after joining the squadron the aircraft was damaged when the port tyre failed after a heavy landing at RNAY Belfast. Fortunately the damage was minor, the Buccaneer returning to Scotland a few weeks later. The aircraft's sojourn with 809 Squadron was short, however, as it was moved to Tengah aboard the RFA *Bacchus*, arriving in October 1963. After preparation XN949 was flown out to join 801 Squadron aboard HMS *Victorious* in December. As with all of this marque XN949 was plagued with engine problems, this being followed by a series of port aileron PFCU problems, the last of which required a diversion to Tengah. The aircraft resumed operations again in September 1964, although it was grounded during the following month after debris from a rocket firing impinged upon the port engine, causing another diversion to a land base.

As this Buccaneer seemed to have more than its share of problems it was shipped back home to the RNAY at Belfast for repairs and overhauling. This was completed by October 1965, the Buccaneer joining 736 Squadron at Lossiemouth for use in preparing crews for the forthcoming Buccaneer S.2. Low flying is always a dangerous business as the crew of XN949 found out in January 1966 when they suffered a bird strike during a toss bombing attack over the sea; flying resumed with 736 Squadron after a few days of repair work. Problems were then encountered with the starboard engine generator which malfunctioned twice in February, on the second occasion as the undercarriage was raising. The starboard undercarriage again caused problems the following month, when the same leg collapsed on landing.

A series of port engine malfunctions followed in April and June 1966, culminating with an IGV failure on approach to the aircraft carrier HMS *Ark Royal*. Reduced to single engine power, the Buccaneer then suffered a tailplane runaway that caused an uncommanded pitch up. As the pilot was unable to regain control the decision was taken to eject, both crew doing so safely while the abandoned aircraft crashed into the sea.

XN950 and XN951

The next two Buccaneer S.1s, XN950 and XN951, were both delivered to 809 Squadron, the former making its first flight on 24 December 1962 and the latter on 26 January 1963. XN950 became part of 809 Squadron in September 1963, being beaten by XN951 by four months. During its service with 809 Squadron XN950 was a fairly reliable aircraft; though it suffered from the usual range of defects, none was serious enough to

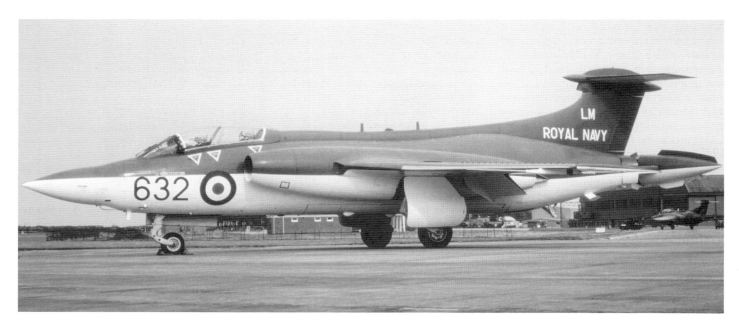

This view of XN950 reveals the demarcation of the early colour scheme as applied to the type. BBA Collection

ground the aircraft for more than a few days at a time. From March 1965 XN950 served with 736 Squadron, the Buccaneer training unit. Having previously endured no more than the normal range of in-flight defects, XN950 ended its career by crashing on 28 March 1966. The cause was later traced to a massive instrument failure that left the crew with no other option but to eject; unfortunately only the observer survived.

In contrast, XN951 was a source of perpetual trouble to the aircraft maintainers. Its first major malfunction occurred in December 1963 when, on a transit flight from RNAY Belfast to Lossiemouth, both engines lost power, forcing the crew to make an emergency diversionary landing at RAE West Freugh. Repairs kept the Buccaneer there until January 1964 when the aircraft finally made it to Lossiemouth. Instead of rejoining 809 Squadron XN951 was transferred to 800 Squadron, which had formed as a Buccaneer unit in March 1964. The aircraft blotted its copybook again the following month when, following a fuel transfer problem, the crew had to make an emergency landing at the Armament Practice Camp at Acklington. Unfortunately this runway was short and had no arrestor gear, so the pilot applied maximum braking which resulted in both tyres bursting. Repairs completed, the Buccaneer resumed operations with 800 Squadron.

The squadron arrived aboard the carrier HMS *Eagle* in August 1965, as this vessel was due to depart to the Far East to relieve HMS *Victorious* as Flag Ship Far East. During this deployment XN951 endured the usual range of engine problems, which occasionally resulted in the aircraft making emergency landings at Changi where the carrier's shore engineering party was based. When HMS *Eagle* returned to British waters in December 1966, XN951 was flown off to RNAY Belfast for overhaul and modifications. These completed, the aircraft was returned to Lossiemouth in August 1967 joining 736 Squadron in November. The aircraft behaved impeccably until 1 December 1970 when the port engine failed to throttle up after a practice overshoot. As the Buccaneer was struggling to accelerate and gain height, the crew were left with no other option than to eject, which both did safely.

XN952

Buccaneer S.1 XN952 had a flying career that could be measured in minutes. Departing on its test flight on 12 February 1963, the aircraft undertook its initial shakedown manoeuvres, carrying out other gyrations before entering a half loop at the end of a LABS attack. At the apex the controls became cross-coupled, the pilot losing control temporarily after

blacking out. With the Buccaneer heading towards the ground the ejection sequence was initiated, but both crew were killed when they landed in the burning wreckage of their aircraft.

XN953

The next aircraft, XN953, first flew on 22 February 1963, but was retained by the manufacturers and the C(A) for flight trials so its entry into naval service was delayed until October 1964 when 800 Squadron became the Buccaneer's new owners. HMS *Eagle* was the unit's home from December 1964 and the cruise was continuing without incident until XN953 was damaged in January 1965 when undertaking a refuelling exercise with a Scimitar tanker. A safe landing was made aboard the carrier, the damage being confined to the canopy and port intake. Repairs were completed quickly, XN953 resuming flying from *Eagle* until transferred to 801 Squadron in April 1966; seven months later it was transferred again, to 736 Squadron.

Having served with little incident with the front-line units, XN953 now ran through a spate of incidents, the first being a malfunction of the starboard engine IGVs in January 1967 that required a single-engined return to base and further investigation. In October 1967 the

Buccaneer was flown to RNAY Belfast for a major servicing, which was completed by January 1970. Flying with 736 Squadron in the training role continued until XN953 was grounded at the beginning of 1971. After a short sojourn at Shoeburyness it moved to St Athan in September 1974 for ground training usage. A move to Culdrose for the same purpose followed in 1975, the Buccaneer remaining in use until July 1983. Eventually the aircraft became a fireman's plaything, finally expiring in 1996.

XN954–XN957

The next four Buccaneer S.1s, XN954, XN955, XN956 and XN957, were all delivered to 801 Squadron in 1963, having undertaken their maiden flights on 8, 13 and 28 March, and 3 April, respectively. All four aircraft joined HMS *Victorious* on 14 August when the carrier departed to the Far East to become the Far East Command flagship. While operating from *Victorious* XN954 had a bird strike that required repairs aboard ship during September. More serious damage was incurred the following month when the aircraft was damaged by fire. As the repairs were beyond the capabilities of *Victorious*, the Buccaneer was craned ashore so that repairs could be carried out at Tengah, Singapore.

XN955 ended up at Changi for repairs twice in January 1964, once after a hydraulic problem and once after a starboard engine flame-out. For three months the Buccaneer was flown without any serious incident, but on 4 April XN955 came close to abandonment when the starboard engine IGV shut completely, reducing the aircraft to single-engined operation; fortunately the fault then cleared itself just as quickly as it had occurred, allowing the crew to bring the aircraft home safely. XN955 did not fly from *Victorious* again as its port wing was damaged aboard the carrier, this being compounded by further damage ashore at Seletar, Singapore, when the starboard wing was damaged.

The Buccaneer was returned to Britain, arriving at RNAY Belfast in November 1964. These were completed by the end of 1966 when XN955 was delivered to the Moor for use by the manufacturers to test proposed engine modifications. A transfer to C Squadron A&AEE took place in July 1967, where XN955 was used for tail warn-ing radar sensor trials and trials of 1,000lb retarded bombs. By February 1968 XN955 had returned to Lossiemouth, being allo-cated to the station for flying duties. Twelve months later XN955 was retired from flying, eventually ending up at P&EE Shoeburyness in March 1970.

The third machine from this group, XN956, only remained with 800 Squadron for three months, transferring to 801 Squadron on attachment after the carrier work-up had been completed. When the time came for 800 Squadron to decamp to *Victorious* in August, XN956 rejoined to complete the inventory. During this deployment XN956 experienced only one major malfunction, when a severe port engine vibration required a landing at Changi in April 1965. Rejoining *Victorious* the following month, the Buccaneer was flown off in July for transit to RNAY Belfast for a major overhaul. At the completion of this the Buccaneer was returned to Lossiemouth where 736 Squadron became the new owners.

The aircraft's greatest claim to fame was during the *Torrey Canyon* crisis in March 1967 when the supertanker struck Pollards Rock, then ran aground on Seven Sisters reef between the Scilly Isles and Lands End. As the waves pounded the vessel it eventually broke in two, allowing 31,000,000gal of oil to escape. The decision was taken to destroy the ship, but the attackers were faced with a problem in trying to set the oil alight, as it was a light oil that was not easily flammable. The first strikes were undertaken by RAF Hawker Hunters that used napalm tanks and rockets in an attempt to set fire to the cargo. Following up on the burning attempt came Buccaneers from Lossiemouth, whose remit was to destroy the ship with 1,000lb bombs. In the case of XN956 its first pass over the ship resulted in a bomb hanging up, although it was released in a second pass.

Although it was afflicted by the usual range of engine malfunctions and hydraulic failures, the Buccaneer continued in service until November 1969. A move to Laarbruch took place soon after-wards where it was used as a weapons loading trainer, eventually ending up in RAF 15 Squadron markings.

The final aircraft in this batch, XN957, moved between the Lossiemouth units, only remaining with 801 Squadron until January 1965 when it was transferred to 809 Squadron. This was a short-term sojourn as 736 Squadron became XN957's new owners in March. Problems with the starboard engine, mainly centred around the IGV, occurred throughout 1965, simi-lar problems also occurring in 1966 and 1967. The aircraft's working life came to an end in February 1971, but unlike others of its ilk which were used as fireman's training aids or scrapped, XN957 ended up at Yeovilton for display at the Fleet Air Arm Museum, where it still resides.

XN958

The following aircraft, XN958, made its first flight on 18 April 1963, joining 801 Squadron at Lossiemouth the following

Buccaneer XN957 wearing the lightning flash markings of 736 Squadron; this aircraft had seen service with 801 and 809 Squadrons previously. At the completion of its flying career the aircraft was sent to the Fleet Air Arm museum at Yeovilton for preservation. Trevor Smith Collection

month. A bird strike in August kept the Buccaneer on the ground for ten days while repairs were effected. An uneventful twelve months followed before the aircraft was detached to RNAY Belfast for a much-needed overhaul and out-standing modifications. This work kept XN958 away from Scotland until August 1965 when 800 Squadron assumed ownership, embarking aboard HMS *Eagle* soon afterwards. The aircraft was lost on 20 November 1965 when the crew decided to undertake a 'bolter' from the deck of HMS *Eagle* and lost control. In trouble, they had option but to eject, both surviving albeit shaken and dampened by the experience.

XN959

Buccaneer S.1 XN959 had its Fleet Air Arm career delayed after its maiden flight on 8 May 1963 as it was required at Boscombe Down for electro-magnetic compatibility trials. Unlike other Buccaneers XN959 then flew to Lee-on-Solent instead of Lossiemouth, arriving in June. From this base flight trials were carried out aboard HMS *Victorious*, the aircraft returning to A&AEE the following month. Lossiemouth finally received XN959 in November, although entry into service with an operating unit – 800 Squadron – did not take place until March 1964. The aircraft behaved impeccably until April 1965 when the tail skid fractured upon landing aboard HMS *Eagle*. As repairs were also required to the tail skid's

surrounding structure, the Buccaneer was flown ashore for repairs at Changi: here it ran off the runway and ended up in a monsoon drain after an IGV failed on approach. As the required repairs were quite extensive, the Buccaneer was returned to RNAY Belfast for repairs.

By July 1965 XN959 had resumed flying with 800 Squadron, this time from Lossiemouth. Preparations were well underway for the squadron to join HMS *Eagle* prior to the carrier departing to the Far East to take up its duties as flagship. All the aircraft were aboard in August, beginning training immediately. XN959's defects were limited to an engine malfunction, a hydraulic failure and a trim problem. It was sent to RNAY Belfast in November 1966 for a much-needed overhaul, returning to Lossiemouth in June 1967 and becoming part of 736 Squadron. In service with the training unit XN959 suffered bomb door problems on two occasions during toss bomb attacks. After rectification it continued flying with 736 Squadron until retiring in November 1969. Eventually P&EE became the aircraft's new owners, keeping it for future use as a target.

XN960–XN962

No.809 Squadron at Lossiemouth received the next three Buccaneer S.1s, XN960, XN961 and XN962. The first undertook its maiden flight on 26 May 1963, although its arrival in Scotland was

delayed as it was required for display at the Paris Air Show in June 1963 and Blackburn retained the aircraft until November, when 809 Squadron finally took it over. In July 1965 XN960 was transferred to 800 Squadron to increase the unit's available aircraft prior to embarking aboard HMS *Eagle*. XN960 suffered the Buccaneer S.1's usual range of engine and hydraulic problems, although all were well within the capabilities of the carrier's artificers. As HMS *Eagle* headed for Britain XN960 was flown off to land at RNAY Belfast for overhaul.

At the completion of this maintenance the Buccaneer was transferred to RAE Farnborough for trails work, which continued until grounding in January 1974. This was not the end of the aircraft's useful life as it gained further employment as a ground trials vehicle until 1976, after which it was moved to Shoeburyness for use as a target.

XN961 arrived at Lossiemouth in July 1963, joining 809 Squadron immediately. An engine failure in December 1963 kept the aircraft on the ground until August 1964, when it rejoined the squadron. A spate of engine problems plagued the aircraft during the remainder of the year, mainly centred around the port engine which suffered IGV malfunctions and spurious fire warnings. An attempt to solve the recurrent faults led to the Buccaneer entering the Aircraft Handling Unit at Lossiemouth in November 1964, from where it was dispatched to 736 Squadron the following April. The aircraft was lost on 25 June 1965 when undertaking a toss-bombing attack during which the aircraft flew into a hill that was obscured by cloud, killing the crew in the process.

The final machine in this trio, XN962, made its first flight on 19 June 1963 and joined 809 Squadron in September. A variety of defects were encountered over the following twelve months, these including problems with the tailplane trim, the fuel feed system and the engines. With these rectified 800 Squadron became the aircraft's new owners in September 1964 for preparation to join HMS *Eagle*. During this cruise XN962 was damaged during a night flight by numerous bird impacts, which required the crew to make a hasty return to the carrier. After rectification the Buccaneer resumed flying only to suffer a severe port engine vibration just after launching from *Eagle*. As the aircraft was carrying a full load of bombs these

XN959 coded 103/E for service aboard the carrier *Eagle*; it was being operated by 800 Squadron at the time. As with many of its compatriots, XN959 was operated by 736 Squadron prior to retirement. BBA Collection

The camera and photoflash crates mounted on the bomb bay door are rarely seen. The forward section housed the cameras while the illumination unit was in the rear section. The carrier aircraft was XN960, which ended its life as a target at Shoeburyness. BBA Collection

were quickly jettisoned while the crew prepared to fly a single-engined diversion to the US Navy base at Sigonella. The severity of the damage required that the Buccaneer return home by ship to RNAY Belfast for repair work.

After extensive repairs, overhaul and modifications XN962 was returned to Lossiemouth in May 1969 to resume flying, this time with 736 Squadron. This period of the aircraft's service was uneventful, finally ending in January 1971 when it was placed in temporary storage. Eventually XN962 was transferred to P&EE for trials work. Eventually the nose ended up with the RAF Display Flight, with whom it still remains.

XN963

Another aircraft that was destined to end its days at Shoeburyness was XN963, which first flew on 5 July 1963 and arrived at Lossiemouth for 800 Squadron in March 1964. The usual selection of faults beset the Buccaneer, the most serious of which was an engine power fluctuation that required the crew to jettison the bomb load prior to the crew making an

emergency landing at Lossiemouth. The aircraft and its operating unit joined HMS *Eagle* in December 1964 for the carrier's cruise to the Far East. In common with the squadron's other aircraft XN963 required the odd diversion to Changi for repairs. At the completion of this cruise the Buccaneer was flown to RNAY Belfast for

an overhaul, arriving in February 1967. Eight months later XN963 had returned to Lossiemouth, becoming part of 803 Squadron upon arrival. The aircraft remained in service with this, its final operator, until November 1970 when it was transferred to P&EE, the aircraft being scrapped the following year.

Closely watched by the aircraft handlers, XN963 taxies out for a training flight. Coded 226/LM, the Buccaneer was on the strength of 809 Squadron, though it moved to 803 Squadron in 1967. The aircraft ended its days as a target at Shoeburyness. BBA Collection

XN965 in transition from one unit to the next: it wears the coding of 736 Squadron while still retaining the badge of 809 Squadron on the intake wall. After its FAA life the aircraft was involved in the MRCA development programme, after which it was withdrawn from use and broken up. Trevor Smith Collection

XN964

Unlike most of the other Buccaneer S.1s delivered to a Fleet Air Arm squadron XN964, which had initially flown on 21 July 1963, was prepared for shipment to the Far East at RNAY Belfast. Arriving at Tengah in January 1964 XN964 was prepared to join HMS *Victorious*, although this was delayed as the Buccaneer experienced tailplane control problems that required a return to Tengah for rectification. The aircraft finally landed aboard *Victorious* the following day, starting training missions almost immediately. Engine problems beset the aircraft during August, these being severe enough to require an engine change. A further trip to Tengah was needed when the port engine flamed out during a rocket training mission, this being followed by the same engine experiencing power fluctuations. These defects kept the Buccaneer grounded throughout much of October and November 1964.

At the completion of the *Victorious* cruise XN964 was transferred to 736 Squadron at Lossiemouth for training duties. Problems with the port and starboard fuel proportioners in early 1966 required diversions to base. These were followed by an engine IGV malfunction which required a single-engined landing at

Lossiemouth. In December 1966 XN964 was delivered to RNAY Belfast for a much-needed overhaul, this being completed in September 1967 when it returned to 736 Squadron.

By February 1970 the aircraft had completed its career with the Fleet Air Arm, moving to RAE Bedford for arrestor net trials and then to the Royal Radar Establishment at Pershore for the trial fitment of ECM systems that were intended for the operational Buccaneer fleet. After a period as a ground training vehicle the aircraft was dismantled and transferred to Brough by road, arriving in October 1976. After use as a test bed for various modifications and repairs, XN964 was disposed of to the East Midlands Airport museum, arriving there during October 1982; its stay was short as it moved to Bruntingthorpe in November 1983. Currently XN964 is on display at Winthorpe Museum, where it arrived in March 1988.

XN965–XN967

Of the next three aircraft one would be scrapped, another would have a second life as a trials machine while the third would have a very short life. Buccaneer S.1

XN965 was the aircraft that had a second life. The aircraft made its first flight on 6 August 1963, being delivered to 809 Squadron that November. Not long after arrival the port engine began to cause concern, suffering a compressor stall and vibration in April and June, respectively. In October it was the turn of the starboard engine to misbehave when vibration was experienced, this being followed by a bird strike later that month. As both engines had given cause for concern the aircraft was taken into the Aircraft Handling Unit at Lossiemouth for deeper investigation at the beginning of March 1965. Once repairs were completed XN965 was transferred to 736 Squadron for crew training purposes.

Although the Buccaneer's engine complaints had been investigated by the AHU, the port powerplant was still causing problems, faults occurred quite regularly throughout 1967; now the experts of the Naval Air Support Unit were called. XN965 entered the care of NASU in September 1967, being returned to 736 Squadron in November. Although it experienced the usual range of defects, none were serious enough to ground the aircraft for an appreciable length of time, so it continued in service until January 1971 when it was withdrawn from flying

Buccaneer S.1 XN965 wearing the code 226/LM, assigned to 809 Squadron when it was based at Lossiemouth. This was one of the few S.1s not to go to sea, remaining a shore-based aircraft throughout its service life. BBA Collection

duties and placed in storage. A transfer to RAE Farnborough was effected in March 1972 at the behest of MOD(PE), to help investigate cockpit noise which was noticeable in both versions of the Buccaneer. Having completed these trials the aircraft was officially struck off charge in February 1974. Even this was not the end of its useful life, as British Aerospace acquired the airframe for use in the devel-

opment of the MRCA/Panavia Tornado. Eventually even these duties ended, and XN965's remains were transferred to the Pendine Ranges in 1988 for use as a target.

XN966 undertook its maiden flight on 1 September 1963, joining 809 Squadron in November. Its short operational life ended on 24 January 1964 when, during as approach to Lossiemouth, one of the engines performed an uncommanded

shut-down. As the aircraft was too low for the crew to safely recover it, they were left with no other option but to eject, which they safely did. The abandoned Buccaneer continued the landing, finally stopping on the runway after a 200yd skid. Originally the aircraft was catagorized as repairable, but further investigation revealed that the extent of the damage was greater than first suspected.

While XN965 was operated by 736 Squadron as 636/LM it was diverted away on at least one occasion for investigation into noise suppression – excessive noise being a problem that plagued the entire fleet. BBA Collection

Eventually the Buccaneer ended up at Lee-on-Solent for scrap.

The third aircraft of the trio was XN967, which had initially flown on 13 September 1963 and joined 809 Squadron in November. In common with the rest of the Buccaneer S.1 fleet, the engines of XN965 gave the usual selection of problems including flame-outs and vibration. A transfer to 736 Squadron was effected in March 1965. During its time with 736 Squadron only one serious fault occurred: an almost complete jamming of the aileron control circuit in July 1967. During the recovery the crew reported that the control column could not be moved to starboard, while movement to port was limited. Investigations on the ground revealed that a loose article had become jammed in the control run, which in turn required the Lossiemouth engineers carry out a deeper investigation to determine whether there were any other foreign objects in the aircraft. These investigations kept the Buccaneer grounded for a few days until it was cleared for a return to flight.

Eventually XN967 was retired from flying in January 1970, being transported to Culdrose for the School of Aircraft Handling by ship. Retired from this task in June 1978, the aircraft was towed to the Cornwall Aero Park as a museum exhibit. Eventually the airframe's corrosion became too great to control so the airframe was scrapped, though the nose was transported to Norfolk for further preservation.

XN968–XN971

Of the final six aircraft from the Buccaneer S.1 contract, four were delivered to 800 Squadron. The first was XN968, first flown on 27 September 1963. Prior to flying to Lossiemouth the aircraft was bailed to A&AEE for carrier trials beginning in January 1964; XN968 was in Scotland with 800 Squadron by March. The unit embarked aboard HMS Eagle in December 1964. Changi was the main diversion airfield, as the shore-based engineering unit was based there. XN968 landed there twice with problems in April 1964: first, IGV problems with the port engine and second, a hydraulic system failure. At the completion of the Eagle cruise XN968 was flown to RNAY Belfast for overhaul, arriving in March 1967. At the completion of this work the Buccaneer was returned to Lossiemouth, joining 736 Squadron in March 1969.

XN968 continued in use until 8 December 1970 when both engines caught fire at an altitude of 2,000ft (600m). Although the fire suppression system was operated, fumes entering the cockpit forced the crew to eject. The pilot survived but unfortunately the observer's seat failed to operate correctly and he was killed.

Also destined to end its service career by crashing was XN969, which first flew on 16 October 1963 and joined 800 Squadron in March 1964. In company with the rest of the unit's aircraft, XN969 was embarked aboard HMS Eagle for its tour as flagship for the Far East. Only one fault – a hung-

up bomb load – bothered the crew enough to require a diversion to a land base, Cubi Point NAS in the Philippines. Once a shore party had dealt with the aircraft's fault it returned to Eagle to resume operations. On 9 October 1965, after a launch from HMS Eagle, the hydraulic bay access door came adrift. This was followed by the failure of both fuel system proportioners, which interrupted the fuel supply to the engines. As the crew were experiencing difficulties in keeping the Buccaneer airborne they decided to eject. Both did so safely, being recovered by the SAR helicopter from HMS Eagle while the stricken machine crashed into the sea.

The next aircraft in the sequence, XN970, also ended its career in a crash. It first flew on 1 November 1963. joining 800 Squadron in March. Bird strikes seemed to plague this aircraft as it was badly damaged by collisions in April and October 1964, both of which incidents required repair by the Lossiemouth AHU. When 800 Squadron embarked aboard HMS Eagle XN970 went with them. During this cruise the aircraft was constantly plagued by engine problems that culminated in the complete failure of the port engine on approach to Eagle on 25 March 1966. As the crew were unable to land the aircraft aboard the carrier they elected to eject which both did, suffering minor injuries in the process.

The last aircraft in this series assigned to 800 Squadron was XN971, which undertook its maiden flight on 20 November 1963 and joined 800 Squadron in April 1964. Joining HMS Eagle for its Far East cruise in December 1964, XN971 was forced to make an emergency landing at Tengah after a loss of engine thrust occurred during a flight refuelling exercise. Other defects that were encountered included the usual range of engine and hydraulic problems, though none was serious enough to ground the Buccaneer for any length of time. 800 Squadron returned to Lossiemouth in May 1965; shore time was limited as the unit re-embarked aboard HMS Eagle in August, departing to the Far East again soon afterwards.

Once Eagle had returned to British waters XN971 was flown off to RNAY Belfast for major servicing. This was completed in July 1967 when the Buccaneer returned to Lossiemouth to join 736 Squadron. This was a short-term sojourn as the headquarters unit, 803 Squadron, assumed ownership a month

Destined to end its career in the sea after hydraulic and fuel problems, Buccaneer S.1 XN969, 106/E, crashed while returning to HMS Eagle after a launch problem, although the crew did eject safely. BBA Collection

XN970 taxis out from the Lossiemouth flight line. It was on the strength of 800 Squadron, which was working up prior to embarking aboard the carrier HMS *Eagle*. The impressive collection of fins and folded wings in the background belongs to two Scimitars, two Sea Vixens and a Hunter. BBA Collection

With rocket pods mounted on the inboard pylons plus the first type of Carrier Bomb Light Store (CBLS), on the outer ones Buccaneer S.1 XN972 of 736 Squadron prepares to land at Lossiemouth. BBA Collection

later, with whom XN971 remained until withdrawal in July 1968. After a period in storage it was transferred to West Freugh for use in the ground training role until February 1971. After use as a spares source the remains were placed on the fire dump in 1976, for use as a fireman's plaything.

XN972 and XN973

The final two aircraft, XN972 and XN973, both made their initial flights in December 1963. XN972 joined 809 Squadron in May 1964 although it was soon transferred to 800 Squadron in September, joining HMS *Eagle* with the remainder of the unit in December. By April 1965 the Buccaneer had joined 801 Squadron, later flying to HMS *Victorious*. On the completion of this cruise XN972

returned to Lossiemouth, joining 736 Squadron in July 1965. While the aircraft encountered the usual selection of engine and hydraulic problems, none was particularly serious, so it continued in service until withdrawn in July 1966. After periods spent at the Aircraft Weapons Research Establishment at Foulness and St Athan its remains eventually ended up at P&EE Shoeburyness.

The last Buccaneer S.1 began its flying career at A&AEE in July 1964 for a variety of trials including electro-magnetic compatibility and deck landing trials. At the completion of these trials the aircraft was loaded aboard HMS *Eagle* for onwards transit to join 801 Squadron, serving aboard HMS *Victorious*. After acceptance checks at Tengah XN973 landed aboard *Victorious* in February 1965. At the completion of the cruise aboard HMS

Victorious XN973 returned to Lossiemouth, joining 736 Squadron in July 1965. Although afflicted by the usual range of Buccaneer problems the aircraft was never grounded for long. In March 1966 XN972 was delivered to RNAY Belfast for an overhaul; this was completed three months later, the aircraft rejoining 736 Squadron upon returning to Lossiemouth.

During the following twelve months the port engine and fuel system gave most cause for concern, but much of this was cured by an engine change and in-depth investigation by NASU. By October 1970 XN972 had been retired from flying duties, ending up on the fire dump by June 1972 although the nose was removed and transported to Warton for use as a simulator, the remainder being scrapped.

XK529 streaking fast and low across the countryside, resplendent in the second naval Buccaneer colour scheme. This aircraft still needs the fin fairing to be fitted while the fibreglass panel on the dorsal fairing still needs painting in gloss white. BBA Collection

Buccaneer Carrier Operations

The Buccaneer spent much of its early service on aircraft carriers, so an overview of their operations aboard each carrier is order.

HMS *Ark Royal*

HMS *Ark Royal* recommissioned on 28 February 1962, adding the Buccaneer S.1s of 801 Squadron to the already embarked air wing. The Buccaneers disembarked on 16 March after taking part in the NATO Exercise *Dawn Breeze*, and *Ark Royal* did not see the Buccaneer again until the vessel recommissioned on 24 February 1970 at Devonport. After work-up the carrier and its air wing took part in Exercise *Northern Wedding*, this being followed by Lime Jug 70 in the Mediterranean during November 1970. During this exercise *Ark Royal* carried out a close 'reconnaissance' of a shadowing Soviet Kotlin-class destroyer by colliding with it. Further exercises that involved *Ark Royal* included *Royal Knight* in September 1971, *Westward Ho* in July 1972, *Strong Express* in September 1972, *Corsica* in November 1972, *Sunny Seas* and *Med Train 73* in February 1973, *Ruler* in March 1973 and *Northern Merger* in September 1974.

A period in refit followed, this being completed in June 1975. After work-up *Ark Royal* resumed its round of exercises beginning with *Ocean Safari* in November 1975. Film stardom in the BBC series *Sailor* occupied *Ark Royal*'s time throughout January 1976, after which the vessel returned to Devonport. Sea duties resumed in September 1976 with Exercise *Display Determination* being the ship's first duty, this being followed by a return to Devonport for its final refit. A moment of spick-and-span glory took place in June 1977 when the Queen reviewed the fleet for the Silver Jubilee. A final spread of exercises began with *Ocean Safari* in September 1977, followed by *Iles d'Or. Ark Royal* undertook its last deployment in April 1978 before

heading to Devonport to pay off in December, during which the air wing including the Buccaneers flew off to land at St Athan.

HMS *Eagle*

HMS *Eagle* first operated the Buccaneer on 1 December 1964 when 800 Squadron joined the air wing for a cruise to the Far East. Seven days after departing Britain the carrier passed through the Suez Canal, beginning its work-up off the coast of Aden immediately afterwards. In March 1965 the carrier took part in *FOTEX 65* off Singapore, after which the carrier departed for Britain. A short period in Devonport for repairs followed, *Eagle* returning to sea in January 1966. Once at sea the carrier departed for the Middle East to relieve the *Ark Royal* on the Biera patrol; this had been put in place to cut off supplies from Rhodesia, which had recently unilaterally declared independence from Britain. Four months later *Eagle* had arrived in Singapore, having been at sea for seventy-one days, having flown 1,880 sorties and having steamed 30,000 miles (50,000k).

The Singapore deployment ended in July 1966 and *Eagle* arrived at Devonport in August to begin a refit. This was complete by April 1967, the carrier putting to sea immediately with an air wing that included 800 Squadron and its Buccaneers. After working up, the carrier group took part in the NATO Exercise *Silver Tower* in September 1968.

By October 1968 the carrier was in port at Devonport for improvements to the catapult and arrestor systems so that the Phantom could be operated. The carrier

continued overleaf

HMS *Ark Royal* smashes its way though a rough sea – the waves are strong enough to wet the deck and its parked aircraft. Under normal circumstances the air wing would remain in such weather, though under wartime conditions the aircraft could be launched, should it be required. BBA Collection

Buccaneer Carrier Operations *continued*

returned to sea duty in March 1969 for normal operations and Phantom carrier trials. On the completion of these trials HMS *Eagle* departed for the Mediterranean where it arrived in September 1969 to take part in Exercises *Peace Keeper* and *Deep Furrow 69*. The carrier returned to Britain in December, carrying out exercises in the English Channel. A return to the Mediterranean followed in February 1971, although Gibraltar was its only port of call as the carrier was required in the Far East where it arrived in July. *Eagle* remained in the Far East before returning to Britain in November 1971. By January 1972 *Eagle* had been paid off and decommissioned, acting as a spares source for *Ark Royal* until being sold for scrap in 1978.

HMS *Hermes*
HMS *Hermes* first operated the Buccaneer in January 1967 when 809 Squadron embarked as part of the air wing. Its first task was to join the Far East Fleet, which was covering the withdrawal of British forces from the Aden Protectorate. After a return to Portsmouth in October 1967, *Hermes* rejoined the Far East Fleet in June

1968, this time with the Buccaneers of 801 Squadron. The carrier arrived off Singapore in September and Exercise *Coral Sands* in conjunction with the Royal Australian Navy occupied most of October before the ship returned to Portsmouth in April 1969.

After re-storing and repairs, HMS *Hermes* returned to sea in September 1969, joining the Western Fleet. After work-up exercises with HMS *Eagle* the carrier took part in Exercise *Dawn Patrol* during June 1970. This was the carrier's last stint as a carrier of conventional aircraft as it was paid off in October for conversion to a commando carrier. However, alone of the four ships to operate the Buccaneer, *Hermes* had a substantial later career, being modified to operate Sea Harrier V/STOL fighter/attack jets at the end of the 1970s, serving as flagship of the Falklands task force in 1982 and going on to join the Indian Navy.

HMS *Victorious*
Originally commissioned in 1941, HMS *Victorious* was host to the NA.39 development aircraft in January 1961, during which thirty-one launches and recoveries were successfully achieved. She recommissioned after a major reconstruction in 1963 with the Buccaneers of 801 Squadron amongst her air group. The carrier departed to the Far East to carry out a series of flag-waving exercises before returning to Britain in July 1965. Resuming sea duties, one of her first tasks took place in April 1966 when the Buccaneers of 801 Squadron undertook a round trip to Gibraltar to carry out a simulated strike. The launch point was in the Irish Sea, the entire trip encompassing 2,300 miles (3,700km).

In July HMS *Victorious* departed to join the Far East Fleet although her progress was stopped at Malta in case British intervention was needed in the Six Day War between Israel and the Arab states. When hostilities ceased the carrier was ordered to return to Britain, finally arriving at Portsmouth for a refit in June 1967. It was during this overhaul that the vessel was slightly damaged by fire and the order was given to withdraw the ship from service two years earlier than had previously been planned. Many in the Royal Navy regarded this as a serious mistake by the government of the day, as *Victorious* was a proven, successful ship.

HMS *Eagle* travelling a speed with Buccaneers, Sea Vixens, Gannets and Wessex on the flight deck. Although *Eagle* was big enough to operate the Phantom, only *Ark Royal* received the necessary modifications. BBA Collection

With a Soviet Navy cruiser in attendance, HMS *Eagle* cruises with part of its Buccaneer force on the flight deck. BBA Collection

CHAPTER FIVE

The Buccaneer Described

The prototype aircraft designed to fulfil Specification M.148 was described as a low-level, long-range naval strike aircraft that was powered by a pair of De Havilland Gyron Junior D.GJ.1 turbojet engines.

Fuselage

The fuselage consisted of three main sections, the first being the cockpit; this was located between the front and rear bulkheads, which were held apart by heavy-duty longerons. Within the cockpit were four console panels, two per position, while the pilot and observer were faced with instrument panels respective to their tasks. The pilot's controls consisted of a control column – a horizontal slide assembly which formed part of the central pedestal – and a pair of rudder pedals. The rudder pedals were adjustable for leg reach by means of an adjuster wheel located below the control column.

The fuselage was shaped by heavy-gauge frames, these in turn being connected by longerons. The outer covering was alloy panelling held in place by rivets, the whole being topped by a single-piece sliding canopy that was fronted by a three-piece windscreen assembly. Mounted within the cockpit was the pressure floor that provided a mounting for the two ejection seats. Underneath the pressure floor was the nose wheel bay, housing an aft-retracting undercarriage leg that carried a single nose wheel.

The next fuselage section was the main load-bearing structure and consisted of three separate compartments. The first was an upper compartment that ran the length of the section and housed the integral fuel tank compartments. Although these compartments were well sealed against leaks, throughout the aircraft's life the stresses placed upon the airframe would result in rivets pulling, leading to small fuel leaks. When each airframe was stopped for major or an equivalent type of servicing one of the first tasks was to pressurize the fuel tanks to discover where the leaks were. Once these were identified and marked the aircraft was defuelled, the lower access panels were removed, the tanks were vented and the difficult task of curing the leaks began. Much of this task required the removal of the PRC sealant and replacement of the loose rivets. After the PRC had cured fully the tanks were refuelled, fingers were crossed, and pressure was applied. If the repairs were unsuccessful, the whole process had to be repeated.

Under the fuel tanks were two other compartments, the forward one being divided into the hydraulic and electrical equipment bays. Aft of this is the area that housed the bomb bay. As with the forward fuselage section, there were heavy-gauge bulkheads between which were two heavy-duty longerons that also carried the attachments for the catapult launching bridle. Although the longerons were designed to withstand the stresses generated by carrier launches and landings, at

This is the pilot's office in the Buccaneer. The primary instruments dominate the panel while other indicators are quite small; these included the flap and aileron droop gauges. BBA Collection

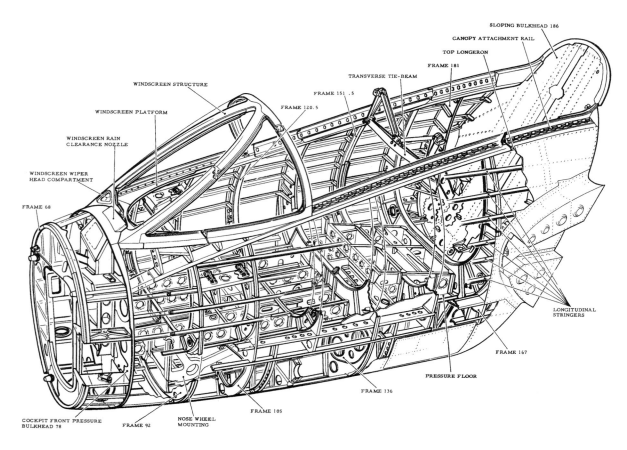

SLOPING BULKHEAD 186
CANOPY ATTACHMENT RAIL
TOP LONGERON
FRAME 181
TRANSVERSE TIE-BEAM
FRAME 151 .5
FRAME 120.5
WINDSCREEN STRUCTURE
WINDSCREEN PLATFORM
WINDSCREEN RAIN CLEARANCE NOZZLE
WINDSCREEN WIPER HEAD COMPARTMENT
FRAME 68
LONGITUDINAL STRINGERS
FRAME 167
PRESSURE FLOOR
FRAME 136
FRAME 105
COCKPIT FRONT PRESSURE BULKHEAD 78
FRAME 92
NOSE WHEEL MOUNTING

The Buccaneer cockpit assembly was, like the rest of the airframe, quite a meaty affair, as this diagram illustrates. BBA Collection

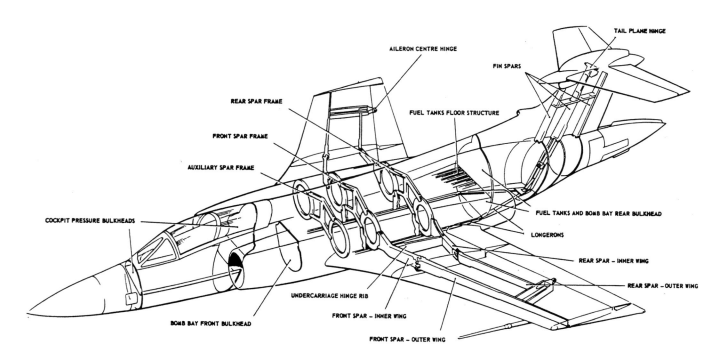

TAIL PLANE HINGE
AILERON CENTRE HINGE
FIN SPARS
REAR SPAR FRAME
FUEL TANKS FLOOR STRUCTURE
FRONT SPAR FRAME
AUXILIARY SPAR FRAME
COCKPIT PRESSURE BULKHEADS
FUEL TANKS AND BOMB BAY REAR BULKHEAD
LONGERONS
REAR SPAR – INNER WING
REAR SPAR – OUTER WING
UNDERCARRIAGE HINGE RIB
BOMB BAY FRONT BULKHEAD
FRONT SPAR – INNER WING
FRONT SPAR – OUTER WING

This diagram illustrates the location and layout of the main structural components of the Buccaneer. BBA Collection

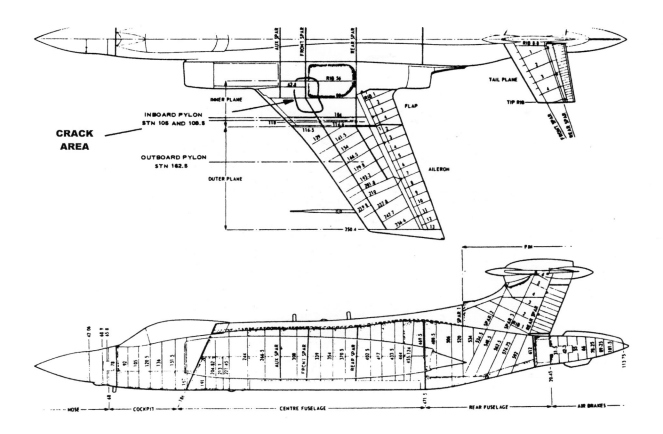

CRACK AREA

ABOVE: **Not only does this diagram show the layout of the frames and spars of the Buccaneer, it also indicates quite clearly the area in which the wing spar failed in February 1980. After a fleet-wide inspection it was decided to rebuild as many of the aircraft as possible. As this required donor, aircraft the overall force was reduced in size. It is not known whether the SAAF aircraft underwent any such programme.** BBA Collection

RIGHT: **Although this diagram illustrates the primary failure area in the wing spar, further investigations revealed that the spar rings were also afflicted by cracks. Depending on the severity of the damage, the spar section and ring would both be replaced.** BBA Collection

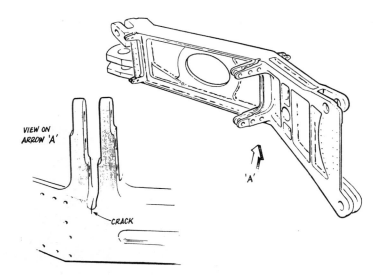

least one aircraft ended up with distorted longerons after the pilot became afflicted by target fixation. The resultant hasty 12g pull-out caused deformation of the longerons and the attached structure. Between the fuel tank bay floor and the longerons were reinforced frame sections that acted as mountings for the front, rear and auxiliary wing spar attachments.

The remaining centre-fuselage compartment was bulbous in shape and housed the radio bay. This section also housed the attachments for the air brake assembly, the arrestor hook, the rudder PFCUs and the LOX venting point.

The final section of the fuselage was the radome, which housed the radar and the folding nose section. Held in the closed position by three latches, the nose section could be unlocked and swung to port, being held in position by the use of a built-in jury strut. Mounted above and below the folding nose section were emergency arrestor barrier cutters, whose purpose was to slice through the horizontal nylon tension rope, thus protecting the engines from damage.

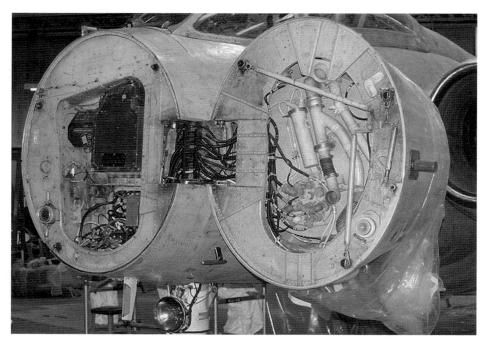

This view shows the nose in the open position. The various pipes relate to the in-flight refuelling probe and air conditioning equipment for the avionics in the nose. BBA Collection

Wings

The wings consisted of two separate structures, the inner and the outer. The inner section was mounted onto the fuselage at the front, rear and auxiliary spar points. These were intended to be an integral part of the airframe and were circular in form, housing as they did the engines and jet pipes. Attached to the aft spar were small plain flaps, these being hydraulically powered. Unlike other aircraft, the Buccaneer used a 'master and slave' jack system for its flaps, which required that the flaps be left in the lowered position otherwise the flap surfaces would go out of synchronization. The power for the flaps was provided by the general services hydraulic system, while synchronization was achieved by linking the port jack selector slide valve to the starboard jack.

The outer wing panel was constructed around two spars and covered by milled stressed-skin panels. Mounted on the trailing edge were the ailerons, these being powered by a PFCU. Wing tip fairings were attached to the wing ends, whilst at the other end of the wing panel were the hinge points and the locking pins, the latter being hydraulically driven. Sometimes the hinge pins would become seized in the bearings and require the careful application of extreme violence, normally involving a road jackhammer. Integral with the outer wings were reinforced points for the carriage of pylons and on the inner wings, fuel tanks plus the associated plumbing.

Fin

The fin was mounted on the rear fuselage section, carried on four mountings. At the top of the fin was the all-moving tailplane, whose PFCU was mounted in the fin. The fin was built around three spars for structural strength, with an auxiliary heavy-duty frame at the front for the forward attachment point. The swept tailplane was built around two spars covered by milled skins, under which were located four formers. Attached to the rear spars were the tailplane flaps.

Landing Gear

The landing gear was hydraulically driven and consisted of two main legs mounted into which are combined wheel and brake units, these being held within a forked lower leg assembly. Upon retraction these legs folded up and retracted inwards under large single piece doors. Occasionally problems arose with these wheels; on at least one instance at Honington a marksman was required to deflate a main wheel assembly whose tyre inflation valve could not be removed.

The noseleg assembly was also hydraulically actuated and incorporated nose wheel steering, the whole being housed under a single door. The steering jack had a range of 50 degrees each side of central,

This view of the wing break point reveals the pipework for the BLC system, and the wing fold and locking units. The front spar locking pin was mounted vertically while the aft spar pin was mounted horizontally. Visible just behind the front spar is the front hinge pin; on at least one occasion a pneumatic jackhammer was used to remove it. BBA Collection

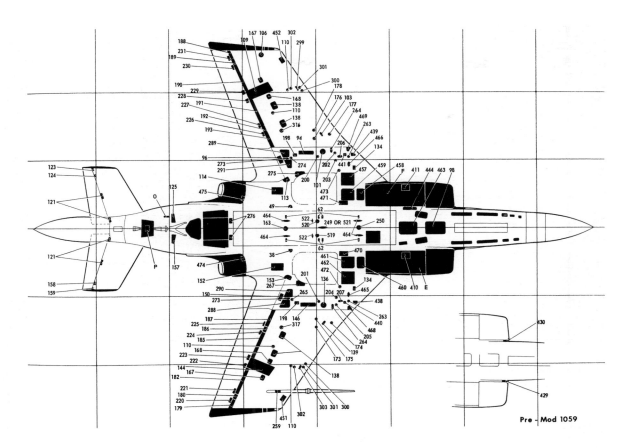

Both versions of the Buccaneer were well provided with access panels, many being reachable without the use of step ladders. BBA Collection

Pre - Mod 1059

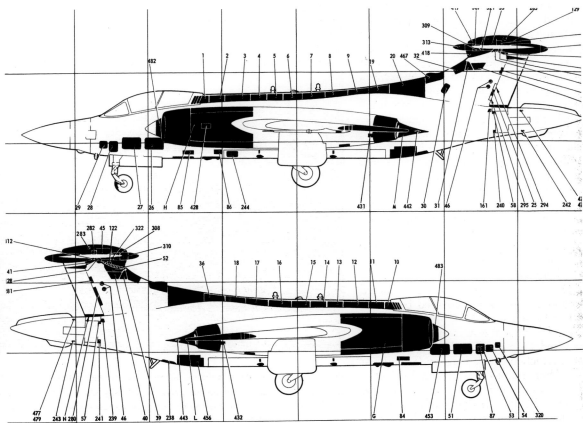

This side view illustrates the access panels on each side of the fuselage. It would be mainly the nose panels that were removed frequently, as much of the avionics equipment was housed here. BBA Collection

this being powered by the general services hydraulic system. Control of the steering jack used an electrical drum switch that incorporated input and follow-up levers operated by the rudder pedals in the cockpit.

Other hydraulically powered systems included the brake units – which incorporated anti-skid units – the arrestor hook, a tail skid and the wing fold and latching mechanisms. When the Buccaneer was operated by the Fleet Air Arm the catapult launch hooks were also hydraulically powered, although they were disconnected for use in the Royal Air Force. Whilst in Fleet Air Arm use the Buccaneer, after Modification 689 had been embodied, could have its under-carriage selected to 'up' prior to launch, this being carried out using the deck take-off button. This allowed quick undercarriage retraction after a catapult launch, although the crew were warned not to use this it from an on-shore establishment as its use rendered the emergency retraction inoperative.

ABOVE: **To improve the airflow over the tailplane, fairings were installed fore and aft of the tailplane. This location was found to be a good place to house the ARI 18228 radar warning receiver heads.** BBA Collection

LEFT: **Both versions of the Buccaneer were fitted with undercarriage legs capable of absorbing the impact of landing on a carrier deck and covered by a single main door. This view shows the air intake located in the wing leading edge of the S.1, which supplied supplementary air to the aircraft's systems.** BBA Collection

BELOW LEFT: **The view looking forward along the main undercarriage bay. The BLC ducting runs to the aft part of the system, while the larger tube is in fact the jet pipe tunnel covering, which passes through the forward spar ring.** BBA Collection

BELOW: **This view towards the rear of the main undercarriage bay shows the jet pipe and the BLC pipework passing through the rear spar.** BBA Collection

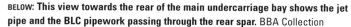

The nose leg carried a landing lamp that illuminated when the leg extended. Above the nose bay was a second pitot head that fed air pressure to the air data system. BBA Collection

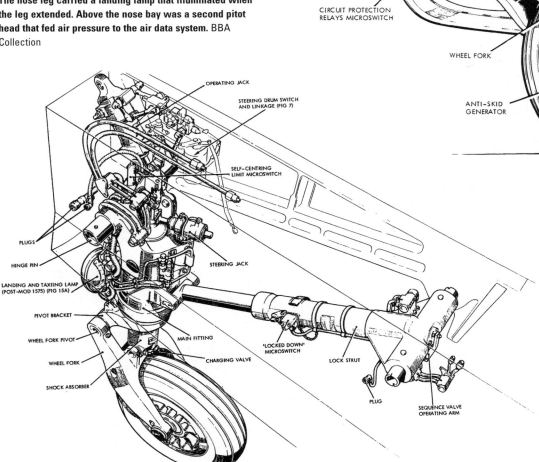

OPERATING JACK

FORWARD PIVOT PIN

DOWN-LOCK PLUNGER

A T O HOOK MECHANISM
PRE- MOD 1538 OR
POST-MOD 1409

REAR PIVOT PIN

CROSSHEAD

UNDERCARRIAGE DOOR

DOOR LOCK LATCH

SHOCK-ABSORBER

CHARGING VALVE

CIRCUIT PROTECTION
RELAYS MICROSWITCH

WHEEL FORK

ANTI-SKID
GENERATOR

OPERATING JACK

STEERING DRUM SWITCH
AND LINKAGE (FIG 7)

SELF-CENTRING
LIMIT MICROSWITCH

PLUGS

HINGE PIN

STEERING JACK

LANDING AND TAXIING LAMP
(POST-MOD 1575) (FIG 15A)

PIVOT BRACKET

WHEEL FORK PIVOT

MAIN FITTING

'LOCKED DOWN'
MICROSWITCH

WHEEL FORK

CHARGING VALVE

LOCK STRUT

SHOCK ABSORBER

PLUG

SEQUENCE VALVE
OPERATING ARM

ABOVE: The Buccaneer main undercarriage was built to withstand the shock of a high sink rate landing onto a pitching carrier deck, hence the solidity of its construction. BBA Collection

LEFT: The nose undercarriage retracted aft into its bay. Although much of the impact of landing was absorbed by the main legs, the nose was still subject to a certain amount of shock loading, hence the forked nose wheel installation. BBA Collection

Trim Control

The aircraft was trimmed by electrical actuators connected to the primary flight control circuits. Two other actuators, controlled by a single switch, operated the aileron droop mechanism and the tailplane flaps. As the Buccaneer used PFCUs, the use of hydraulically powered artificial feel units was mandatory, these gaining their input from the pitot static system. These gave simulated feel to the rudder and tailplane in relation to altitude and forward speed, power being supplied by the starboard hydraulic system. PFCUs were fitted to the ailerons, rudder and flying tailplane, each being a tandem unit powered by a flying-control hydraulic circuit. As with most hydraulically powered flight control systems, there was no manual reversion available to the pilot.

To improve the low-speed handling in the NA.39 the concept of aileron droop was introduced, a maximum of 30 degrees being available; this did not affect the operation of the ailerons. The aileron circuit had an electrical actuator mechanically connected to the system, this comprising of two identical motors, one for normal use and one for emergency purposes. Normal control was via a selector switch with 5-degree increments available, there being definite gates at the 20-degree and 30-degree positions. The pilot's notes warned that the aileron droop system could not be used should the boundary layer system be switched off or inoperable, nor should it be operated when the autopilot was engaged or when the hydraulic system was unpressurized. Should the aileron droop normal circuit fail for any reason, the

emergency system was available for one use only and could not be raised after use.

Control of the PFCUs as installed in the Buccaneer S.1 had three available modes: manual, auto stabilizer and autopilot. Under manual demand the input from the pilot was transferred mechanically to the control valves, which were opened as required to the appropriate side of the jacks; this allowed fluid to enter and operate the relevant flight control surface. Once the selected position was reached, a follow-up movement closed the relevant valves. In auto stabilizer mode the input signal was transmitted electrically to the relevant actuator, which in turn operated the control valves; as before, there was a mechanical follow-up to close the valves, and there was also an electrical feed-back that controlled the position of the actua-

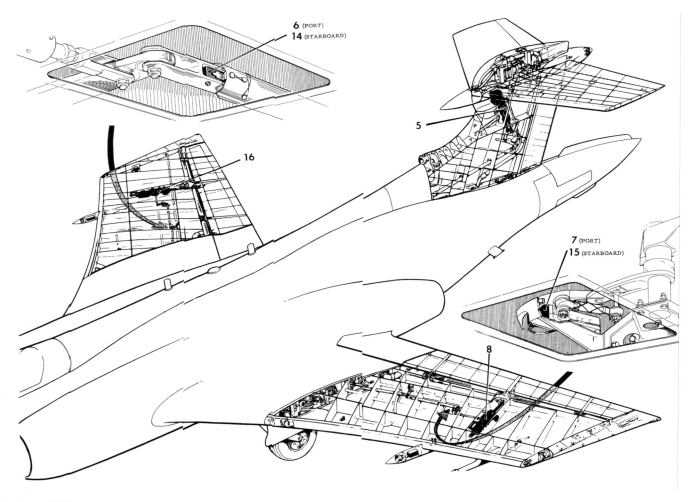

6 (PORT)
14 (STARBOARD)

16

5

7 (PORT)
15 (STARBOARD)

8

The aileron PFCUs were housed in their own bays in the outer wing panels. Being substantial items, they required at least two persons for installation and removal. They were also not very good at bouncing when accidentally dropped from a wing in the folded position! BBA Collection

tor. The autopilot mode also transmitted its signal to the actuator electrically to operate the relevant actuators. In this mode the mechanical follow-up was inoperative, so a second electrical feed-back was provided to control the position at which point the actuator control valves would return to the neutral position.

The artificial feel system was applicable to all three flight control runs, these being double-acting spring units mounted in the control linkages that led to the PFCU control valves. In operation, the use of the control column or the rudder pedals was met by an increasing spring force. The airspeed feel component was applicable to the rudder and the tailplane circuits only, these being hydraulically powered units that were incorporated in the control runs. Each unit consisted of a feel simulator control and a hydraulic jack: the former metered the amount of fluid entering the control jack, this being governed by the pitot and static pressures, thus resisting the pilot's control movement. In operation, the resistance force increased in proportion to the square of the aircraft's speed. To give additional resistance to control movements from neutral on the ground, the feel simulator exerted a base pressure even when there was no pitot pressure being applied.

Trim control for the rudder and ailerons was effected by an actuator attached to each control system by a lever and a double acting spring link. Alteration of the either trim was effected by altering the position of the spring link lever, which altered the neutral position of the control surface. The tailplane was also trimmable across a range of 28 degrees, this being achieved by movement of the control column and the datum shift trimmer. The 28 degrees of range consisted of 8 degrees nose down and 20 degrees nose up. Use of the control column in trim mode gave a range of 12 degrees nose down and 10 degrees nose up while a separate trimmer switch gave a range of 4 degrees nose down and 13 degrees nose up, although when Modification 1123 was embodied the nose-up range was decreased to 9 degrees.

Incorporated into the aileron control run was a gear change unit. This system was a range-limiting device, thus in high-speed selection the range of movement was 12.5 degrees each side of neutral on post-Modification 793 aircraft; unmodified aircraft had a range of 17.5 degrees each side of the neutral datum. When the

selector was set to low speed, the aileron range of travel was 17.5 degrees either side of the neutral datum, these figures being applicable to all aircraft whether they were pre- or post-Modification 793.

Prior to the installation of the autopilot in the NA.39, the flying control surfaces were held in place by mechanical locking devices; after the fitment of the autopilot, control locking was through the PFCUs. Trimming of the ailerons and rudder was by electrically actuated spring bias mechanisms connected to the primary control circuits. The tailplane circuit was provided by an electrically actuated datum shift mechanism, this being incorporated in the gearing unit at the aft end of the tailplane control system. Each trim system was controlled by a single switch mounted on the port console, labelled 'Tail Plane Trim Rate: High – Low'. The 'high' selection came into operation when the flaps were lowered, this occurring irrespective of the tailplane flap position. When the system was switched over to the standby circuit the high rate selection was inoperative. Tailplane trimming was operated by a thumb switch on the control column – 'forward' was down while 'back' was aft. Should the normal motor or circuit fail for any reason, the standby circuit was selected by the operation of the standby switch.

Rudder Stop System

To ensure that the Buccaneer's rudder system did not exert excessive loads upon the airframe, a rudder stop system was installed, this being especially needed when the aircraft was travelling at high speed. Mechanical stops were fitted into the rudder's mechanical control circuit. The system used air pressure piped from the air bleed system, this being selected by a two-position switch located in the port console, near the throttle levers.

Flaps

The tailplane flap system as fitted to the Buccaneer was powered by the general services hydraulic system. Only two selections were available, 'normal' and 'up'. In the normal position the tailplane flaps were in line with the tailplane, while in the up position they were deflected by 30 degrees, although this was limited to 20 degrees in the prototype, XK486. In the

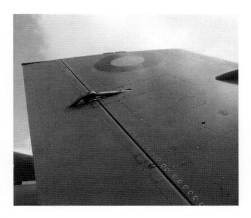

This view shows the location of the wing PFCU and the aileron hinging. It was possible to cross-connect the hydraulic pipework leading to the PFCU, which resulted in some impressive displays of hydraulic fluid blasting out of every orifice when the internal seals in the PFCU blew! BBA Collection

fully up position the flaps were hydraulically locked in position. The flaps' position was selected using a switch mounted in the port console panel. Should there have been a failure of the electrical or hydraulic systems, the emergency system was capable of providing one movement to the up position only, where it stayed until the aircraft had landed. Once on the ground the tailplane flap was reset on the ground using the hydraulic manual reset.

The two flap sections mounted on the trailing edge of the inner wing sections were operated by electrically selected hydraulic jacks powered by the general services systems. The flap switch was located on the port console, labelled 'Up', 'Take Off' and 'Down'. The flap switch had seven positions, each of which would give a steady rate of raising of lowering. Should there be a failure of either the electrical or hydraulic systems, the flaps could be lowered for one use only by the emergency switch. The flaps could not then be reselected up, or otherwise operated, until the ground release switch was operated on the ground. As the flaps operated in synchronization, only the port flap gave indications of position in the cockpit.

Air brakes

The air brakes were mounted at the aft extremity of the fuselage, where they formed the rear fuselage when closed. The

The airbrakes were normally mounted into the airframe using a crane, as they frequently were delivered as a complete assembly. BBA Collection

In the closed position the airbrakes reveal that there were two parts to each side: the main petals and the fairings that covered the operating arms. BBA Collection

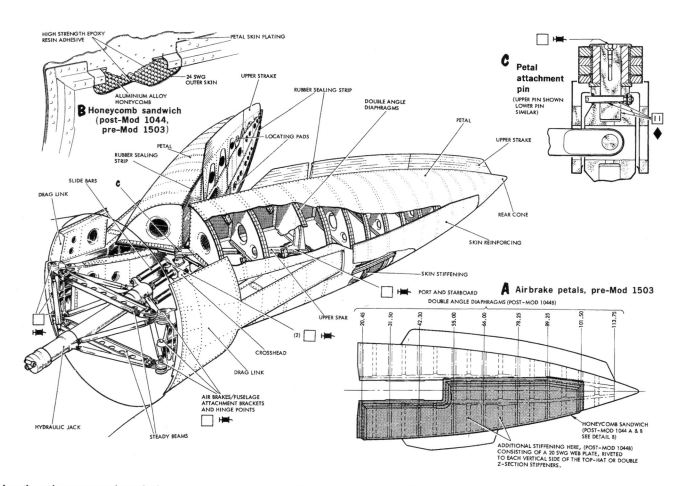

Unless the maintenance work required was minor in nature, it was easier to remove the entire airbrake assembly from the aircraft for refurbishment. Sometimes the major servicing team would be lucky and acquire a ready-to-fit set. BBA Collection

The bomb bay door was capable of housing a transit pod, which is seen hanging off the rotated door of this Buccaneer S.2. BBA Collection

air brakes were operated by a double-acting hydraulic jack which took its power from the general service hydraulic system. The control switch mounted in the starboard throttle lever and had two positions, 'In' and 'Out'. To select the air brakes to an intermediate position the pilot had to select 'Out', then return the switch to neutral when the required position was reached. In the event of an emergency, the standby selection allowed for either one extension or retraction. As with other standby circuits, the air brake system's could only then be reset on the ground.

Bomb Door

Another system that gained its power from the general service system was the single-piece bomb door. When in the closed position the door completely covered the weapons bay. The inner face was a rigid structure capable of carrying a range of weaponry. The door was mounted on pivotal bearings mounted fore and aft, and driven by a single hydraulic double-acting jack powered from the general services system. The bomb door was controlled by

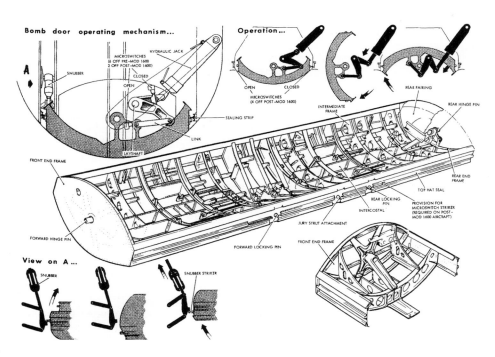

One of the cunning parts of the Buccaneer design was the rotary bomb bay, which operated in a similar manner to that of the Martin B-57. Many critics though that the Buccaneer's bomb load was small for an aircraft of its size, but it should be borne in mind that improved delivery made each bomb more effective. The era of mass carpet bombing was waning fast. BBA Collection

a gated switch that could be selected to either 'Open' or 'Closed'. To ensure that the door remained undamaged the made selection had to be completed before another one could be made. Should there be any system failure of the bomb door circuits, there was a standby system that gave a single operation, either open or closed, although the circuit would then have to be reset manually on the ground.

Anti-Spin Parachute

Unlike the production machines, the prototype aircraft were fitted with an anti-spin parachute that was located in the port air brake petal. Until required for use the parachute was housed under a blister cover which, when released, allowed the parachute to be pulled out into the airflow. Control of the parachute was via an electrical switch on the pilot's port console. To prevent an inadvertent selection of the switch there was a spring-loaded safety stop fitted. To prevent the parachute being jettisoned by mistake before it was streamed, the cover was fitted with a microswitch that controlled the jettison circuit.

Autopilot

The autopilot system in the NA.39 – as distinct from the Buccaneer S.1 – integrated the auto stabilizer and flying control units, and was operated by a control unit mounted in the starboard console and a grip unit incorporated into the control column. Power to this system was drawn from either the No. 1 or No. 2 flight instrument inverters. The switches on the control unit were autopilot, force stick/lock and the auto stabilizer switch. The control column grip had three selections: engage, disengage and cut-out. Should the cut-out or the limit switches be operated the autopilot could be reset using a gated switch on the port console. Application of electrical power to the aircraft would cause the autopilot fail lights on the centralized warning panel to illuminate. To counter this the reset switch had to be reset to re-arm, the cut-out circuits restoring the system to normal mode.

Once the autopilot system was engaged the following modes became available: height lock, Mach number lock, force stick with auto stabilizer and force stick without auto stabilizer. To engage height lock the force stick lock switch was moved to 'lock' and the height Mach switch to 'height', after which the 'engage' switch on the control grip could be depressed. Once in operation the aircraft's height was governed by the prevailing barometric height. When Mach lock was required the force stick lock was selected to 'lock' while the height/Mach switch was set to 'Mach'. Again the engage switch on the control column grip needed to be engaged to operate this selection. The use of force stick required that 'force stick' be selected on the control unit, this being followed by the 'engage' selection on the grip. In this mode there was no height, heading or Mach monitoring.

Should the pilot need to change the autopilot mode, the current selection had to be disengaged using the control column grip switch. To ensure that there was no inadvertent selection of the autopilot at an inopportune moment, such as take-off or landing, there was a gated switch on the control column that had to be in the 'off' position until required for use. The pilot also had to be aware of keeping the tailplane and the aircraft trimmed correctly even in autopilot mode; failure to monitor this system could result in operation of the tailplane limit switches.

The autopilot fitted to the Buccaneer S.1 was a more sophisticated device than that in the NA.39. The computer at the heart of the system gained its data from the air data system, the maximum rate gyro (MRG) and the compass. Once the computer had gained its data input it then made the required computation; this effected the necessary switching in the auto stabilizer and the autopilot modes, which in turn controlled the PFCUs. When in auto stabilization or manual mode the system relied on three rate gyros, which monitored the yaw, pitch and roll channels. Signals produced by an angular rate of movement were fed into the computer, where they were amplified and fed onto the relevant actuators of the PFCUs; this in turn moved the attached control surface. As the control surface movement was dependent upon airspeed, the pilot was provided with the capability to select either high- or low-speed gearing for the yaw and roll channels.

When the autopilot mode was engaged a failure of the auto stabilizer could be limited by engaging a yaw damper, which controlled any lateral or directional oscillations. The downside of any yaw channel failure was that it was extremely difficult to detect on the ground. When the autopilot was engaged the rate of bank was limited to 10 degrees per second, while the tailplane trim was not to be engaged during a turn. When flying below 5,000ft (1,500m) the longitudinal trim had to be maintained at 0.25 degrees either side of the neutral datum. The autopilot could not be used should the temperature in the radio bay exceeded 60°C, although this increased to 70°C once Modification 1019 was embodied.

Protecting the aircraft from damage or destruction were four safety devices that were developed for the NA.39 and incorporated into the Buccaneer S.1; three of these were automatic while the other was manual. All were designed to prevent autopilot runaway which, if unchecked, could cause major structural damage to the aircraft. Should any of the automatic protection devices be triggered a light on the CWP illuminated to warn the pilot. The automatic protection devices were fitted to the aileron and tailplane systems. In the case of the ailerons, the runaway limits were set at 3 degrees either side of neutral, although this was reduced to 2 degrees upon the incorporation of Modification 670. Tailplane limits were set at 0.75 degrees and –1.5 degrees. Should any of the safety devices be operated, the autopilot and auto stabilizer became disengaged, this occurring even with the manual safety device.

The NA.39 was fitted with the Mk 5 FT compass system, which provided heading reference data for the autopilot. Heading selection was via a heading selector knob that placed a pointer on the required heading. To place the aircraft on the required heading the pilot could turn the aircraft either manually or through the autopilot using the force stick mode. To protect against malfunction there was a cut-out fitted to the grip on the control column. Protecting against aileron system runaway, each side was protected by spring boxes fitted between the aileron inputs. The tailplane was protected by a control surface angle-limit switch that would disengage the autopilot automatically. Should any of these back-ups be operated, the aircraft reverted to manual control while the relevant lights on the CWP illuminated and the autopilot electrical supply was switched off.

Engines

The engines were mounted forward of the front spar rings, one each side of the forward part of the centre section. Mounting the engines onto the fuselage required an inboard trunnion mounting on the engine centreline and a forward upper mounting attached to a cantilever beam that extended from the fuselage, while there was a rear mounting link attached to a transverse beam in the upper nacelle structure. The engines each had two accessories gearboxes, one driven by gearing from the low-pressure compressor shaft and one from the high-pressure compressor shaft, these being termed the right and left gearboxes, respectively. The right-hand gearbox drove a constant-speed drive unit that provided power to turn the AC alternators, while the other drove the hydraulic pumps.

The engines also provided pneumatics, for which three tappings were taken from the engine casing at the seventh stage of the HP compressor. This system supplied air to the blowing system, fuel tank pressurization, negative 'g' recuperators, fuel- no air valves, windscreen rain clearance, hydraulic reservoir pressurization, constant speed drive unit (CSDU) pressurization, engine and radio bay cooling, cabin pressurization and air conditioning. Further services included windscreen demisting, anti 'g' suit pressurization, accessories bay cooling, radome conditioning and pressurization. A further tapping from the HP compressor supplied air for the engine anti-icing system.

Should there be a failure in the air conditioning system, the NA.39 was fitted with an emergency ventilation system that could be selected via a control on the starboard console. Operation of this control opened a ram-air valve that allowed air to enter the cabin at ram-air pressure, this being drawn into ducting via two small intakes close to the engine intakes. To compensate for any possible cabin over-pressurization, the cabin discharge valve was opened to vent any excess pressure. Pilots were warned quite strongly about opening this valve rapidly at altitude, which would cause a sudden cabin decompression.

The engines fitted to the Buccaneer S.2 were a pair of Rolls-Royce Spey Mk 101 engines. The Spey was a two-spool bypass turbojet that had a four-stage low-pressure compressor and a twelve-stage high-pres-

The engine was housed behind three removable panels and an intake assembly, although in normal practice it was only the upper and lower doors that were opened for maintenance purposes. BBA Collection

This view of a severely stripped Buccaneer on the Abingdon fire dump reveals the engine bay installation and the horizontal mounting beam. BBA Collection

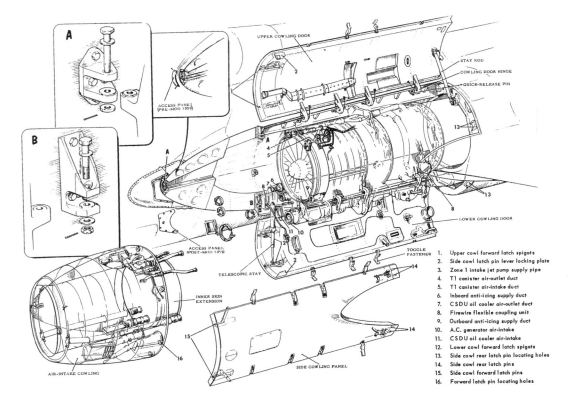

A

ACCESS PANEL
(PRE-MOD 1059)

B

ACCESS PANEL
(POST-MOD 1059)

TELESCOPIC STAY

INNER SKIN
EXTENSION

AIR-INTAKE COWLING

UPPER COWLING DOOR

STAY ROD
COWLING DOOR HINGE
QUICK-RELEASE PIN

LOWER COWLING DOOR

TOGGLE
FASTENER

SIDE COWLING PANEL

1. Upper cowl forward latch spigots
2. Side cowl latch pin lever locking plate
3. Zone 1 intake jet pump supply pipe
4. T1 canister air-outlet duct
5. T1 canister air-intake duct
6. Inboard anti-icing supply duct
7. CSDU oil cooler air-outlet duct
8. Firewire flexible coupling unit
9. Outboard anti-icing supply duct
10. A.C. generator air-intake
11. CSDU oil cooler air-intake
12. Lower cowl forward latch spigots
13. Side cowl rear latch pin locating holes
14. Side cowl rear latch pins
15. Side cowl forward latch pins
16. Forward latch pin locating holes

Installation of the Spey and the earlier Gyron Junior was fairly straightforward in comparison with other aircraft as the entire intake and cowling panels could be removed, giving unprecedented access to the engine. BBA Collection

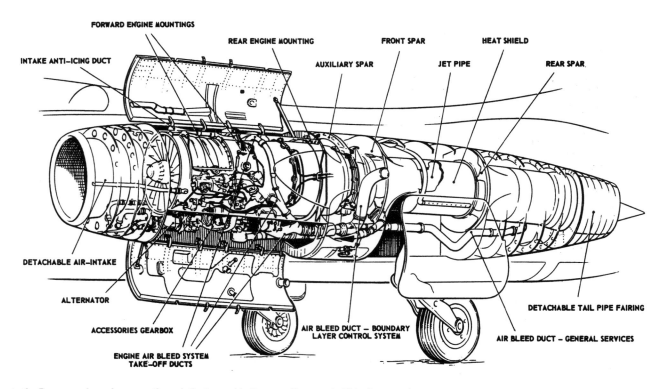

FORWARD ENGINE MOUNTINGS

REAR ENGINE MOUNTING

FRONT SPAR

HEAT SHIELD

INTAKE ANTI-ICING DUCT

AUXILIARY SPAR

JET PIPE

REAR SPAR

DETACHABLE AIR-INTAKE

ALTERNATOR

ACCESSORIES GEARBOX

ENGINE AIR BLEED SYSTEM
TAKE-OFF DUCTS

AIR BLEED DUCT – BOUNDARY
LAYER CONTROL SYSTEM

DETACHABLE TAIL PIPE FAIRING

AIR BLEED DUCT – GENERAL SERVICES

Access to the Buccaneer's engines was through the top and bottom cowling panels. This diagram also illustrates the connections for the various services. BBA Collection

sure compressor, each being driven by a two-stage turbine. The compressor stages operate independently, the low-pressure shaft rotating within the high-pressure shaft.

Air, on entering the engine face, passed through the low-pressure compressor; some of it then passed through the high-pressure compressor while the remainder passed through the bypass ducting. The air that had passed through the high-pressure compressor was ducted to the combustor part of the engine, where it entered the ten combustion liners where fuel was added. At this point the mixture was ignited by the high-energy ignition units, the resultant gas passing at high speed and temperature over the turbines. Having passed the turbine the gas entered the gas mixer, where it mixed with the bypass air expelled from the low-pressure compressor, after which the gas was ejected through the convergent propelling nozzle and out through the jet pipe. In order to minimize damage to the turbine and to

Looking down the intake shows the front face of the Spey compressor and the inlet guide vanes which, on the Gyron version, gave endless trouble. BBA Collection

The BLC system installed in the Buccaneer. Testing for correct operation on the ground required that selected personnel stand a safe distance behind the wings holding flags. Once the BLC was engaged the flags should stream directly aft. Obviously this could only be done on a virtually windless day. BBA Collection

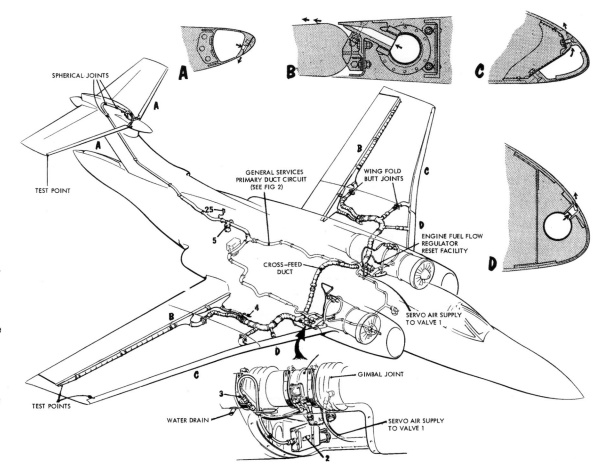

extend its life, the aircraft was fitted with a temperature monitor located just aft of the turbine which, when a preset value was reached, automatically reduced the fuel flow to the engine, this being achieved by the use of an actuator in the fuel system.

As the Buccaneer was designed to operate in numerous different environments, the engines incorporated variable IGVs in an effort to smooth the airflow into the compressor, these being supplemented by high-pressure air bleed valves. When the IGV was in the open position the bleed valve allowed air from an air take-off tapping from the compressor's seventh stage to enter the bypass duct. This tap-off also provided air to the general services system for the BLC system. The twelfth stage of the compressor provided air to pneumatically controlled air shut-off valves that controlled the BLC system. All personnel were warned that the BLC system should not be operated with the wings folded, as damage to the wing fold

seal could result and it was hazardous to personnel in the vicinity. This tapping also supplied air to the engine anti-icing system when needed.

Further engine services operated an engine-driven high-pressure pump that supplied fuel to the combustor liner spray nozzles. This pump was controlled by a single lever that also operated the throttle valve. The high-pressure drive was also coupled to a low-pressure starter for engine starting. Once the external starter trolley was supplying air, the remainder of the start sequence was controlled automatically through the starter control circuit.

Flight Controls

The flight control system installed in the Buccaneer consisted of the primary surfaces: ailerons, rudder and tailplane; and the secondaries: mainplane flaps, air brakes and tailplane flaps. Operation of

the flight control surfaces was by powered flying control units, these being controlled either by manual inputs from the pilot or by inputs from the autopilot system. Modes available to the autopilot were short-term auto stabilization around all three axes and automatic altitude holding at any desired altitude. The system also incorporated a heading lock, although this was only available when either the height lock or Mach lock was engaged. Should there be a failure of the auto stabilisation yaw mode, the system was fitted with a standby yaw damper that became available only when the primary had failed.

Fuel System

Fuel was carried in eight tanks in the upper fuselage. These were coupled in pairs for feeding purposes: four acted as masters while the others acted as feeds to the masters. Fuel movement required an air

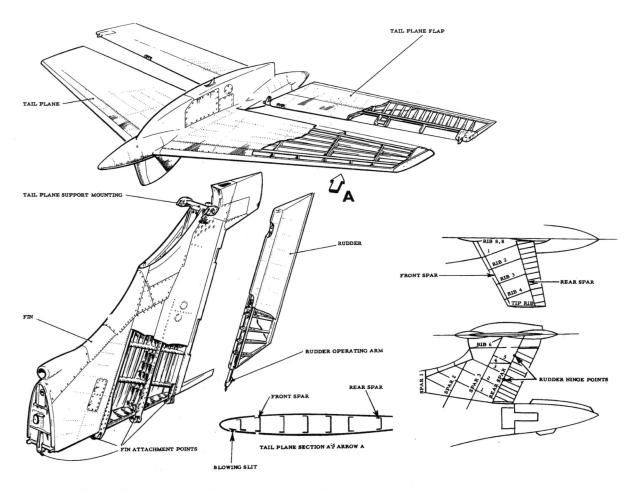

This diagram illustrates the fin and tailplane assemblies. Of note is the ram air cooling intake mounted on the dorsal panel. BBA Collection

pressurization feed to push the fuel to the master tanks. When the aircraft was refuelled care needed to be taken to ensure that the sequence was followed correctly, otherwise the Buccaneer would quite happily sit backwards onto its tail skid. Actual fuel feed to the engines used electric pumps mounted in the master tanks.

As the Buccaneer design progressed extra tanks were developed to increase the aircraft's range. The first of these were the jettisonable slipper tanks that were carried under the inner wing sections. A further fuel tank was introduced by the RAF as part of Modification 1600, this being the bomb door tank. Fuel transfer from this tank used electrical pumps, while the underwing tanks used air pressure to feed fuel into the master tank.

Refuelling of the aircraft was through a single pressure point on the port side of the nose, while for refuelling in flight a demountable in-flight refuelling probe was available, which was introduced by Modification 881. The probe was connected to the ground refuelling gallery, the system being controlled by a 'Flight Refuel On/Off' switch. When this switch was moved to 'on' it isolated the external fuel tanks, and the bomb door tank if fitted. Another action caused by this operation was to open the fuel transfer circuits, which operated the refuel solenoids for the refuel/defuel valves. Once the aircraft was plugged into the tanker's drogue and fuel transfer had started the refuel continued automatically, being governed by the tank high-level float switches. Once the fuselage tanks were full the system then switched across to allow the external and bomb bay tanks to be refuelled. At the completion of the refuel the flight refuel switch was returned to the 'off' position, allowing the fuel in the external tanks to be utilized.

The fuel system in the aircraft was quite unique as the fuel passed through hydraulically driven fuel proportioners mounted in the bomb bay, from where the fuel passed through flow meters and low-pressure fuel cocks to the engines. This system, coupled with pneumatically driven anti-g fuel recuperators, ensured that a fuel supply could been maintained for a period should the normal supply be interrupted for any reason.

One final option was available for the crew, this being four electrically operated jettison valves that allowed fuel from the fuselage tanks to be jettisoned through a fuel mast under the rear fuselage, although

until Modifications 880 and 1091 were applied this was for emergency use only: prior to these being embodied there was a danger of the radio bay being flooded. Fuel jettisoning had to be monitored until 4,000lb (1,800kg) of fuel remained, at which point the procedure had to be stopped. Dumping fuel from the underwing tanks could be achieved either by jettisoning the tank completely or by operating the jettison valves at the rear of each tank. Fuel in the bomb door tank was dumped through the same point as the main fuel tanks.

When the M.148/NA.39 was constructed the fuel system was controlled by a cock, mounted on the starboard side of the pilot's cockpit, which in turn controlled the four air-operated fuel transfer valves situated in the bases of Nos 1, 3, 5 and 7 tanks. The high-pressure fuel cocks were controlled by a lever that was combined with the throttles. When the levers were pushed forward the initial stage opened the high-pressure cocks prior to engine starting. The low-pressure cocks were manually operated, their controls being located on the pilot's port console. Indicators for the fuel system were located on the starboard side of the instrument panel and console. Those on the panel concerned the fuel proportioners, the equipment that showed a white doll's eye when failed, while the console housed the gauges for fuel inlet pressure indication.

The aircraft pressure refuelling point was located on the starboard side of the fuselage, just forward of the nose wheel bay. Located alongside the coupling were

eleven red lamps, of which only eight were initially used; the others were later connected to the underwing and bomb bay fuel tanks. Just forward of this group was a panel of eight refuelling switches, these being marked for 'Refuel' and 'Defuel' and controlled by a master switch that was labelled ON–OFF. (In the first prototype these switches were located alongside the pressure refuelling point.) During a refuelling operation the master switch was set to 'ON' while the required refuel switch was set to 'Refuel': this illuminated the relevant indicator lamp. When the selected tank was filled the indicator light went out. Defuelling was carried out in a similar manner. When neither operation was being undertaken the master switch had to be in the 'OFF' position.

The fuel tanks were vented to the atmosphere through an outlet located on the underside of the fuselage, just forward of the air brakes. When the aircraft was refuelled the air displaced during this operation was pushed through the tank vent shuttle valves, whose pipelines joined together at the inward/outward vent valve and into a common vent pipe, which led to the vent outlet. When the aircraft was defuelled, air at atmospheric pressure was fed into the fuel tanks via the common vent line, passing through the inward/outward vent valves and into the tank. These valves were operated when the evacuating fuel caused enough of a vacuum to open the valves.

The fuel tanks were pressurized by air drawn from engine tappings that entered the fuel system via the tank venting

Mounted on the lower port rear fuselage was the defuel mast, through which fuel could be dumped in an emergency. BBA Collection

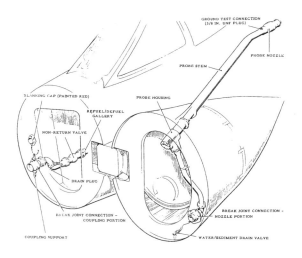

ABOVE: **The folding nose section allowed the aircraft to fit into aircraft carrier hangars; it was also home for the demountable in-flight refuelling probe and its associated plumbing.** BBA Collection

LEFT: **This nose-on view shows the offset angle of the detachable refuel probe, as fitted to both versions of the Buccaneer. The original probe was a neat fold-away affair, but its extension and subsequent coupling to a drogue caused airflow problems with the starboard engine as the intakes are close to the fuselage.** BBA Collection

system. To prevent any chance of air pressure leaking back to the engine system, the air passed through non-return valves. Should the system pressure exceed 6psi, the excess air was vented to the atmosphere. To indicate the state of the fuel tank pressurization, indicators mounted on the starboard console showed black when the system was operating correctly and white when any pair of tanks fell below the normal operating level.

The Buccaneer could also act as an in-flight refuelling tanker, should this be needed. A Flight Refuelling Ltd Mk 20C or E pod could be carried on a special pylon under the starboard wing. The pod gained its fuel from the aircraft's fuel system and would act as a fuel tank when not in use for tanking duties. Once the pod had been selected for refuelling, a self-contained hydraulic system operated the hose drum unit and the hose brake. The pod also incorporated a pneumatic system for release of the emergency brake and a fuel pump to dispense the fuel to the receiving aircraft. Both this pump and that for the hydraulics were powered by a ram air turbine mounted in the nose of the pod.

Most of the pod's operations were automatic, only the extension and retraction of the hose being under manual control once the correct switch selections had been made. The first required that the master switch on the observer's port console be selected to 'on': this changed the role of the pod from fuel tank to that of dispenser, after which the contents had to be verified as full. Selecting trail on the trail/wind switch allowed the hose and its drogue to run out to its full extent, at which point the hose brake was applied. When the receiver aircraft plugged into the drogue its forward motion was normally enough to force the hose to wind approximately 7ft (2m), which in turn allowed the fuel-flow valve to open. As fuel emptied from the refuel pod it was replenished from the

The RAF were not frequent users of the under-wing refuel pod, preferring to use dedicated tankers instead. Even so, some training with the pod was required. BBA Collection

aircraft's system. In order to maintain the aircraft's balance during this operation the port underwing fuel tank transfer valve needed to be on. Once refuelling was completed the hose could be rewound into the pod, after which the master switch was selected to 'off', allowing the pod to act as a fuel tank once again.

Hydraulic System

The hydraulic system installed in the M.148/NA.39 aircraft was equipped with four pumps. Two of these running at 3,000psi drove the flight control surfaces, though this was increased to 3,300psi in the production versions. Both pumps drove the surfaces and were capable of reduced-rate operation in the event of an engine or pump failure. The port pump drove the auto stabilizer, autopilot and the forward jack attached to the aileron and tailplane PFCUs. Power was also supplied to the rudder control unit, as this is not integrated into the autopilot unit. The starboard pump supplied power to the rear jacks of the flight control surfaces, but unlike the port circuit it had no connection to the autopilot or auto stabilizer. This meant that should the port services fail for any reason, the autopilot and auto stabilizer units were inoperative.

The flying control circuit pumps were supported by accumulators whose purpose was to cater for any sudden upsurge in control surface requirements. The accumulators, two per system, were located on each side of the bomb bay. One accumulator in each pair contained hydraulic fluid charged by the engine-driven pumps, while the other was pressurized to 3,000psi and was used to push the fluid back into the hydraulic operating system. So that the pilot had some idea of the behaviour of these pumps, there were indicators incorporated into the centralized warning panel that illuminated in the event of a failure.

The other two pumps mounted on the engines were responsible for providing the general service requirements of the aircraft. Fluid supplies for this system were provided by the common main reservoir. The purpose of this system was to supply power to the remaining hydraulic circuits and its operating pressure was 4,000psi. Should the reservoir that supplied the general services fail for any reason, such as excessive leakage, hydraulic power could be supplied by two emergency hydraulic

---

Main System Fuel Tank Operation

When the NA.39 was constructed its fuel system tanks had the following capacities:

No. 1 tank 170gal (770ltr)	No. 5 tank 170gal (770ltr)
No. 2 tank 205gal (930ltr)	No. 6 tank 205gal (930ltr)
No. 3 tank 170gal (770ltr)	No. 7 tank 205gal (930ltr)
No. 4 tank 170gal (770ltr)	No. 8 tank 205gal (930ltr)

When the fuel system is operating normally Nos 1, 3, 6 and 8 tanks fed the starboard engine and Nos 2, 4, 5 and 7 the port engine. The hydraulically powered fuel proportioners mounted on the bomb bay walls regulated the amount of fuel drawn from each fuel tank group. Should an emergency occur, the fuel flow could be redirected via an inter-tank transfer system through a cross-feed pipe that connected the port and starboard engine fuel feed pipes. When the aircraft was inverted or under negative 'g' conditions, fuel supply could be maintained for a short period by two air-operated recuperators.

The fuel system controls were located on the standby control panel located on the starboard side of the pilot's cockpit. The switches operated an electrically controlled cross-feed cock that was situated in the bomb bay and linked the port and starboard engine fuel lines.

When the Buccaneer S.1 was introduced it retained the same fuel system as the NA.39, but the contents had changed thus:

No. 1 tank 205gal (930ltr)	No. 5 tank 180gal (818ltr)
No. 2 tank 220gal (1,000ltr)	No. 6 tank 198gal (900ltr)
No. 3 tank 183gal (832ltr)	No. 7 tank 192gal (873ltr)
No. 4 tank 168gal (763ltr)	No. 8 tank 184gal (836ltr)

Extra fuel tankage was fitted under the inner mainplanes in jettisonable fuel tanks, each of which contained 250gal (1,137ltr) each.

The development of the Buccaneer S.2 resulted in a further revamp of the fuel system contents thus:

No. 1 tank 214gal (973ltr)	No. 5 tank 191gal (868ltr)
No. 2 tank 224gal (1,018ltr)	No. 6 tank 192gal (873ltr)
No. 3 tank 174gal (791ltr)	No. 7 tank 193gal (877ltr)
No. 4 tank 169gal (768ltr)	No. 8 tank 203gal (923ltr)

As before the S.2 featured the 250gal underwing fuel tanks, while the bomb door tank contained 440gal (2,000ltr). When the external refuelling pod was fitted it contained 140gal (636ltr) of fuel.

---

reservoirs; each of these contained enough fluid to cover one undercarriage down selection, mainplane flaps down, tailplane flaps up, air brakes in or out once only, bomb bay door one open and close only, fluid proportioners until the reservoirs are empty while nose wheel steering became inoperative.

Supporting the wheel brake requirements were two accumulators, one for normal operations and one for emergency back-up, both operating at 1,500psi. Pilot indication was via a triple pressure gauge mounted above the port console, which showed the overall accumulator pressure and that of the individual brake units. Monitoring of the emergency system required the pilot to study the gauge on the starboard console. Should there be a pump failure, a flow indicator in the relevant circuit transmitted a signal to the general services warning indicators on the pilot's starboard console. While both pumps were

behaving normally the indicators show black; when one failed the indicator showed white.

The hydraulic system was driven by two engine-driven pumps, one per engine. Each pump drove the PFCUs on its side of the aircraft, and an interchange system allowed either pump to drive all the power controls. The Buccaneer was also fitted with a second set of pumps, one per engine, that provided power to the general services hydraulic systems. Components served by these pumps included the landing gear, nose wheel steering, brakes, flaps, bomb door, air brakes, wing fold, arrestor hook, tail skid and the fuel flow proportioners. Given that the flying controls were the most important systems aboard the Buccaneer, the general services hydraulic systems could be switched across to supplement the flying control systems. Only one other hydraulic system was fitted to the aircraft, this being the completely

This view shows the solid affair that was the tail bumper. The jack not only absorbed any launching and landing shocks, but it also retracted and extended the bumper. BBA Collection

Located in a specially shaped trough in the lower rear fuselage was the arrestor hook, which was a solid affair. The main component in this assembly that required replacement was the hook, which was inspected for cracking using NDT techniques. BBA Collection

independent windscreen wiper, whose pump was driven by two electric motors.

One of the most innovative ideas applied to the production Buccaneers was hydraulic system integration. Should an emergency arise, the port and starboard flying control systems could be separately supplied from the general services systems through the integration valves. In such an event the port flying control circuit was supplied by the starboard general services supply, while the starboard flying controls were supplied by the port. The crew were warned that, should one flying control system be operating satisfactorily, the integration valves should not be opened until the aircraft was in the landing circuit. The crew were also warned that the complete loss of fluid in a flight control circuit should not be compensated for by opening a integrated valve, as the connected general service system would probably empty as well. In a worst-case scenario such as the partial failure of a PFCU, the crew were warned that the general service supply would continue to supply fluid at a reduced rate.

Other failures that could cause problems for the crew centred upon the main hydraulic reservoir which, should it empty, would cause the piston to bottom while the control valves moved to the neutral position and shut down all of the supplied circuits except for the fuel proportioners, which continued to operate until the emergency reservoirs were empty. The fluid remaining in the emergency reservoirs was deemed to be capable of providing one complete cycle to operate the built-in flight refuelling probe, although this was deleted during Modification 881. Further services available in this mode included a single undercarriage 'down' selection, the flaps could be selected and full complete cycles were available for the bomb door and the air brakes, while the hook was available for a single lowering only; the tail skid was inoperative.

Provisos for use of the emergency system concerned the operation of the integration valves: their use meant that less fluid would be available to operate the aircraft. During the use of the emergency selection system the entire hydraulic system remained in emergency mode until the air brakes or bomb door had completed their cycle. During any part of this phase the emergency selection could be cancelled and the systems reverted to normal operation. It was recommended that the under-carriage selection remain unaltered, as hydraulic pressure would be removed from the down locks, although this could be altered should the brake pressure fall to 'low'. The change of the undercarriage system back to normal would allow the accumulator to be recharged.

Other services operated by the general services hydraulic system included the wing fold mechanism, both the folding and spreading being accomplished using the normal side of the system. To ensure that the wings were not moved when a jury strut was fitted or when the aircraft was on jacks, a locking solenoid was installed.

Communication System

The radio bay was home to the greater majority of the radio and electrical equipment. The NA.39's radio installation consisted of twin VHF radios and an integrated intercommunications system. The radio transmitter/receiver units were mounted in the radio bay. Control of the VHF sets was through the pilot, the controls being located on his port console; between these units was a change-over switch.

The communications installed in the Buccaneer S.1 included a tele briefing that was mounted in the starboard undercarriage wheel bay, and an intercom system that incorporated a centralized audio selector system. Primary communications

with the outside world was by an ARC52/TR5 transmitter/receiver set that provided up to 1,750 frequencies, of which nineteen could be preset. Supporting the primary UHF set was a standby system that held two channels only, one for emergencies and one for test purposes. In addition to the UHF set-up, the aircraft was equipped with an HF set that had a voice communications range of up to 1,500 miles (2,400km) and a frequency selection of 1,750 channels. The Buccaneer S.2 used a similar communications system to the earlier version, with the addition of a tape recorder introduced by Modifications 1258 and 5209; Modification 1314 introduced a playback facility. The tape deck was installed on the starboard side of the observer's cockpit and was used to record communications traffic.

Should there be a failure of the primary electrical supply, emergency supplies could be selected by use of a switch near the radio control boxes. The aerials for the radio sets were located on the dorsal fin structure; the No.1 set was connected to the forward aerial while No.2 was connected to the aft installation.

Instrumentation and Avionics

Electrical power was provided by two engine-driven alternators, each rated at 30kVA, 200V, 400Hz AC, the drive for which was through an engine-mounted CSDU. From the initial 200V AC supply

the voltage was stepped down to 115V AC via a step-down transformer, while two transformer rectifier units provided a 28V DC supply. Back-up electrical supply was provided by a 24V DC battery located in the radio bay in the rear fuselage, which was kept fully charged from the DC bus bar. In the event of a generator failure, the battery was automatically isolated from all but the essential electrical services.

Pitot and static pressures for the air-operated instruments were gained from a pressure head that was mounted under the port outer wing panel. A second pitot head located under the nose fuselage provided air pressure services to the standby instruments and the hydraulic flight control feel systems. Static pressures were provided by two static vents located on each side on the folding nose.

The NA.39 aircraft were fitted with the Mk 5 FT gyro-magnetic compass, which comprised of a Type A detector unit mounted on the starboard wing tip, a Type A amplifier unit in the fuselage, a Type A heading indicator on the pilot's instrument panel and a Type A repeater unit mounted in the observer's starboard console. The heading indicator was provided with a conventional course-setting knob and synchronization knob. Should there be a failure of the primary compass system, the crew were provided with an E2B magnetic compass.

Other avionics brought most of the remaining instrumentation, automatic pilot and other electronic systems together

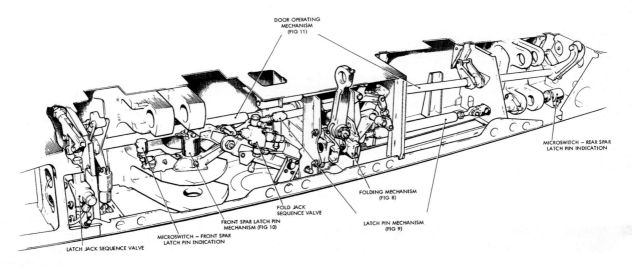

When the wing fold and locking mechanisms were operating under hydraulic power great pains were taken to ensure that all personnel were clear of the moving parts. There is a strange propensity for humans to put their hands in the way of moving objects, and quite a few fingers were lost in the early days of Buccaneer operations. BBA Collection

to provide a control and navigation system that also provided an attack weapon system.

As the NA.39s were produced primarily for development purposes, the flight instrumentation system in the production machines consisted of the Air Data System (ADS) and a dynamic reference system that was later developed as the Integrated Flight Instrument System (IFIS). The purpose of IFIS was to present information and navigation data to both crew members; it had a secondary role as a data supplier to the integrated weapons systems. The ADS provided information regarding the speed of the aircraft and the atmosphere through which it was flying. It provided centralized measurement, computation, corrections and electrical inputs to the pitot/static transducer, static transducer, height lock transducer, Air Data Computer (ADC), IAS and Mach number indicator and the height indicator.

The ADC comprised of a number of servo units, each of which was capable of resolving a mathematical equation when the previous initial value had changed. Outputs from this computer were sent to the crew's flight instruments as well as to the strike sight, autopilot and the Doppler navigation system. The information provided by the ADC was displayed on three separate instruments these being the ASI and Machmeter, the height and vertical speed indicator, and the height and True Air Speed indicator.

The second part of the IFIS was the dynamic reference system which comprised the master reference gyro (MRG), the detector unit, attitude indicator, navigation display and navigation repeater. The MRG provided pitch, roll and heading information for the attitude indicator and the compass system of the navigation display. The detector unit was mounted in the starboard wing tip and measured the horizontal component of the earth's magnetic field, the outputs from this unit being fed to the navigation display on the instrument panels. The attitude indicator was of roller blind format and was operated by signals generated by the MRG. It gave a continuous indicator of pitch on the roller blind and the roll indication using a pointer at the base of the blind frame. To assist the crew in understanding the pitch position the frame was painted half black and half grey, the divider being the natural horizon. The

navigation display could be used as a conventional compass indicator and could also be used, by switch selection, for direct TACAN and offset TACAN facilities.

Other instrumentation installed in the operational Buccaneers included a deck landing ASI, an airstream direction detector system for angle of attack indication and a Mk 6D artificial horizon and a flight director, for use in the event of an IFIS failure.

Ejection Seats

Prior to development of the definitive ejection seats for the production aircraft, the prototypes were fitted with the Mk 4M fully automatic lightweight ejection seat, this being designed to provide a safe escape option for the crew at all altitudes and speeds within the aircraft's operating range. Once the seat had been operated the parachute deployed automatically and lifted the occupant clear of the seat. When operated at high altitudes, a barostatic control mounted on the seat delayed opening the main parachute and the subsequent separation until the altitude has decreased to 10,000ft (3,000m). A 'g' control switch was also fitted to the seat to delay the main parachute deploying until a safe speed was reached. The seat was launched out of the aircraft by a cartridge-operated jettison unit attached to the seat and operated by the face screen handle; there was a 1-second delay between the canopy departure being initiated and the seat cartridge firing. The escape sequence could also be initiated by seat pan handle. Should the crew decide to stay with the aircraft a manual canopy ejection system was installed.

The seat parachute was a 24ft Irvin canopy that acted as the seat back of the ejection seat; mounted in the base of the seat was the survival pack which formed the seat. Inside the pack was a Type K single-seat dinghy and a Type P survival pack. The dinghy was inflated by a CO_2 cylinder carried in a sleeve on the side of the buoyancy chamber. The prototypes encountered problems with the canopy jettison system, the main cause initially being a defect in the observer's canopy jettison unit. Prior to modification action the interconnection between the seats and the canopy was disconnected, both requiring manual operation for escape purposes. To counter this a modification was carried

out that rendered the observer's jettison unit inoperative and removed the jettison handle. To improve the aircraft's escape capabilities the pilots ejection unit was improved and a handle installed for use by the observer. Aircraft XK488 was the first to be modified, with XK486 and XK487 being modified subsequently.

When the Buccaneer S.1 entered service the crew positions were fitted with Martin Baker Type 4MSA seats. These were fitted with a combined safety and parachute harness mounted into a single quick release box. The Mk 37A horseshoe-shaped, back-mounted parachute was augmented by a Type R personal survival pack. Seat height could be adjusted by an electric motor whose switch was on the starboard side of the seat. To eject, an 80ft/sec (24m/sec) ejection gun was initiated by either the face blind or the seat pan handle. To ensure that the seats cleared the aircraft safely, canopy breakers were mounted on the head box; this allowed a quicker ejection time instead of waiting for the canopy to depart the airframe.

Supporting the more conventional escape systems was an automatic underwater escape system that was installed as Modification 631. This system was capable of ejecting an unconscious occupant from the aircraft, after which the sequence separated him from his seat and inflated the life jacket to take him to the surface to await rescue. The major components in this system included the water pressure sensing unit that activated at a depth of 13ft (4m), a main air bottle pressurized to 3,000psi that operated the escape mechanism, and an auxiliary CO_2 bottle that forced the occupant forwards and upwards, after which the life jacket inflated.

The Buccaneer S.2 was fitted with a pair of Martin Baker Type 6 ejection seats. Originally these were of the MSB1 Mk 2 variety, but when the Martel missile system was introduced the Mk 3 with splayed thigh guards was brought into use, to provide greater clearance for the missile system's TV display unit. Following the two earlier versions came the Mk 4 that introduced an extra Miniature Detonating Cord (MDC) unit behind each seat that complemented the navigator-initiated MDC system. When the Mk 5 seat was installed it was similar in nature to the Mk 4, but featured the splayed thigh guards of the Mk 3. To drive the seat out of the Buccaneer a multi-tubed rocket pack was fitted under the seat pan. The use of this

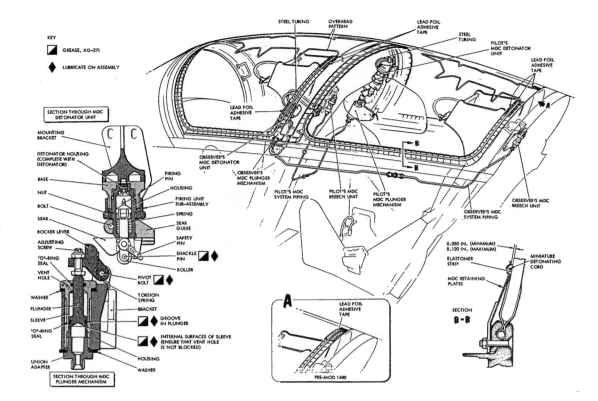

KEY

GREASE, XG-271

LUBRICATE ON ASSEMBLY

SECTION THROUGH MDC DETONATOR UNIT

MOUNTING BRACKET
DETONATOR HOUSING (COMPLETE WITH DETONATOR)
BASE
NUT
BOLT
SEAR
ROCKER LEVER
ADJUSTING SCREW
"O"-RING SEAL
VENT HOLE
WASHER
PLUNGER
SLEEVE
"O"-RING SEAL
UNION ADAPTER

FIRING PIN
HOUSING
FIRING UNIT SUB-ASSEMBLY
SPRING
SEAR GUIDE
SAFETY PIN
SHACKLE PIN
ROLLER
PIVOT BOLT
TORSION SPRING
BRACKET
GROOVE IN PLUNGER
INTERNAL SURFACES OF SLEEVE (ENSURE THAT VENT HOLE IS NOT BLOCKED)
HOUSING
WASHER

SECTION THROUGH MDC PLUNGER MECHANISM

STEEL TUBING
OVERHEAD PATTERN
LEAD FOIL ADHESIVE TAPE
STEEL TUBING
PILOT'S MDC DETONATOR UNIT
LEAD FOIL ADHESIVE TAPE
LEAD FOIL ADHESIVE TAPE
OBSERVER'S MDC DETONATOR UNIT
OBSERVER'S MDC PLUNGER MECHANISM
PILOT'S MDC SYSTEM PIPING
PILOT'S MDC BREECH UNIT
PILOT'S MDC PLUNGER MECHANISM
OBSERVER'S MDC SYSTEM PIPING
OBSERVER'S MDC BREECH UNIT

A
LEAD FOIL ADHESIVE TAPE
PRE-MOD 1480

0.050 IN. (MINIMUM)
0.120 IN. (MAXIMUM)
ELASTOMER STRIP
MDC RETAINING PLATES
MINIATURE DETONATING CORD
SECTION B - B

The earlier NA.39 and Buccaneer canopies relied on a cartridge system to throw the assembly clear of the airframe during an ejection. In the event of a low-level escape, clearing the canopy took precious seconds, so the process had to be speeded up. The answer was to install MDC as shown here. BBA Collection

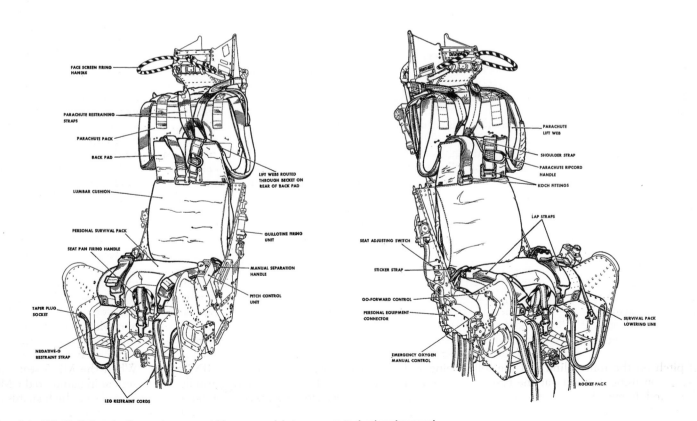

FACE SCREEN FIRING HANDLE
PARACHUTE RESTRAINING STRAPS
PARACHUTE PACK
BACK PAD
LUMBAR CUSHION
PERSONAL SURVIVAL PACK
SEAT PAN FIRING HANDLE
TAPER PLUG SOCKET
NEGATIVE-G RESTRAINT STRAP
LEG RESTRAINT CORDS
LIFT WEBS ROUTED THROUGH BECKET ON REAR OF BACK PAD
GUILLOTINE FIRING UNIT
MANUAL SEPARATION HANDLE
PITCH CONTROL UNIT

PARACHUTE LIFT WEB
SHOULDER STRAP
PARACHUTE RIPCORD HANDLE
KOCH FITTINGS
LAP STRAPS
SEAT ADJUSTING SWITCH
STICKER STRAP
GO-FORWARD CONTROL
PERSONAL EQUIPMENT CONNECTOR
EMERGENCY OXYGEN MANUAL CONTROL
SURVIVAL PACK LOWERING LINE
ROCKET PACK

The original Martin Baker ejection seats were cartridge powered, but as escape technology improved rocket packs were installed instead, which improved the occupant's chance of survival. BBA Collection

system in place of the earlier cartridge type gave this seat a true 'zero speed, zero height' capability, as the rockets increased the seats trajectory. Each seat tube contained a solid propellant that was initiated by a firing mechanism. Upon initiation via the seat pan handle the MDC shattered the canopy, after which the seat restraint cords pulled the occupant's legs back towards the seat to stop them flailing about when departing the aircraft.

Canopy

When the NA.39 prototypes were built the early-build machines were provided with a canopy that could be inched back from fully closed to fully open, although pilots were warned to utilize this facility with care as constant operation would damage the operating mechanism. Aircraft fitted with this system had an operating switch marked 'Normal–Stop–Reverse', instead of the usual 'Open–Close'. To use the inching facility the canopy should be selected to 'Stop', then the 'Reverse' option could be used to adjust the position of the canopy.

The Buccaneer canopy was a single assembly that in normal operation slid backwards and forwards using an electric actuator that was controlled either by a lever in the cockpit or an external open/close handle. Jettisoning the canopy could be achieved using switches located at the pilot's and navigator's positions, and externally. The canopy was shattered, originally, by a reinforced section on the ejection seats although the introduction of MDC as part of Modifications 1480 and 1596 improved the crew's escape chances. Each system was independent, being operated when the seat handle sequence was activated. When the handle was pulled the MDC fractured the transparency above the relevant seat.

Crew Services

The seats were fitted with a demand oxygen regulator set and a multi-service personal equipment connector that catered for the crew's needs. Breathing oxygen was provided by a removable LOX pack – introduced by Modification 917 – mounted in the radio bay, which could either be removed for replenishing or filled

in situ, though replenishment outside the aircraft required that the pack be allowed to stabilize for at least five hours prior to crew usage. The vent for this system was also located in the rear fuselage, close to the fuel system dump pipe. The liquid oxygen was converted to gaseous via a series of coils and was delivered to the crew via Mk 17F or 'g' pressure regulators.

While the production aircraft were fitted with a LOX system, the prototypes used a gaseous installation with a maximum capacity of 750ltr (165gal), which was housed in four cylinders located in the radio bay. Should it be required, there was provision for the installation of a fifth cylinder. The Mk 17D regulators were mounted on the starboard console for the pilot and on the port side for the observer. In common with others in this series of regulators, the Mk 17D was controlled by a manually operated air inlet shutter marked 'Normal Oxygen–100% Oxygen'. There was an emergency switch which also acted as a press to test for the mask. This particular version of the regulator delivered 100 per cent oxygen automatically above 30,000ft (9,000m). The supply feed was separated into two sections that fed into each cockpit separately, although there was a cross feed that connected them together so that in the event of a failure a supply would be available to both cockpits.

Lighting

Lighting as installed in the prototypes was initially limited to external usage only, as the aircraft were not fitted with internal cockpit lighting – this was rectified at a later date. In fact, the engineers gained more from illumination in the early days of the Buccaneer as a single cockpit-type lamp was installed in the roof of the accessories bay. The weapons bay was also illuminated, although there were four cockpit-type lamps that were operated by the rotation of the bomb bay door, being turned off by the action of an isolating microswitch. Other lamps were installed in the radio bay, controlled manually by a switch located in the tele-communications panel in the radio bay. In the early days of NA.39 development flying no external lighting was installed, although this was rectified as the programme progressed. The production machines had navigation lights, formation lights and rendezvous lights externally while, inter-

nally, lighting was available for the IFIS, instrument panels and the various maintenance sections of the aircraft.

Radar

In the early prototypes no radio altimeter or radar system was installed. In the Buccaneer S.1 the radar was housed behind a nose cone radome manufactured from resin-bonded glass fibre cloth. The radar unit itself was a podded unit that housed the search radar scanner and was normally maintained under pressure. The radar fitted to the S.1 was the *Blue Jacket* Doppler system, which was a twin-beamed, pulsed Doppler X Band unit that was capable of indicating position, wind, track and ground speed, and driving a roller map. The system consisted of the aerial, a transmitter/receiver, a navigational computer and an indicator. Height input was originally provided by a Mk 7 radio altimeter that covered two separate ranges, these being 0–500ft and 0–5,000ft (0–150m and 0–1,500m). The altimeter switched out automatically when an altitude of 20,000ft (6,000m) was reached, being restored when the aircraft dropped below this height. An improved altimeter, the Mk 7B, was introduced by Modification 1146, to give greater accuracy at low altitudes.

Giving the Buccaneer S.1 some measure of protection against radar detection was the wide-band homer that could detect pulsed radar transmissions. This system was capable of detecting transmissions from any altitude, the results being displayed on a CRT mounted in the observer's cockpit. When Modification 5020 had been embodied, the detector heads were mounted in pods under each wing.

Safety Equipment

The NA.39 aircraft were reasonably well equipped with fire safety equipment. In the cockpit the observer's compartment housed a hand-operated fire extinguisher. Engine fire protection and suppression was provided by an automatic extinguisher bottle equipped with a dual head, this being mounted on the inside of each engine's outboard nacelle housing. Detection was by a firewire sensing element that was looped around the engine and heat shield, and was connected to a relay box in the radio bay. Should the system detect a fire, a warning light would illuminate in the centralized warning panel. Supporting the lights on the CWP were a second pair mounted within the fire extinguisher buttons. Should the aircraft end up crash landing, there were crash switches installed that caused the engine fire extinguishers to fire automatically; these were subsequently rendered inoperative as part of STI/Bucc/151B in 1966.

The fuel tanks were protected by an automatic detection and suppression system that also covered the weapons bay. The fire extinguishers were located in the radio bay and were connected to a gallery pipe, which were connected in turn to a series of smaller pipes that projected into the space around each fuel tank. Firewire elements were included in this set-up, one being attached to the spray delivery pipes and one mounted in the weapons bay. Fire warning lamps were mounted in the CWP and illuminate on detecting a fire. All the fire extinguishers installed in the suppression systems used methyl bromide – the fumes of this are toxic, so all personnel were warned not to inhale them.

The CWP provided visual and audio warning should there be a fire anywhere in the areas protected by the fire detection and suppression systems. The CWP also provided warning coverage for the autopilot, cabin pressurization, DC electrical supplies and the port and starboard hydraulic pumps for the flying control systems. The CWP panel consisted of a twelve-lamp unit located on the starboard console. Should any of these lamps illuminate a further pair of warning lamps located on the coaming would flash intermittently, being backed up by an audible warning played in the pilot's helmet. Further warning lamps were incorporated into the CWP, although these could only activated by using the master push/pull switch. When engaged, warnings for oxygen, cabin pressure, the port and starboard generators, autopilot and the port and starboard controls became available. Should the master switch be pulled these indications were not available, this being indicated by a warning lamp on the switch. This selection was only to be used on the ground.

The introduction of the Buccaneer S.2 saw further failure and warning lights introduced into the CWP, which now covered excessive heat warnings in the area of the engines, fuel tanks, bomb bay and radio bay. Other areas covered by this system included the autopilot, cabin pressurization, flying control hydraulic systems, generators, wing and nose fold locks and DC(TRU) failure. A second warning panel mounted on the pilot's starboard console indicated failures in the DC supplies, radio bay cooling, cabin pressure, port and starboard generator, port and starboard powered flying controls, autopilot and auto stabilizers, wing and nose fold locks, fire in port or starboard engines, fire in the fuel tank area and fire in the bomb bay or other equipment bays.

Engines

Engine management and services provided by the Gyron Junior Mk 101 powerplant included BLC, engine de-icing, fuel tank services and various cockpit services. Control of the engines' fuel system was managed by a Dowty spill-type system that managed each engine automatically; the only manual controls were the combined throttle and HP levers. Starting of each engine required that an external air supply be attached, normally a Palouste air starter, that was controlled electrically from the aircraft starter circuits.

The spill valve system controlled the amount of fuel that entered the combustion chamber and consisted of the following sub-units that were known as the fuel metering unit: the HP pump, HP cock, maximum speed governor, top temperature control, all-speed governor, acceleration control, low-pressure control valve, minimum pressure valve, and the high- and low-pressure filters. The control exerted by the spill valve ensured that there was an increase in idling RPM above 15,000ft (4,500m), while above 35,000ft (11,000m) the idling speed settled at 80 per cent of available thrust. Also depending on the fuel system were the inlet guide vanes and the row of stator blades that varied automatically according to engine speed and intake temperature, this ranging between 68–94 per cent of RPM. The guides and stators were moved by a variable-stroke, plunger-type fuel pump

---

In-Service Modifications

Buccaneer S.1
During its service life the Buccaneer S.1 was subject to many modifications to improve its capability, reliability or safety. The important ones applied to this version were:

Mod. 497	Standard warning system improvements
Mod. 631	Introduction of underwater escape system
Mod. 751	Improvements to armament and jettison selectors
Mod. 780	Introduction of simultaneous jettisoning of all conventional stores
Mod. 824	Introduction of AC power indicator lamps for 2,000W power installation
Mod. 839	Introduction of improved autopilot computer
Mod. 871	Introduction of improved observer's windscreen
Mod. 880	Introduction of fixed in-flight refuelling probe
Mod. 1044	Introduction of strengthened air brake petals
Mod. 1123	Introduction of reduced tailplane trim authority
Mod. 1125	Increase in stroke of bomb door jack
Mod. 1232	Introduction of improved tailplane PFCUs
Mod. 5030	Introduction of Bullpup missile removable items

Buccaneer S.2
The Buccaneer S.2 also underwent modifications to improve its capabilities and other operational aspects:

Mod. 951	To implement the Bullpup adaptive control
Mod. 1045	Increase in rudder trim
Mod. 1105	Provision of fittings for 600lb store (WE177)
Mod. 1123	Reduction in tailplane in trim
Mod. 1143	To introduce multiple stores carriers
Mod. 1157	To introduce Sidewinder provisions
Mod. 1188	To make provision for Martel missile
Mod. 1190	General improvements to weapons systems
Mod. 5139	To introduce modified underwing tanks
Spey Mod. 2187/2214	To implement changes in IGV movement range
Mod. 3039	Bang bang Bullpup controlled
Mod. 3061	To modify stores release sequence

attached to the operating jacks, which in turn were attached to the operating mechanism and the follow-up mechanism.

The inlet guide vanes caused trouble throughout the life of the prototypes and the Buccaneer S.1. An IGV failure was indicated by a disparity between the IGV position for the set RPM, or by a failure to accelerate while the jet pipe temperature rose rapidly. Should the IGVs fail to fully open in the range 84–88 per cent RPM, it was possible to achieve maximum acceleration if the throttles were opened carefully. However, if the engine failed to accelerate it was suggested that the pilot open the throttles to achieve the highest RPM possible while monitoring the JPT limits carefully. Failure of the IGVs to fully open at an RPM below 84 per cent meant that no engine acceleration was available, though the crew were enjoined to treat the engine in a similar manner as before. Should the failure occur at idling RPM, the engine could not be accelerated

beyond 60 per cent, but it should be kept running for the services it provided. If the IGVs failed in the fully closed position the engine could not be accelerated above 50 per cent RPM due to the lack of airflow, therefore the JPT would be low.

When the Buccaneer S.2 was developed this version was fitted with a pair of Rolls-Royce Spey Mk 101 engines that were more reliable and powerful and the earlier Gyron Juniors. Like the S.1's, the engines of the S.2 featured variable incidence inlet guide vanes, these being augmented by an air bleed at the seventh stage of the HP compressor to ensure stability during acceleration and deceleration. Fuel flow control was via the combined acceleration and speed control unit (CASCU), which managed the fuel flow from the HP pump. As the pilot made throttle movements the flow of fuel was managed by the CASCU and the LP shaft governor. To protect the engine from overheating, a turbine gas temperature control system was installed.

Its purpose was to reduce the flow of fuel to the engine when the engine reached a predetermined figure. The only time this setting was breached was during use of the BLC, when the setting automatically increased.

Weapon System

The Buccaneer S.1's fire control system consisted of two parts, the radar and sighting systems. The radar allowed the observer to locate the target and provided the sighting system with the target range and bearing. The sighting system also computed and displayed the required information to the pilot, allowing him to select his aiming point and to undertake the required release manoeuvre. This latter phase could be accomplished either by the pilot or autopilot, except when depressed line of sight attacks were being undertaken. The fire control system

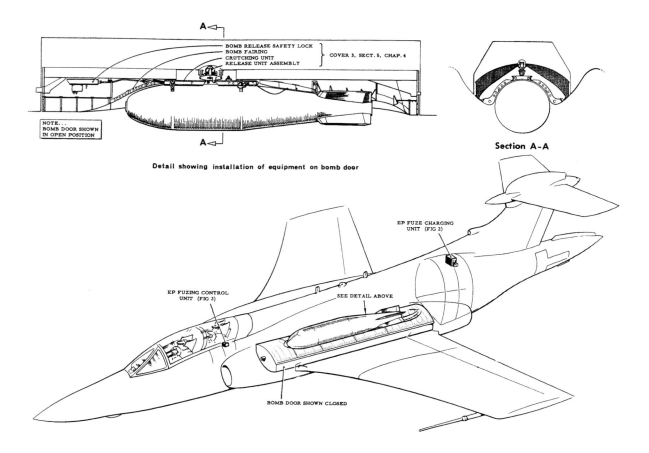

This diagram illustrates the *Red Beard* weapon installation and its associated aerodynamic fairings. Originally *Red Beard* was known as the 'Target Marker Bomb' in an effort to disguise its real purpose. BBA Collection

Blackburn NA.39 XK530 spent the period from 1978 to February 1983 as the gate guard at Honington before being replaced by XK526, after which the original incumbent was scrapped. BBA Collection

ABOVE: Buccaneer S.1 XN970 undergoing preparation for deployment on the Lossiemouth flight line. The aircraft was lost in a crash in February 1966 during the Beira patrol. Trevor Smith Collection

RIGHT: XK534 was the aircraft displayed to the West German Navy in August 1961. Here it is seen in the white anti-flash finish applied to the Buccaneers early in their service. BBA Collection

ABOVE: **XT286 served with the Royal Navy before joining the Royal Air Force. In this guise the Buccaneer was on the strength of 800 Squadron as 112/E.** Trevor Smith Collection

LEFT: **Sporting the fin badge of 736 Squadron and the associated 653 coding, XV866 taxies out for a sortie. After service with the RAF, the Buccaneer was scrapped at Shawbury in 1991.** Trevor Smith Collection

BELOW: **XN965 had served with 809 Squadron before passing to 736 Squadron as 636/LM in March 1965.** Trevor Smith Collection

ABOVE: **XX894 wears the 020/R coding of 809 Squadron operating from** *Ark Royal*. **The aircraft later joined the RAF and is currently preserved at Bruntingthorpe.** Trevor Smith Collection

RIGHT: **Buccaneer S.50 414 sports the first colour scheme applied to the South African aircraft. To the front of the aircraft sits a spread of Nord AS.30 missiles.** Trevor Smith Collection

BELOW: **Although the RAF Buccaneers could carry their own refuelling pod, the preferred option was to use another tanker in this case a Victor K.2 of 57 Squadron at Wyton.** Trevor Smith Collection

ABOVE: Having operated Hunters in an earlier incarnation the Buccaneers of 208 Squadron carried on the tradition of sporting the unit's flying eye motif, as seen here on XT278. Adrian Balch

LEFT: Complete with both access ladders in place, XW528 'C' of 15 Squadron sitting in the sunshine. This aircraft was finally grounded after the crash in February 1980, being stripped for spares for the remainder of the fleet. Trevor Smith Collection

BELOW: Pictured soon after delivery, a pair of Buccaneers with XN983 leading practise a low-level approach over the sea. After service with 12 Squadron XN983 spent two years in Germany with 15 Squadron. BBA Collection

ABOVE: **This Buccaneer of 12 Squadron carries a Martel missile under the starboard wing. Just inboard is the special pylon used to carry either the training or data link pod used in programming or simulating the missile.** BBA Collection

RIGHT: **The markings applied to the Buccaneers of 16 Squadron were the more colourful of the two Laarbruch-based squadrons, reflecting the days when the unit flew Canberra B(I)8s.** Trevor Smith Collection

BELOW: **XN976 of 208 Squadron sports one of the most colourful schemes applied to a Buccaneer. The aircraft was later lost in a crash on 9 July 1992 after a PFCU failure.** Via Robbie Shaw

ABOVE: **XV353 underwent the ASR1012 upgrade process, returning to 208 Squadron with whom it stayed until the unit disbanded, after which it was scrapped.** Via Martyn Chorlton

LEFT: **XZ432 was the final aircraft built, being delivered in October 1977. It was finally retired from service in October 1992.** Trevor Smith Collection

Sporting the markings of 12 Squadron over a wraparound scheme, a pair of Buccaneers on patrol, each with a full load of Sea Eagles. Via Martyn Chorlton

ABOVE: **XW986 was a popular performer at the Kemble air shows although it was limited to high-speed taxi runs only. This Buccaneer is currently located in South Africa.** BBA Collection

RIGHT: **Trials Buccaneer S.2 XW987, resplendent in an immaculate raspberry ripple finish, on a flight from West Freugh. Close to the end of the aircraft's career it had gained parts from other machines and looked a bit messy.** Via Martyn Charlton

BELOW: **XV332 sporting the desert ARTF scheme. This Buccaneer was prepared for Gulf use and even sported the name 'Dirty Harriet', but in the event it was not deployed to the Gulf, being retained at Lossiemouth.** Via Martyn Chorlton

ABOVE LEFT: **XX899 'P' of the Muharraq detachment seen from above. After returning home the aircraft remained in service until the Buccaneer fleet was retired.** BBA Collection

ABOVE RIGHT: **Another aircraft that deployed to the Gulf as part of second wave was XV863, which sported 'Sea Witch'/'Debbie'/'Tamnavoulin', plus six mission symbols on the nose. The aircraft is currently preserved at Lossiemouth.** BBA Collection

LEFT: **After service in the Gulf the returnees were highly sought after for air displays and photocalls. To the latter end XV863 was sent to Brize Norton.** BBA Collection

BELOW: **The final colour scheme applied to the Buccaneer fleet was overall medium sea grey. This is XX895, which still sports the pirate flag on its nose and the 'L' coding applied during its service in the Gulf.** BBA Collection

Mounted under the nose of the Buccaneer was a camera gun, aft of which were the twin aerials for the *Violet Picture* radio homing system used in the detection of tanker aircraft. BBA Collection

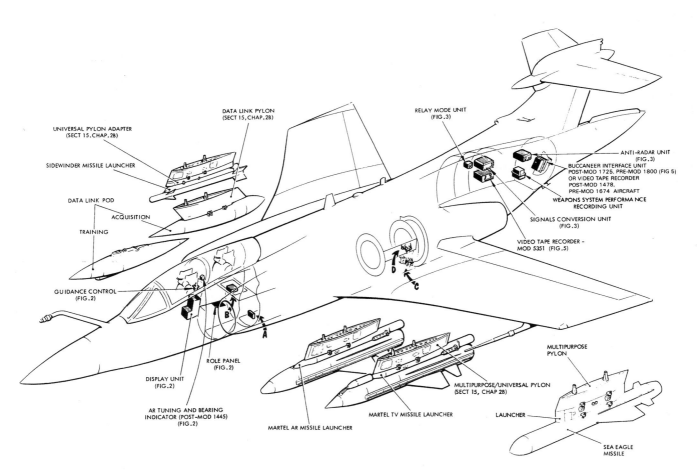

This diagram illustrates the layout of both the Martel and Sea Eagle missile installations. BBA Collection

One final modification applied to the Buccaneer before it left service was the mountings for chaff and flare dispensers. BBA Collection

Not normally seen under the wing of a Buccaneer is a missile simulator that pretended to be an AIM-9 Sidewinder air-to-air missile. The pod was basically a seeker head that gave audio warnings to the pilot. BBA Collection

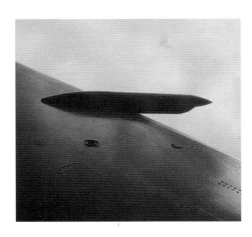

The pods on the wing housed passive warning systems. The first was ARI 18154, which operated in the S band and was used to detect the radar of the ships that were to be attacked. This system was later replaced by the ARI 18126 unit, which covered both the S and X bands and was capable of passively interrogating ships to determine whether they were friend or foe before launching a missile. BBA Collection

incorporated nine different sub-units these being based around the *Blue Parrot* radar unit and the *Blue Jacket* Doppler radar operating modes.

The sighting system covered four modes: the long toss and over the shoulder modes for the so-called 'Target Marker Bomb' (actually the *Red Beard* nuclear bomb); dive toss for conventional bombs; and depressed sight line, which was reserved for rocket firing and as the standby mode for conventional bomb dropping. The introduction of the Bullpup missile to the Buccaneer S.2's inventory required a depressed line of sight launch technique with manual release; this weapon could be selected via a post-Modification 1190 armament selector mechanism.

The conventional weapons cleared for use by the Buccaneer included: 1,000lb Mk 10 bombs, both conventional and retarded; 500lb Mk 21 bombs; 540lb Mk N1 bombs; 1,000lb Mk N1 bombs; and 100gal Mk 1 fire bombs; the latter two could only be carried externally. The remainder of the bombs could be carried on the Nos 1–4 external pylons and stations 5–8 on the bomb bay doors. After the introduction of Modification 1143, an increased number of bombs could be carried externally by fitting a special carrier to each pylon. This allowed the carrier to mount two 500lb Mk 21 and two 540 Mk N1 bombs in tandem per pylon. The same modification also allowed up to eight reconnaissance flares to be carried.

Buccaneer S.2 aircraft prior to the introduction of Modification 1188, the introduction of the Martel missile system, could operate Bullpup missiles. Up to four of these weapons were carried, one per pylon. Selection and fuzing of any missile was via a selector in the observer's cockpit. Guidance used the Bullpup guidance control selector, and two types of control systems could be installed: the 'bang bang' unit or the adaptive unit that was post-Modification 951 only. The bang bang selector consisted of a hand grip on top of which was a thumb switch that could be selected to up, down, left or right; the missile was controlled and manoeuvred in the direction selected. The adaptive control selector used a knob-type handle that altered the DC signal strength. After each movement the signal decayed to zero, which minimized any tendency of the missile to drift off course due to over-controlling of the handle.

To give the Buccaneer S.2 some measure of self defence Modification 1157 was embodied, which allowed the carriage of one Sidewinder missile on the port or starboard outer wing pylon.

The Buccaneer also had a day and night photo reconnaissance capability, although only the daylight facility was used in service. The F95 cameras were carried in a crate that was mounted on the bomb bay door and that was provided with heating and demisting systems. Up to six cameras can be carried, three mounted vertically and three obliquely.

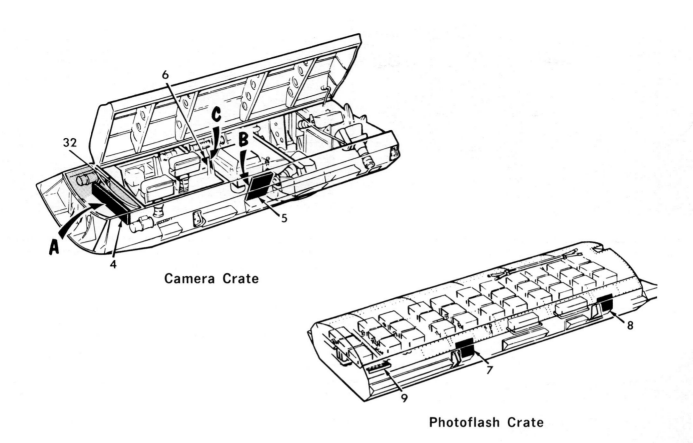

Camera Crate

Photoflash Crate

The reconnaissance installation in the bomb bay consisted of two sections; one housed the cameras while the other provided illumination. BBA Collection

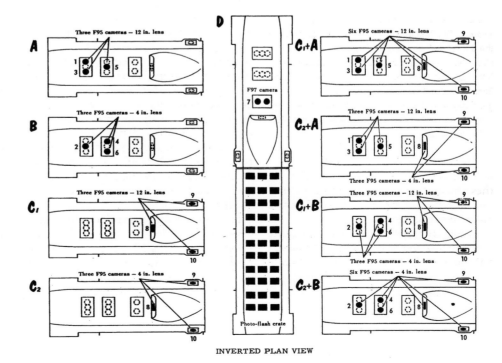

This diagram illustrates the various camera permutations that were available to the reconnaissance crate. BBA Collection

INVERTED PLAN VIEW

CHAPTER SIX

Flying the Buccaneer

Prototypes

Take-Off and Landing

Getting the M.148/NA.39 into the air began with external inspections that started at the starboard nose. The walk-around covered the entire aircraft and required the crew to check the security of panels, removal of any control locks, checking for leaks and ensuring that the power supply was plugged in. Following the inspections the crew entered the cockpit, checking that the seat pins for the ejection seats were in place and that external power was switched on. Successfully installed in their relevant seats, they pushed the various system press-to-test switches to ensure that all warning lights were available. Having tested the warning lights, the pilot selected the engine master switch to 'on' and then selected the radio to 'on'. With the various system switches set correctly,

the throttles were pulled back to ensure that the HP cocks were shut. One check that did not feature in the production aircraft were the two green rubbing lights that were illuminated when the compressor blades touched the engine casing. When production versions of the engine became available the make up of the blades had been altered so that their rate of expansion was better controlled.

Once the pilot was satisfied that all was in order the process of starting the engines could begin. With the aircraft powered up, the battery master switch was set to 'on', as was the engine master switch. With the engine fuel bypass set to 'off', the throttle was set to 'ground idling'; at this point the engine start button had to be pushed for 3 seconds. Once the selected engine began turning over, the oil pressure began to rise as did the RPM, the engine speed stabilizing between 2,000–2,200rpm. During this phase, manipulation of the engine fuel bypass valve switch was sometimes required to prevent compressor stall on

acceleration, to achieve stable idling RPM. Once both engines were running within limits, the hydraulic systems and the generators were checked for correct operation, after which external power could be removed. Should there be a failure during the start phase, the relevant throttle lever had to be closed and a period of 36 seconds allowed for excess fuel to drain away before another start was attempted.

With all systems within limits, post-start checks were undertaken: the oil pressure had to be at a minimum of 10psi; the fuel tank pressure and proportioners had to be indicating black to confirm that they were functioning correctly; while the brake accumulators had to indicate 4,000psi. All systems required for flight such as the flight controls, navigation systems and the BLC were tested for functionality. Once all were complete. those systems not needed immediately were set to 'off' and the NA.39 prepared for taxi. With chocks removed, the throttles were advanced to overcome the aircraft's inertia before

ABOVE: **XV359 of 208 Squadron outside its shelter, waiting for its crew. At this point the various hatches under the aircraft have been locked shut, although all the bungs and blanks are still in place.** Trevor Smith Collection

LEFT: **On the pilot's walkround, careful inspection of the nose locking latches was required, and the various blanks and covers were confirmed as removed.** BBA Collection

being pulled back to idle, as this was enough for ground movement. Getting the aircraft to turn was achieved by nose wheel steering and the wheel brakes, this being preferred method to asymmetric engine handling.

Having reached the runway threshold, the crew prepared the NA.39 for take-off. Their first action was to place the rudder to neutral while the rudder override stops were set to off, the aileron was set to neutral and the tailplane rate switch was selected to high. The air brakes were shut, the flaps set to 'take-off' and the aileron droop set to neutral, although with the BLC engaged the aileron droop was to selected as required.

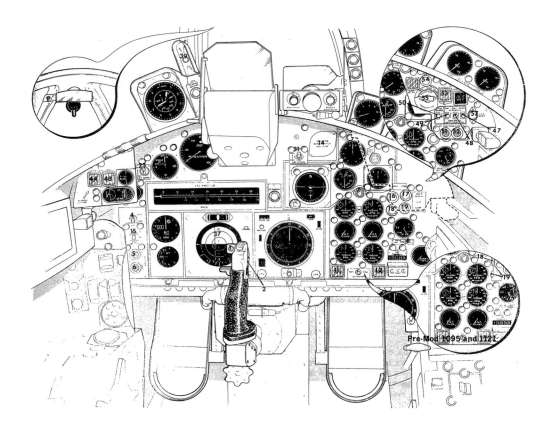

This is the pilot's main panel, dominated by the strike sight mounted on the coaming and the strip gauge in the centre. BBA Collection

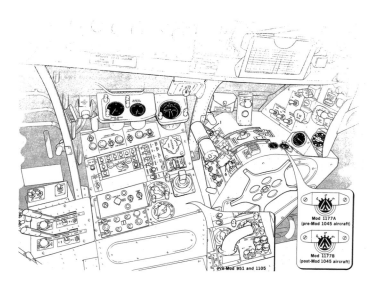

The pilot's left-hand console was mainly engine orientated – the throttle levers immediately catch the eye. BBA Collection

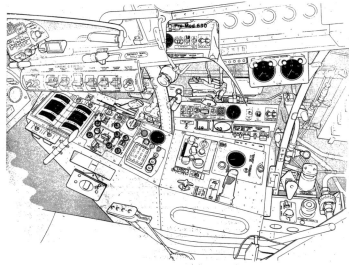

The starboard console in the pilot's cockpit concerned itself with environmental duties, amongst others. BBA Collection

Having carried out all of their pre-flight checks the aircraft was ready for take-off. One of the most obvious checks prior to advancing the throttles was to confirm that the nose wheel was facing in the correct direction, after which the brakes were set to on. Held on the wheel brakes, the throttles were smoothly opened to take-off power. Just before releasing the brakes the pilot confirmed that the engine RPM was stable and within limits, that the IGVs were set correctly, that jet pipe temperatures were within limits, that oil pressures were correct and that the BLC was indicating the correct selection. After brake release the aircraft was controlled by the nose wheel steering and the brakes until a speed of 50kt was reached, this being the point at which the rudder became effective.

Once the aircraft was safely airborne the main wheels needed to be braked before the undercarriage was selected up. Once the undercarriage was up and locked, the tailplane flaps were to be set to neutral, aileron droop deselected, BLC to off and the wing flaps selected up. Once the aircraft had achieved a speed of 400kt, the fuel cross-feed cock was to be placed in the closed position while the auto stabilization system had to be activated. Engine power was then to be reduced to 8,550rpm. 400kt had to be maintained throughout the climb, although above 20,000ft (6,000m) the engine speed had to be reduced to 8,390rpm.

The pilot had to be aware that the flight controls had certain limitations: excessive use of the rudder could induce Dutch rolling, though with the auto stabilizer engaged this behaviour was negligible; and at low speed the movement of the tailplane was sluggish, especially when it was fully negative as in the approach, without the tailplane flaps in operation. Trim changes were also noted and the pilot had to be aware of the trim reactions to his actions. The undercarriage moving through its cycles produced no trim changes whereas the flaps gave a nose-down reaction for flaps down and the opposite upon retraction. The aileron droop system also produced marked trim changes, although it had to be noted that the droop was not to be used without the BLC engaged. With the droop down there was a strong nose-down reaction, while in the normal position a strong nose-up reaction would be experienced. In contrast, movement of the tailplane flaps was

described as moderate, the trim deflection following the natural movement of the surfaces, although a warning was given that three seconds would elapse before any change was noted.

As the first issue of the NA.39 pilot's notes was being written as experience was gathered, some sections were by necessity incomplete. This affected the aircraft's stalling behaviour, especially in the approach configuration with the BLC on, where no warnings were given. In contrast, the BLC-off notes were ready: in approach configuration with alighting gear down, 30-degree flap selected and engine speed at 7,000rpm the aircraft would stall between 138–142kt, the indications being severe buffeting and the dropping of either wing. When the aircraft was set to dive, it was noted that the speed built up quickly, while very steep angles of attack could be achieved with the throttles closed and the airbrakes open.

Prior to landing, the autopilot was to be switched off and the rudder auto stabilizer engaged. Two types of normal landing could be carried out: with and without the BLC system. Using BLC, the brake pressures were checked first; the gauge needles had to read 1,500psi while the emergency

accumulator required an operating pressure of 4,000psi. Next the airbrakes were to be deployed, as needed, to slow the NA.39 to below 200kt, after which the undercarriage could be lowered. At the time the NA.39 was being tested the minimum fuel requirement was 1,500lb (680kg), especially as the aircraft used at least 1,200lb (540kg) in undertaking a full circuit. With the aircraft now below 200kt the flaps were selected to 45 degrees, at which point the aircraft's speed was to be reduced to 160kt. Next the BLC was selected on, after which aileron droop was set to 15 degrees. To counter the pitching induced by the ailerons drooping the tailplane flaps were selected to up, although this was restricted to 20 degrees below 175kt.

Should the crew elect to carry out a landing without BLC many of the procedures were similar; aileron droop and the tailplane flaps were not on the list, but a flap selection of 45 degrees was needed.

On the final approach under BLC conditions the speed was to be 145kt with ailerons and flaps fully drooped and the air brakes fully out. As the point of touchdown approached the speed had to be progressively reduced to 130kt while the engine power had to be maintained at

This view of a Buccaneer S.2 turning in towards the camera shows the gaps that appeared when the wing fold doors were removed. Flight testing revealed that their removal was not detrimental to the performance of the aircraft. Trevor Smith Collection

7,500rpm. In the non-BLC configuration the approach speed had to be maintained at 165kt with the flaps fully lowered and the air brakes out. Just prior to touchdown the speed was to be progressively decreased to 150kt, although should turbulence be encountered the approach speed should be increased by up to 10kt. On touchdown the power needed to be eased off completely so that touchdown would happen at 120kt while the nose was lowered at 110kt and braking progressively applied. In all cases, full 'Maxaret' braking was not to be applied above 120kt.

From the outset the NA.39 exhibited little problem when landing in a crosswind, but the crew were warned that a crab-like offset approach was the recommended method of landing up to a maximum crosswind component of 25kt. Missed approaches could be carried out from any altitude, while overshoots required that the throttles be advanced smoothly, the undercarriage retracted and the air brakes retracted. Once an altitude of 300ft (100m) minimum had been achieved, the tailplane flaps were to be reset to normal and the flaps retracted to fully up. The only outstanding services left in use at this point were the aileron droop and the BLC; the former was to be retracted in stages, which required retrimming of the aircraft after which the BLC could be switched off. The preferred fuel contents for this operation was set at 3,000lb (1,400kg). One point stressed to the pilots was that the throttles be advanced and retarded smoothly, as the early Gyron Juniors were sensitive to mishandling – a common problem amongst early turbojets.

When the aircraft had finally landed it was recommended that the pilot stop it on the runway to undertake a series of post-landing checks. These included checking the brakes for operating pressures and temperature, setting the aileron droop to normal, flaps to up, tailplane flaps to normal, BLC to off, air brakes to in, trims to neutral, pressure head heaters to off and the same for the de-misters. Once on the

LEFT: **XV353 of 208 Squadron inbound to Lossiemouth, complete with CBLS carriers under the outer wing pylons. The nearest range to Lossiemouth, at Tain, received its fair share of Buccaneer bombs – and in some cases the aircraft themselves – upon its battered soil.** Trevor Smith Collection

BELOW: **XV361 of 12 Squadron sitting on the flight line with the starter trolley and electrical power supplies plugged in. By this time the aircraft had the definitive ARI 18228 system fitted.** Trevor Smith Collection

XV864 of 809 Squadron; the nose section, including the radar package, has been removed for repair. Trevor Smith Collection

pan the nose wheel had to be centred, at which point the parking brake was to be applied. With the chocks in place and the undercarriage ground locks in place the engines were to be shut down one at a time by closing the throttles fully, this shutting the HP cocks. Once the engines were shut down the final checks were required: to pull the CWP master switch, engine master cocks to off, electrical services to off, battery switch to off, ejection seats and canopy to safe, and the brakes to release.

Emergency Procedures

The crews test flying the NA.39 were also well briefed on emergencies. In the event of an engine fire in the air the first move was to warn the observer of the situation, after which the relevant throttle lever had to be pulled fully back to close the HP cock. With the engine master cock shut the aircraft was to be slowed down so that the relevant fire extinguisher could be operated – these were slightly more effective against flames that were not being fanned by high-speed wind. The crew were then to select 100 per cent oxygen and open the emergency ventilation valve. On the ground the actions were the same, except for the oxygen and ram air intake.

Engine failures were also dealt with – the early machines were vulnerable to failures at awkward moments. During take-off, should flying speed not be achieved it was recommended that the aircraft be stopped

on the runway, at which time the brakes were to be applied fully and the anti-spin parachute streamed. Should the available runway be too short, the crew were recommended to run the aircraft onto the grass and retract the undercarriage. Should the take-off speed of 175kt be reached, this being below the flaps and aileron droop retraction speed, both surfaces need to be retracted and a shallow climb undertaken until a safe height was reached. Once the situation had been stabilized the aircraft should undertake a single-engined landing. An engine failure in the air required that the defective powerplant be shut down and the fuel cross-feed cocks opened to allow fuel balancing to continue. One outcome of an engine failure was the reduction in hydraulic power systems availability; in addition, should the port engine fail the hydraulic feeds to the autopilot and auto stabilizer also shut down.

In the event of both engines failing it was possible to keep the aircraft flying; if both engines were windmilling this would allow a measure of hydraulic power to be available to operate the flying controls. In these circumstances minimal control movement was recommended, while holding a descent speed of 260kt.

Should the aircraft become uncontrollable for any reason the crew would have to abandon it. The recommended method of escape was to use the ejection seats, though instructions were also given for a free bale-out. This required the canopy to be jettisoned and each occupant to manu-

ally separate from the seat. The notes baldly state that the crew should 'leave the aircraft', though it is highly likely that an attempt to invert the aircraft, thus allowing the crew to drop clear, would be made. Instructions were also given for ditching, although the chances of surviving such a landing was minimal. Optimistically, the crew were recommended to jettison the canopy, abandon the aircraft and undertake the specified dinghy drill.

Flight Limitations

The first limitations for the type were issued for XK486 just prior to its preview by A&AEE at Boscombe Down. The engine limitations applied only to the engines fitted to this machine, these being serial nos 3220 and 3222. Maximum thrust with or without air bleed was 9,000lb (40kN) while the maximum military thrust (a type of engine governor) was given as 8,550lb (38kN), dropping to 8,300lb (37kN) for maximum continuous. Minimum thrust for a blown landing was 6,000lb (27kN), this dropping to 4,500lb (20kN) with BLC switched off. Both could be used without a time limit. Ground idling speed was given as 4,200lb (19kN) thrust.

The airframe was also subject to speed limitations, these being 450kt or Mach 0.9. Minimum air speeds were also given and centred around the operation of the flaps at various weights. With flaps at 0 degrees the speeds at 30,000, 35,000 and 40,000 feet were given as 150, 160 and

Strongly displaying its loyalty to its operators, XX891 of 12 Squadron carries out a flypast, the pilot cleaning up the airframe in the process as evidenced by the hook retracting and the airbrakes closing. Trevor Smith Collection

170kt respectively. At the same heights with BLC off and flaps at either 30 and 45 degrees of flap, the limiting speeds were 142, 152 and 162kt. With the BLC on and aileron droop at 15 degrees the speeds reduced to 128, 138 and 148kt, respectively. During all these test flights the crew were warned not to take the aircraft past its maximum altitude of 30,000ft (9,000m).

The NA.39 was also subject to manoeuvring limitations, the first being the rate of roll which was set at 100 degrees per second for a 360-degree roll. Maximum angles of sideslip were 17 degrees at 260kt, 11.5 degrees at 300kt and 6.5 degrees at 400kt. The maximum angles of climbing and diving were not to exceed 60 degrees, while maximum speeds for bomb door opening and air brake operation was 350 and 400kt respectively. The pilots were warned that operation of the air brakes while yawing the aircraft was prohibited. Maximum take-off weight was set at 40,000lb (18,000kg), while the maximum landing weight was set at 34,500lb (15,650kg).

As it was a new system the autopilot was also subject to limitations. The minimum speed given for autopilot engagement was Mach 0.6 while the maximum speed for continuous cruise was Mach 0.85. This latter figure also applied to the climbing speed while the maximum speed permissible was Mach 0.95. One limitation that was quickly removed from the auto stabilizer was that of the minimum engagement speed, which had originally been set at Mach 0.3 but was soon altered to any speed.

The aircraft's electrical system was also subject to limitations, the first being the aileron droop that had to be rested for two minutes before another cycle was undertaken. The aileron trim was also subject to a rest period, although this was limited to one minute only; a similar set of conditions applied to the rudder trim system.

The rest period applied to the tailplane trim were a bit more complicated, as it was divided between high and low rates of operation. In high-rate range the system was to be rested for at least five minutes after moving through the full range, while in low-rate the movement was limited to short bursts of three seconds that required a cooling period of eighteen seconds before being used again. Two other limitations were applied to the NA.39, these being a three-minute cooling period for the canopy while the BLC could only be ground-run for three minutes only.

Buccaneer S.1

The appearance of the Buccaneer S.1 introduced numerous improvements to the basic M.148 specification. As before, the usual fire warning indicators were built into the standard warning panel although these were augmented by indicators for the autopilot, cabin pressurization, flying controls, hydraulic systems, generators, and the wing and nose fold locks. Warnings could be given both visually and audibly, with power being supplied from the emergency battery.

Flight Limitations

Production aircraft fitted with production Gyron Junior engines were cleared for service use with a range of limitations. Fuel

XX901 of 208 Squadron approaches Lossiemouth with everything out and down. If the crew had been undertaking toss bomb manoeuvres one hopes that the underwing slipper tanks were empty, otherwise the airframe would have been over-stressed. Trevor Smith Collection

Just showing off, a Buccaneer from 237 OCU shoots past the camera into a climb. Of note are the streamlined CBLS carriers on the outer wing pylons. BBA Collection

cleared for this type of aircraft included AVTUR 50 and AVTAG without anti-icing additives, although the latter was for use in emergencies should AVTUR not be available. Non-additive fuels that were cleared for this type included AVTUR 50, AVTAG and AVCAT 48. Thrust ratings were set at 97.3 per cent with a JPT temperature of 805°C this being with BLC engaged. With BLC switched off the RPM rating increased to 98 per cent; the allowable JPT dropped to 635°C with a caveat that a rise to 99 per cent was allowable above 400kt. The maximum time allowed for operating under negative 'g' conditions was ten seconds, after which three minutes had to be allowed for the recuperators to refill. Should the Buccaneer encounter icing conditions the minimum RPM was 82 per cent, although after ten minutes the throttles were to be opened to 90 per cent for thirty seconds to assist in keeping the engines clear of ice.

Various failures involving the flight controls were dealt with in depth, as a failure to understand the signals and consequences of such behaviour could result in the loss of the crew and aircraft. Should there be a failure of the rudder trim system after a trim actuator runaway, the airspeed had to be reduced to below 300kt as this would reduce the loading on the fin, thus protecting the structure. Unfortunately there was no standby rudder trimmer. Another rudder fault that could cause fin failure involved rudder artificial feel failure, which was indicated

by failure of the starboard flying control hydraulic system and caused the rudder feel to become light. The response by the pilot was to use the surface sparingly while any slipping- and skid-type manoeuvres were to be avoided if possible. Should the Buccaneer be forced to fly at low speeds it was recommended that the speed be held at 250kt with the flaps set at 15–10–10 degrees for the flaps, aileron droop and tailplane flaps, with BLC on. In this condition the auto stabilizers should be selected to 'approach' for roll and yaw, with the aileron gear change selected to low speed. Use of BLC in this condition was limited to a maximum of twenty minutes.

Other handling limitations covered low-speed handling and stalling, the first being that deliberate stalling was prohibited. Should the aircraft approach the stall, the obvious warnings were buffet or intake banging while the ADD warning would also sound. At this point corrective action needed to be taken.

Spinning of the Buccaneer intentionally was prohibited, though should the aircraft enter a spin the normal swept-wing recovery techniques were effective. During a spin the aircraft would descend at a rate of 20,000ft/min (6,000m/min), during which the engines might flame-out, causing a loss of flying control hydraulic power. If the aircraft entered a spin the pilot was to apply full opposite rudder, centre the ailerons and progressively push the control column forward; the forward movement was to be restricted to 50 per cent of the

range, otherwise the aircraft might enter an inverted spin. Should they be deployed, the undercarriage, flaps and air brakes were to be retracted and external stores jettisoned. While the Buccaneer was in a spin the behaviour of the aircraft was oscillatory in nature, so full recovery had to be maintained until the rotation had ceased. Once the rotation had ceased the rudder was to be centralized.

Rolling of the Buccaneer had to be monitored, as maintaining the rate of roll could result in a loss of control, severe structural damage or total destruction of the aircraft. Outside of monitoring the rate of roll, the pilot had to be aware of the slight tendency to yaw that was to be expected, as use of the rudder or tailplane to counter this behaviour could cause severe damage to the airframe. Above 500kt manoeuvres had to be carried out with care and the use of excessive rudder was to be avoided, as damage could occur. If the aircraft was being flown without external stores normal rates of roll could be used up to 300kt, although the auto stabilizers had to be engaged and the ailerons' gear change had to be set to high speed.

When the aircraft was flying with empty external fuel tanks rolling manoeuvres could be undertaken using the normal clean aircraft limitations, although their fitment did reduce the aircraft's directional and longitudinal stability. Fuel tanks containing fuel limited the Buccaneer's angle of bank to a maximum

Wearing the first colour scheme applied to the RAF Buccaneers, 15 Squadron's XV530 touches down at Honington. When 'tone down' started in the mid-1970s the gloss finish was replaced by a matt finish. BBA Collection

Caught just after take off, XV888 of 12 Squadron, which sports a *Pave Spike* pod on the port inner wing pylon. Trevor Smith Collection

of 60 degrees, although during a toss-bombing run a half-roll off the top was allowed. The pilot also had to be aware of the possibility of inertia cross-coupling, which could be induced by a coarse application of aileron or by exceeding the maximum permissible angle of roll: the Buccaneer's inertia would override the effect of the controls and generate violent gyrations in both yaw and pitch. This could occur without warning and could result in a loss of control and possible structural damage. Should it occur the pilot was to centralize all controls smoothly by releasing them. During this phase the rudder and tailplane were not to be used to control the pitch and yaw, as this could aggravate the situation and induce a stall.

When landing the Buccaneer S.1 at least 1,000lb (450kg) of fuel had to remain for the downwind leg prior to landing; should an overshoot and its subsequent circuit be required at least 500lb (225kg) of fuel would be consumed. When the aircraft was in the final approach the flaps, aileron droop and tailplane flaps needed to be extended one stage at a time, being checked for synchronization at each stage. Prior to the embodiment of Modification 756 the pilot was instructed to check that there was no pressure in the brake system, otherwise a cycle of the undercarriage was required to disperse the pressure.

During an approach with an asymmetric store loaded the crew were warned that the aircraft had a tendency to bank in the

XV334 of 12 Squadron. Unlike those of many aircraft, the access ladders of the Buccaneer could be clipped into mounts on either side of the nose, which aided access in more confined spaces. Trevor Smith Collection

direction of the store at approach speeds, so a small amount of opposite flight control was needed. Should a 'bolter' off an aircraft carrier be required, a small amount of corrective rudder would be needed to counteract the drag of the store. Landing in a crosswind also required some care: although the aircraft was cleared for 25kt it was recommended that a crosswind component of 20kt be observed until the upper limit was cleared for service use. During such a landing the crew were recommended to allow for a slightly longer approach, and upon touchdown to lower the nose to the ground slowly. Nose wheel steering was not be used until the aircraft was firmly on the ground and the rudder bar centred.

After taking off the crew was warned not to operate the wheel brakes, otherwise it could lead to a failure of the pre-shortening mechanism in the main undercarriage units that in turn could result in a failure of an oleo on landing. The preferred alternative was to allow the auto braking system to stop the wheels spinning prior to retraction.

Once the Buccaneer S.1 was airborne the aircraft was to undertake its climb-out at a maximum speed of 400kt, the pilot all the while maintaining a watch on the JPT. The crew were warned that when switching the BLC on and off whilst airborne, a muffled thud would be heard as the turbine cooling valves were operated. Given the propensity of the IGVs to misbehave it was important that the indicators match the position of the actual vanes. While it was not physically possible to check the positions of the IGVs, the performance of the engine itself would indicate whether the indicators and vanes were synchronized or not.

There were also limitations to certain ground operations. On aircraft prior to Modification 82A part 1 the wings were to be spread and folded using a hydraulic ground test rig only, with the aircraft stationary. Once the aircraft had been modified the wings could be folded or spread at speeds up to 40kt, and this increased to 55kt when the wind was within 30 degrees of the nose heading. When underwing stores were fitted the wings could be folded without restriction, but during spreading of the wings with Bullpup missiles or 1,000lb bombs the wings were to be spread with care, using the interrupt positions to ensure that the locking pins engage properly. At the next wing fold the pins had to be inspected for any damage. After the wing fold doors had

The ground crew wheel an air-transportable starter pod away from an 809 Squadron Buccaneer as the pilot spreads the aircraft's wings prior to departing from the flight line for its next sortie. BBA Collection

been deleted from the aircraft, no restrictions on the performance of the aircraft were imposed.

General flying restrictions applied to the Buccaneer S.1 included a maximum angle of dive or climb of 60 degrees. Maximum acceleration with no aileron applied was 6g at 37,000lb (17,000kg), this reducing linearly to 5g at 42,000lb (19,000kg). During flight either the rudder auto stabilizer or the standby yaw damper had to be engaged at all times. The boundary layer control system was not to be used for more than 45 minutes during any sortie. Negative 'g' aerobatics were limited to 10 seconds, while deliberate sustained inverted flying was prohibited. Looping was restricted to no more than a half loop followed by a roll off the top. The aileron was not to be used in low-speed gear above 300kt, although full aileron control was available with the system in low-speed gear. The aircraft's avionics also had some restrictions placed upon their operation: the Type M4 standby UHF set was not to be used for longer than thirty minutes except in an emergency. Given the microwave generation of the radar system, the *Blue Parrot* had to be switched to standby mode for landing.

For the Buccaneer to be refuelled in flight, Modifications 881, 992 and 5089 had to be embodied. During the engagement the aircraft had to flying in the speed range of 230–290kt, although 250kt was the recommended speed. Maximum height for this operation was set at 35,000ft (11,000m) and the aircraft could receive fuel from Sea Vixen, Scimitar, Buccaneer S.2 and Victor tanker aircraft.

Should there be a need to jettison fuel from the internal fuselage tanks, any aircraft that was pre-Modification 880 could only dump fuel in an emergency due to possible flooding of the radio bay. Aircraft that were post-Modification 880 were able to jettison fuel throughout the flight envelope. External tanks could be emptied at any point of the flight envelope as long as the aircraft was flying straight and level. Should there be a need to jettison the external tanks, the limitations were 300kt with the undercarriage up and 160kt with the undercarriage down.

The canopy was not to be opened in flight; should it be lost in flight for any reason the flight could continue, although the crew were advised to land as soon as possible. In the latter case, aircraft that were pre-Modification 871 with both seats occupied were limited to 250kt; with just the pilot aboard the speed increased to 450kt. After modification the speed increased to 550kt, there being no limitations concerning the number of occupied seats.

General aircraft limitations included the ability to operate world-wide at ambient temperatures not exceeding 40°C (104°F). While operating ashore the maximum take-off weight with BLC on or off was 46,000lb (21,000kg) while the maximum weight for a normal landing was 36,000lb (16,000kg). The aircraft's emergency landing weight was not to

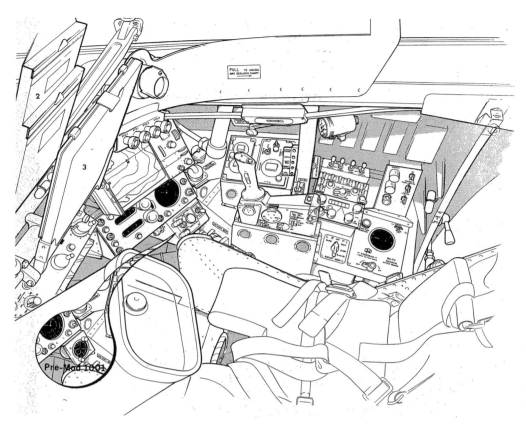

LEFT: **The observer's cockpit looking towards the starboard side. From the outset this was a cluttered environment; when the Martel and, later, Sea Eagle missiles were added space was reduced even more.** BBA Collection

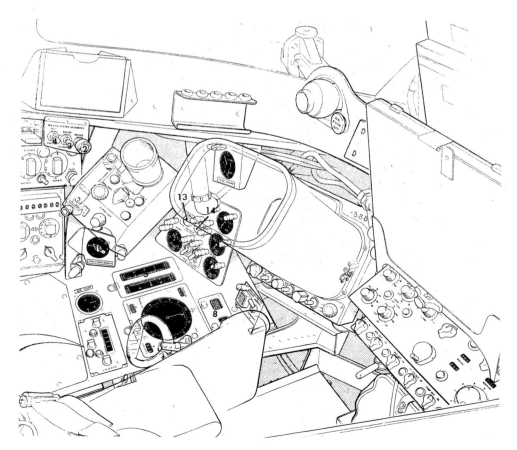

RIGHT: **The port side of the observer's cockpit was concerned mainly with navigation and weapons delivery.** BBA Collection

Scattered all around and under this Buccaneer are the jacks to support the aircraft and the various tool kits needed to fix it. BBA Collection

exceed 40,000lb (18,000kg).

When the Buccaneer was flying above 30,000ft (9,000m) the maximum speed in level flight was between Mach 0.89–0.92; this left just enough leeway for the maximum diving speed of Mach 0.95 to be attained. The aircraft might experience some slight buffeting between Mach 0.88–0.91, but handling above this figure was very smooth. During the recovery from a dive, especially in a turn, some airframe buffet and intake banging would be experienced. Should the latter occur severely the engines would probably flame-out. Therefore, if there was any intake banging the pilot was to reduce altitude, incidence or engine speed as required until the engine started to behave normally. When the aircraft was flying at low level the limiting speed was 580kt, this being achievable at less than full power. In this part of the flight envelope the Buccaneer was reported as being pleasant to fly and capable of undertaking manoeuvres up to 6g without inducing buffet.

Further limitations included the rate of descent, especially when the air brakes were deployed. With the air brakes deployed the engines should be set at 85 per cent thrust, giving a maximum speed of 300kt. This gave a rate of descent of 12,000ft/min (4,000m/min). At the maximum rate of descent with air brakes fully out the engines had to be throttled back to 60 per cent. Maximum speed for this operation was 400kt, this giving a high rate of descent although the crew were warned against such a course under conditions of low visibility. Severe turbulence also had to be considered.

Although the production version of the Buccaneer had undergone rigorous testing before entering service there were a few areas that needed further development. One of these was rain clearance, as neither the wiper nor the air jet were fully effective during flight in heavy rain. The limitations for the wiper were that it must not be used on a dry screen nor above 350kt, while the air jet was not to be selected until rain was encountered otherwise screen damage could result.

XX883 of 12 Squadron starting its roll down the runway. It is quite clean under the wings, a most unusual state for the type. Trevor Smith Collection

Emergency Procedures

Engine failure in flight was always a possibility with the Buccaneer S.1, a trait it inherited from the prototypes. After the obvious mechanical failure of an engine the HP cock had to be fully closed, the master cock and generator switched to off while the inter-tank transfer valve was to be opened to allow the fuel load to balance. As the mechanical failure of an engine could be accompanied by fire, the aircraft was to be slowed down and close observation of the fire warning system maintained.

Flame-outs were also a persistent problem with these early Buccaneers, though in most cases a successful relight could be carried out almost immediately while the RPM was decreasing. A double flame-out required similar actions, the first being to press both the relight buttons for twenty seconds. Should both relight attempts prove unsuccessful, all unnecessary services were to be switched off while the aircraft was to descend below 27,000ft (8,000m). Once past this point a further relight attempt could be undertaken; should the procedure be unsuccessful again, the crew were to glide to a suitable area and abandon the aircraft. It was not unknown for crews to try to bring their stricken aircraft back to a suitably close airfield, although a minimum speed of 250kt had to be maintained so that basic hydraulic services would be available.

As far as emergency escape went, although there had been a suggestion with the prototypes that some form of manual escape was possible, by the time S.1 entered service the only recognized means of emergency egress was the ejection seat. Those fitted to the Buccaneer S.1 had a limited ground-level capability, although any successful escape also depended on forward motion and attitude. Under the most adverse conditions at least several thousand feet were required for a successful escape. Originally it was intended that the canopy should be jettisoned before ejection, although the aircraft had to flying below 230kt otherwise the wind blast would make use of the intercom difficult and would draw clouds of dust and dirt upwards; should this occur the crew were directed to use the seat pan handles to fire the seats and escape. With the introduction of canopy breakers both crew could successfully depart through the canopy, which made escaping much easier.

Occasionally the airfield barrier had to be used to stop the aircraft in the event of brake failure or fading. The crew had to be aware of the hazards of using this system, which included damage to external fuel tanks: this could allow fuel to spill onto hot brakes, so the tanks should be jettisoned or emptied before the barrier was engaged. During arrested landings the canopy had to be retained to protect the crew, this would allow the barrier top wire to pass safely over the cockpit. Even then, it was suggested that the crew ducked their heads forward just in case the wire penetrated the canopy.

Reconnaissance Equipment

When in the service of the Fleet Air Arm the Buccaneer S.1 was given a reconnaissance capability. Mounted in the bomb bay, the system was capable of both day and night photography using F95 cameras. In daylight mode three cameras were mounted vertically and three obliquely to port, starboard and forward. In night reconnaissance mode only a single vertically mounted F97 camera was installed, this requiring the use of a pyrotechnic photoflash unit to provide illumination. The camera equipment, including any photoflash unit, was mounted in crates on the bomb door, the camera crate being supplied with heating and demisting systems. Control of the reconnaissance equipment was via an interchangeable panel located on the observer's port console, while the pilot used the control column firing switch to control the cameras. Protective relays fitted to the bomb door prevented inadvertent operation of the system with the door rolled shut.

XV350 spent much of its active life as a trials aircraft. In this view a single access ladder is clipped into the port side of the nose while the access doors for the radio and hydraulic bays are open and the bomb door is partially rolled open. BBA Collection

The Buccaneer S.2

Flight Limitations

The Buccaneer S.2, when cleared for service, was allowed to fly in day and night providing the ambient temperature did not exceed 40°C (104°F). As with both earlier versions, the S.2 could not be intentionally spun nor stalled. Deliberate inverted flight was also prohibited, while flight under negative 'g' conditions was still limited to 10 seconds. As the Buccaneer S.2 was a more capable machine, the ability to loop was still limited to a half roll off the top and was used to give the strike sight a 7-degree pitch rate for weapons release. To enter a loop the aircraft had to be flying at an altitude of 7,000ft (2,000m) with an entry speed of 530kt and an all-up weight of 51,000lb (23,000kg). The behaviour of the Buccaneer S.2 under rolling conditions was similar to that of the earlier S.1, so in low-speed gear the maximum speed was 300kt while in high-speed gear weight was a primary consideration: up to 51,000lb the minimum speed was 250kt, while above this weight the minimum speed was 280kt.

The Buccaneer S.2 was also subject to speed limitations: in a clean condition, this including clean pylons without stores, the maximum speed was 580kt. When lowering the arrestor hook the aircraft speed should not exceed 400kt. Flying control integration reduced the aircraft's top speed to 350kt, this also applying to windscreen wiper operation. The use of aileron gearing in the low setting restricted the Buccaneer to 300kt, this reducing to 225kt with the undercarriage down. With the air brakes deployed there was no restriction.

This version of the Buccaneer was equipped with the more capable Rolls-Royce Spey Mk 101 engine. Maximum thrust without BLC was 97.5 per cent, the turbine gas temperature being limited to 655°C (1,211°F) on a pre-Modification Spey 3119 engine, while a modified engine was limited to 585°C (1,085°F). With BLC in use the thrust limit was the same, while the temperature limits were 675°C (1,247°F) and 595°C (1,103°F), respectively. Maximum continuous rating was set at 93 per cent while the temperatures were 585°C (1,085°F) and 520°C (968°F, respectively.

Maximum weight for the Buccaneer S.2 was set at 54,000lb (24,500kg), whether the BLC was engaged or not. Maximum normal landing weight with the BLC either on or not was 39,000lb (18,000kg), while the emergency landing weight was 48,000lb (22,000kg). Should a landing above 39,000lb be needed, the aircraft would require at least 3,000yd (2,700m) of runway and maximum use was to be made of aerodynamic braking. Under normal operations the Buccaneer S.2 required 2,000yd (1,800m) of runway to make a safe landing. The S.2 also kept the same crosswind limitation of 25kt for both landing and take-off. As airfield technology had improved by the time the S.2 entered service, the type had to be cleared to use various types of arrestor gear. Those cleared for the Buccaneer included the rotary hydraulic arrestor gear Mk 1, spray arrestor gear Mk 1, purpose-use arrestor gear Mk 21 and the chain arrestor gear Bliss Mk 500S.

The flight control system of the Buccaneer S.2 was more capable than its predecessors, yet even so it was subject to limitations. The heart of the system was the autopilot which had a range of mode clearances available once a series of airframe modifications had been incorporated and the computer was to Modification 1019, which covered the Type B5 or B6 model, or Modification 1126, which covered the Type B7. In this condition Mach lock mode was available for climb, descent or level flight throughout the speed range of Mach 0.70–0.85, within the height range of 4,000–35,000ft (1,200–11,000m), although bank angles should not exceed 30 degrees. In barometric height lock mode the speed limitation was between Mach 0.70–0.83 with the same speed and height range as before. One limitation applicable to this mode was that the radio height mode was not to be used as it was unreliable. The tailplane auto stabilizer was also subject to a limitation: below 100ft (30m) under high-speed flight conditions, it was recommended that the system remain disengaged as in the event of a tailplane runaway a sudden loss of height could occur. Conversely, during this phase the rudder auto stabilizer or standby yaw damper had to be engaged at all times.

Bomb door operation was also subject to limitations. Pre-Modification 1125, it was not to be rotated if carrying an uneven number of bombs, and should the load be

two bombs they were to be loaded diagonally opposite to each other. Operation of the bomb door in level flight was possible up to maximum speed of 550kt or Mach 0.85. A higher speed was available when the door was locked open, the maximum available being 580kt or the limiting speed of the carried store. On occasion the bomb door would fail to lock fully in either position, though this malfunction did not preclude the aircraft landing either afloat or ashore. The crew were warned that subjecting the airframe to excessive acceleration could damage the bomb door and/or the surrounding structure, though in an emergency such manoeuvres could be undertaken.

When removable LOX packs were introduced to the Buccaneer fleet Modification 5158 introduced the facility for their carriage, though once the removable parts of this Modification were installed the door was not to be rotated in flight. The ground crew were also warned about their responsibilities concerning LOX packs in the bomb bay ,as charging or discharging them could have induced fire and explosion.

Avionics

The Buccaneer S.2 avionics fit comprised: the ARI 18124/1 UHF transceiver; the AN.ARC 52 UHF; the ARI 18120/4 UHF Homer; the ARI 23057 Standby UHF the ARI 23159 Standby UHF D403M after Modification 1117 had been embodied; and the ARI 23090/5 HF SSB, which was cleared for 40,000ft (12,000m), although up to 30,000ft (9,000m) the crew were warned of possible deterioration and during air-to-air refuelling it was to be placed on standby. The remainder of the communications systems was cleared for use under all normal circumstances.

Other systems cleared for normal service use included: the ARI 23099 Centralized Audio Selector System; the ARI 18012 Tele briefing; the ARI 18107 AN/ARN 21 TACAN; the ARI 4848 IFF; the ARI 23172/1 Radio Altimeter Mk 7B; the ARI 5880 Doppler Navigation Radar; the ARI 5930 *Blue Parrot* attack radar; and the ARI 18165 S Band homer. Some of these systems had minor limitations: for example, the *Blue Parrot* had to be switched to standby during carrier landings and take-offs to prevent the disengagement of its azimuth resolver gears. The homer's only limitation was that the cockpit altitude

LEFT: **When not required for flying from its parent carrier, each Buccaneer was securely tied down using numerous shackle points both on the deck and the airframe.** Trevor Smith Collection

BELOW: **A Buccaneer of 809 Squadron based aboard HMS *Ark Royal* caught just before touchdown. At this point the ailerons are drooped, the flaps are down while the tailplane and its flaps are set to counter the effects of the wing surfaces.** Trevor Smith Collection

A Buccaneer S.2 of 809 Squadron caught at the moment of launch. Note the configuration of the wing flaps, ailerons, tailplane and tail flaps. Trevor Smith Collection

was not to exceed 25,000ft (7,600m), while the radio altimeter was limited by speeds, 550kt at 40°C (104°F), or 580kt at 36°C (97°F).

Carrier Launches

Great emphasis was placed upon briefing the crew upon the behaviour of the Buccaneer during carrier launches. Under normal minimum launch speed (MLS) conditions the Buccaneer made a better launch if it departed hands-off, as a manual take-off could result in over-control by the pilot. The settings for a launch included selecting BLC to on while the flaps were set to 45 degrees, and the aileron droop and tailplan to 25 degrees. Auto stabilization and aileron gearing were to be engaged, the latter in high gear unless

launching into turbulent conditions. Selection of pitch auto stabilization was mandatory, otherwise the Buccaneer could not be launched safely.

Having set the aircraft up for launching the pilot was waved into position on the carrier's flight deck by the catapult director. Once close to the loading chocks the director would signal the pilot to slow down until gentle contact was made. Once engaged on the bridle, the BLC was to be confirmed as on and the brakes as off, and the controls exercised fully before acknowledging by hand signal to the director holding the pre-launch check board. At this point the aircraft was tensioned and set back onto its tail skid prior to launch. With all set the pilot would signal the launch director that the aircraft was ready to go.

While a normal launch speed was

preferred, the crew had to be aware of the behaviour of the Buccaneer if MLS was not achieved. Below MLS there was a strong chance of losing the aircraft as the angle of attack frequently moved out of range while the aircraft dropped at least 15ft (5m). Should the aircraft be launched under these conditions the pilot was directed to allow the initial nose nod to take place before gently pulling the stick back to continue the climb away. Launches under normal peace-time operating conditions were to be undertaken at MLS or above, but under wartime conditions launches below MLS could be undertaken should necessity demand it.

Should there be an engine failure on take-off, various methods were given for recovery although the final one was very significant: it just said 'Eject'.

CHAPTER SEVEN

Building a Better Bomber – the S.2

While Blackburn and the Admiralty were reasonably happy with the Buccaneer S.1, both realized that the Gyron Junior's thrust was marginal, especially when all services were running. Blackburn had already began to investigate a more powerful powerplant to increase the margin of safety, and this culminated in a meeting between the Ministry of Aviation, the Admiralty and the manufacturers held at Brough in January 1960. The first contender to put forward a replacement for Gyron Junior was De Havilland, whose proposal was a modified version of the original with an extra turbine stage and an increased thrust of 10,700lb (47.6kN), although there was a weight penalty of 1,800lb (820kg). While the new engine could be developed quite quickly and offered an increase in range of 25 per cent,

the required airframe modifications meant that it was not a viable proposition for the next version of the Buccaneer.

Bristol Siddeley put forward a modified version of their BS.55 Orpheus engine whose rating could be uprated to 9,000lb (40kN) thrust with a 30 per cent increase in range. The downside of this proposal was an uncertain development period and a calculated reduction in thrust to 8,300lb (36.9kN) when the BLC was engaged.

Given the possible size and development problems already facing the two declared contenders, the appearance of Rolls-Royce and their offering was manna from heaven. Originally developed for the new British European Airways airliner, the De Havilland (later Hawker Siddeley Aviation) Trident, the RB163 Spey seemed to be the ideal replacement

engine. Output thrust was put at 11,000lb (49kN), dropping to 9,000lb (10kN) with BLC engaged for a weight penalty of 1,000lb (450kg). Using a set of preliminary drawings and dimensional, data Blackburn determined that the new engine would fit into the existing airframe without too many major alterations. The major changes centred around the intake assembly and the engine casings, the former being required to cope with an increased mass flow of 80 per cent.

To get the new engine into the air it was decided that one of the pre-production aircraft would be used, as all the Buccaneer S.1s were heavily involved in flight trials or introducing the type to the Fleet Air Arm. Although not ideal, the airframe of choice was XK526, which had just finished tropical flight trials in the Far East and was waiting in Singapore for shipment back to Britain. The intended programme had a start date of March 1961 with the first flight due in December and service deliveries beginning in October 1963. In the event XK526 did not return to Brough until November 1962, the conversion taking until April 1963 when engine ground runs began. As well as the new engines, the aircraft was fitted with an improved electrical system developed by English Electric to which was added a Honeywell Inertial Navigation Platform and other improved avionics. As the Spey engines had a greater output than the Gyron Juniors, the modified intakes were matched by reworked jet pipes that were canted slightly outwards.

Although the airframe modifications proceeded with little incident the same could not be said of the engines, which brought with them a whole raft of problems as the twelve-stage compressor of the Spey operated at higher pressure and temperatures; this in turn led to a complete revamp of the air-ducting system to cope with the output. Unlike the Gyron Junior the Spey utilized two tappings, one at the seventh stage and the other at the twelfth. Initially this led to some failure of

This view illustrates the various weapons and other systems that could be carried by the Buccaneer S.2. The only things missing are the various nuclear weapons carried by the type. The Blackburn Archive

116

test bed engines undergoing trials at Derby: the cause was discovered to be an overloading of the compressor blades when air bleed services were selected. The English Electric combined gearbox powered uprated alternators coupled to a modified electrical system, which was developed on test benches prior to installation in XK526.

Other delays were experienced with the microswitches selected for the new variant, which required full certification before service use; Blackburn had decided that the ones fitted to the S.1 were unreliable, being prone to failure at the most inopportune moments. Further clearances were required to permit the engine for use in a military aircraft, as the Spey ran at higher operating temperatures then earlier, lower-output engines. Clearing the Spey required the manufacturers to construct a test tunnel so that the engine could be put through its paces prior to acceptance.

Blackburn also put forward other proposals to develop and improve the initial design. These included electrically signalled flight controls, an electronic warfare fit, a dedicated reconnaissance installation and reheated Spey engines for a possible fighter version of the Buccaneer.

Flight Trials

The first flight of the converted prototype was undertaken on 17 May 1963, the crew being D. J. Whitehead and J. Pearson. Transferred to C(A) charge at the time of the initial flight, XK526 was flown to RAE Thurleigh, Bedford, in November – unfortunately, both main wheels burst on landing, which delayed flying for a couple of days. Notwithstanding this minor hiccup XK526 began to undertake a series of flight trials that were carried out by RAE and the manufacturers.

As the Buccaneer S.2 was intended to be a more capable aircraft than its predecessor, the final ten S.1s from contract KC/2F/05/CB.9(a) under construction on the production line were reworked to the new standard. Serialled XN974 to XN983, many of these machines joined the development programme that was being spearheaded by XK526 and the second S.2 prototype, XK527. The first three aircraft from this batch XN974, XN975 and XN976, were allocated for development duties having made their maiden flights on 5 June, 30 June and August 1964, respec-

The Royal Navy did not often use rocket pods, but here an aircraft from HMS *Ark Royal* lets loose a salvo for the camera. BBA Collection

Having been converted to be the second Buccaneer S.2 prototype, XK527 spent much of its working life as a test bed for various aircraft systems. The aircraft was finally grounded in 1983: eventually much of the airframe was scrapped, although the nose still survives. Trevor Smith Collection

While many of its compatriots joined the RAF, XN974 was used to clear various systems and weapons for both the RN and RAF before retirement. *Trevor Smith Collection*

tively. XN974 remained on free loan to Brough from July for manufacturer's flight trials before moving to RAE Bedford to undertake minimum launch speed, catapult proofing and energy proofing trials. Having completed these, it moved on to the development of multiple rocket launchers, which later featured in the S.2 weapons inventory.

During the initial flight trials with these five aircraft, an annoying buzz was encountered while flying at high speeds. Investigations later revealed that the cause was the disturbed airflow between the fuselage and the enlarged intake. After

a variety of experiments using a number of shaped fairings, a final one was chosen and test flown. However, Rolls-Royce were concerned that the change to the airflow entering the intake could reduce the fatigue life of the engine. After further development in both the wind tunnel and aboard a test airframe, a compromise shape was developed that satisfied all parties. To further reduce the noise problem the cockpit soundproofing was improved, although the Buccaneer S.2 remained a noisy aircraft throughout its service life.

A problem with excessive drag was also experienced at high speeds, the cure being

very simple: Roy Boot stood at the rear of XK527 in the hanger at the Moor, and determined that the outwards and downwards deflection of the jet pipes and their attendant airframe structures was inducing the drag. Some redesign of the area, and changes to the angles applied to the jet pipes, reduced the drag to an acceptable level.

Engine power output was also giving rise to concern, as cruise performance at high altitude was below that required. With the help of the newly commissioned altitude chamber at Derby and some tweaks to both the engine and its control system, this was improved.

A few changes were made to the airframe, the most noticeable of which was the replacement of the original square-cut wing tips by tips that flared out slightly at the trailing edge. This improved the speed of the aircraft, whilst keeping the wing tips within the wing fold clearance dimensions. Calculations of the wing strength with these new tips added revealed that there appeared to be a negligible alteration to the stresses applied to the structure during flight. That conclusion was highlighted and questioned after an RAF Buccaneer suffered a major failure of the front spar, where the stresses of low-speed flight allied to minute cracks in the engine spar rings resulted in a catastrophic failure. Subsequent investigation revealed that the change in role to low-level attack had resulted in the stress paths altering, thus overloading the structure. Amongst other changes following this accident, a reversion to the original wing tip shape was carried out, the loss in performance being acceptable in order to extend the aircraft's fatigue life.

The first three production aircraft devoted their early years to trials and development of the Buccaneer S.2. XN974, having completed the initial shore-based ground catapult launches, was detached to HMS *Eagle* for initial deck landing trials in September 1964, followed by a return to shore-based duties for LOX system testing and trim calibration. A return to sea aboard HMS *Ark Royal* followed in March 1965 for further deck trials, travelling with the carrier to the United States where cross-deck trials were taken aboard USS *Lexington*. XN974 was then displayed to the American public at Elgin AFB and NAS Patuxent River, before undertaking tropical trials at Pensacola NAS from October 1965.

Although nominally on the strength of the Royal Navy, XN974 remained as a trials aircraft for the manufacturers, amongst others, even after being transferred to the RAF. BBA Collection

Originally planned to be an S.1, XN974 was completed as a Buccaneer S.2. Most of its Fleet Air Arm service was spent as a test vehicle, although its future with the RAF was far more violent; it remained in the test role until it was lost in a crash on 14 June 1978 near Brüggen, Germany, while avoiding a civilian helicopter. BBA Collection

The aircraft then undertook a first for an FAA aircraft, that of crossing the Atlantic. Crewed by Cdr G. Higgs and Lt Cdr A. Taylor, the departure point was Goose Bay in Canada; the Buccaneer arriving at Lossiemouth in four hours sixteen minutes, having covered 1,950 miles (3,140km) in the process. From Lossiemouth the aircraft returned to A&AEE, undertaking an endurance flight that lasted just under nine hours during December. HMS *Hermes* saw a lot of XN974 throughout 1966, as it practised various aspects of deck handling, launching and recovery. The manufacturers, by now Hawker Siddeley Aircraft, and 'C' Squadron at A&AEE, then used the aircraft until it was transferred to the RAF in January 1971.

XN975, the second aircraft, spent its early days with the MoA fleet at Brough from July 1964, moving on to Boscombe Down in October for C(A) release trials. Armament trials followed in December, followed by clearance launches for the flight refuelling pod and other external stores, these lasting until February 1965. *Ark Royal* was the Buccaneer's next venue for deck trials and further flight refuelling pod trials. Weapons release, further tanking pod trials and weapons sighting flights occupied XN975 throughout 1965. The following year XN975 was involved in clearing the WE177 nuclear weapon during May, returning to carrier clearance trials later that month. Night catapult launches and recoveries aboard HMS *Hermes* occu-

pied XN975 throughout August. By mid-1967 it was engaged in live weapons release trials at RAE West Freugh, the usual weapon being the 600lb high explosive bomb. Further weapons release trials were the Buccaneer's lot until April 1970 when XN975 was transferred to the RAF.

XN976 was initially retained at the Moor as part of the MoA air fleet for armament and deck release trials. A trip to the SBAC show at Farnborough was undertaken during September 1964, the Buccaneer then moving to Boscombe Down for further weapons carriage and release trials. Modifications at the Moor followed in November, the Buccaneer rejoining Boscombe Down for further deck landing trials. These were completed by

Initially employed in the trials role, XN976 is seen here at Farnborough carrying Bullpup missiles on the outer pylons and rocket pods on the inners. By 1970 it had been transferred to the Royal Navy, although in 1971 moved to the RAF, becoming part of 237 OCU's inventory. BBA Collection

This view shows XN976 sporting Royal Navy titles although the photographic marks along the fuselage betray its trials work.
BBA Collection

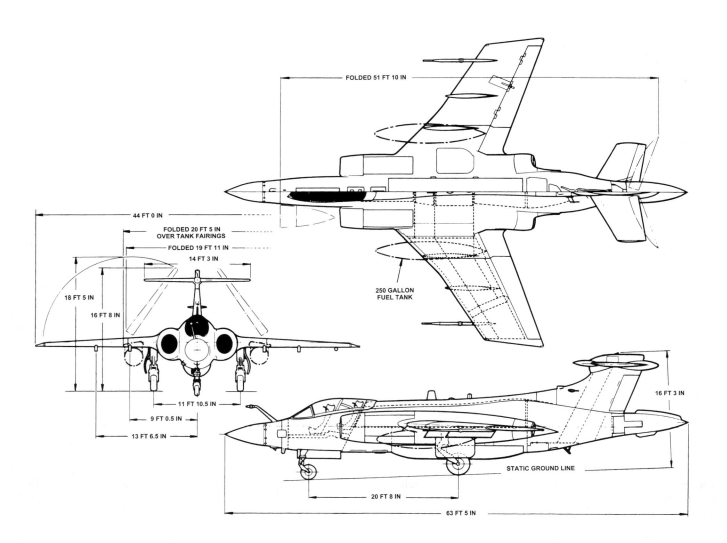

This general arrangement drawing of the Buccaneer S.2 shows the principal dimensions of the aircraft. BBA Collection

May, XN976 returning to the manufacturers for tropical trials preparation. In fact, the Buccaneer was then detached to Iceland to link up with USS *Lexington*, returning to A&AEE by the end of that month. There, trials investigated the test installation of rocket ejection seats, the 500lb single-bomb carrier, maximum all-up weight launches, and the behaviour of the type at high weights whilst flying on a single engine. The tropical trials began in March 1967, the Buccaneer being transported aboard HMS *Hermes* to Sicily and Luqa for the trials, rejoining the carrier a few days later.

Having returned aboard ship to Britain XN976 was used for further bomb release trials by the manufacturers and RAE Bedford. A transfer to Boscombe Down took place during January 1968 for trials of the 1,000lb bomb Mk 10 tail fuzing unit. Weapons trials with conventional bombs continued until April 1970, when the Buccaneer arrived at Brough for conversion to S.2B standard (that is, able to operate the Martel missile). After completing the Martel missile and guidance pod trials, XN976 returned to the manufacturers to be demodded to S.2A standard, in which guise it first flew on 11 March 1971. At the completion of a short series of test flights the aircraft was dispatched to RNAY Sydenham for the incorporation of RAF modifications, finally joining No.237 OCU at Honington on 13 August 1971.

Service Entry

The first unit to equip with the Buccaneer S.2 was 700B Squadron, which formed at Lossiemouth on 9 April 1965 as the type's Intensive Flying Trials Unit. The first aircraft delivered to the unit was XN977, followed by XN978, XN979, XN980, XN981 and XN982.

XN977 had first flown on 24 September 1964, joining the Handling Squadron in February 1965 before moving in March to 700B Squadron, with whom it was coded 725/LM. XN978 undertook its maiden flight on 15 October, going via A&AEE for autopilot assessment before arriving at Lossiemouth, coded 726/LM. The third aircraft to join the IFTU was XN979, which had first flown on 7 November but spent a short period in storage at Lossiemouth before joining the unit in April 1965 being coded 727/LM. Following XN979 down the production

line was XN980, first flying on 20 December and joining 700B Squadron as 728/LM in June 1965, having been in storage at Lossiemouth during the proceeding months. Slightly quicker into service was XN981 which first flew on 14 January 1965 and joined the unit in March as 729/LM. The final machine from this batch to join the IFTU was XN982, which made its maiden flight on 25 January 1965 and joined the squadron in April.

XN978 seemed to have inherited the engine problems of the S.1 version, as failures of the starboard engine required two emergency diversions to base in May and then an emergency engagement with the airfield's arrestor gear after the engine failed again. As the performance of this powerplant was unacceptable it was moved into the hanger for a replacement to be installed. Except for a hydraulic leak in September, no further engine problems arose.

Although 700B Squadron was disbanded on 30 September 1965, it was not until November that XN978 joined its first full operational unit,, 801 Squadron as 231/V. Joining XN978 on the 801 Squadron inventory was XN979, which became 232/V. (The letter V signified a forthcoming cruise aboard HMS *Victorious*.) This particular machine had a tendency to suffer from tailplane trim problems, though the loss of XN979 on 9 June 1966 was caused by an incorrectly wired aileron PFCU torque motor which, coupled to an untried underwing stores combination, caused instability. On launch from the catapult aboard HMS *Victorious*, the aircraft pitched up uncontrollably leaving the crew with no other option but to eject, which both successfully did, suffering slight injuries in the process. To discover the cause of the crash a recovery of the airframe remains from a depth of 60 fathoms was undertaken.

XN980 also ended its service career by crashing. Early on it suffered a starboard engine problem and skin distortion during an air display practise; after repair XN980 rejoined 700B Squadron, staying with them until October 1965 when it transferred to 801 Squadron, with whom it was coded 233/V. This would be the aircraft that was selected to fly over Nelsons Column on 18 October 1965 to celebrate Trafalgar Day. In May 1966 the crew flying XN980 blotted their copybook when the aircraft was allowed to sink too low on approach to HMS *Eagle*; this resulted in a

heavy landing that required repairs back at Lossiemouth.

Upon the completion of the heavy landing repairs, XN980 was transferred to 800 Squadron as 110/E on 8 January 1967. It was one of the aircraft from Lossiemouth that was allocated to the bombing missions planned to destroy the tanker *Torrey Canyon*, which had run aground and had begun to break up and leak oil into the sea. During the bomb run one of the 1,000lb bombs hung up and even the most violent manoeuvres failed to loosen it, so the crew were left with no alternative but to bring the aircraft back to base where a very careful landing was made with the bomb onboard. On 31 March 1967 XN980 was transferred to the Buccaneer training unit, 736 Squadron, with whom it was coded 652/LM. On 3 March 1969 XN980 was involved in combat manoeuvring with Buccaneer XV159 during which they collided. XN980 became uncontrollable so the crew elected to eject, suffering minor injuries before being collected from the sea by a passing fishing boat.

The following Buccaneer, XN981, had an uneventful career with 700B Squadron, which terminated in October 1965 upon transfer to 801 Squadron with whom it was coded 234/V in anticipation of the squadron's cruise aboard HMS *Victorious*. Like any high-performance combat aircraft XN981 suffered the normal range of operational defects, although it did seem to specialize in bomb hang-ups. Only one real scare surrounded the aircraft when, on a sortie from *Victorious* in March 1967, the bomb bay fuel tank failed to transfer its contents to the main system. Having dumped the excess unusable fuel, the Buccaneer had insufficient fuel to return to the carrier so it had to divert to Changi, Singapore, to collect fuel and return to the ship. After a period undergoing modification work at Lossiemouth during May 1968 the Buccaneer was released to join 800 Squadron two months later, being recoded 115/E in the meantime. Its tenure with the squadron was short-lived as in January 1969 the Buccaneer was delivered to the manufacturers for conversion to S.2B standard.

Now Martel-capable, XN981 resumed flying in the last week of October 1969, flying onto RNAY Sydenham in early November for a major servicing. Upon completion of this work the aircraft was released to join the RAF and 12 Squadron at Honington, arriving in July 1970. Three years with the Royal Air Force ended in February 1973. Modifications and maintenance kept the aircraft on the ground until May 1974 when 809 Squadron gained ownership, coding it 026/R. They were the Buccaneer's last naval operator, as it remained with *Ark Royal* until she decommissioned in 1978.

XN981 joined 208 Squadron in April 1979, transferring to 12 Squadron in July 1983 and rejoining 208 Squadron in May 1984. In 1986 the aircraft entered the Sea Eagle modification programme, returning to RAF service and 12 Squadron in February 1986. XN981 was selected for the ASR1012 avionics upgrade programme, which was undertaken at the manufacturers from November 1987. Fully upgraded, XN981 departed Woodford for 12 Squadron at Lossiemouth in July 1988, remaining on charge until withdrawn for scrapping in early 1994.

The penultimate Buccaneer S.2 from this batch, XN982, finished its time with 700B Squadron in June 1965, moving into the hangars at Lossiemouth for modification work that lasted until October. From this date the aircraft's new owners were 801 Squadron, who coded it 235/V in preparation for a cruise aboard the aircraft carrier HMS *Victorious*. During its period with 801 Squadron the aircraft suffered the usual range of mishaps, although none were serious. It flew into Lossiemouth for maintenance in November 1968. After this period XN982 was transferred to 800 Squadron as 110/E prior to joining HMS *Eagle*. A short period with 736 Squadron for crew conversion duties lasted from February to July 1973.

Conversion and maintenance at the manufacturers followed before the aircraft joined 809 Squadron in May 1974. During its deployment aboard HMS *Ark Royal* the Buccaneer suffered a major hydraulic leak in January 1975. As the leak could render the Buccaneer difficult to land aboard an aircraft carrier it was diverted to Roosevelt Roads, Puerto Rico. Although the undercarriage seemed to select 'down' correctly, the port wheel and noseleg collapsed on touchdown, the observer electing to eject. As the aircraft could not be recovered by *Ark Royal*'s maintainers it was returned home to Britain aboard the assault ship HMS *Fearless*. Its final destination was RNAY Sydenham, where it underwent a full rebuild and modifications. 809 Squadron resumed control of the aircraft in March 1978, it remaining on their charge until transfer to the Royal Air Force in August.

The final aircraft from this initial batch, XN983, made its first flight on 8 March 1965. Instead of being delivered to the FAA the aircraft was held on C(A) charge for use by Rolls-Royce for Spey 101 engine development, this being followed by thrust measurement checks at the Rolls-Royce base at Hucknall in July 1966. A transfer to 'C' Squadron Boscombe Down followed in March 1968 for clearance of the windscreen washer tanks to complete C(A) clearance. By October 1969 XN983 was at the Hawker Siddeley facility at Brough for preparation for FAA service and conversion to S.2B standard. This was completed in June 1970 when the Buccaneer joined the RAF at Honington. By March 1978 the aircraft had returned to the care of the Royal Navy and 809 Squadron as 032/R. Its time with *Ark Royal* was cut short in July when it was damaged in a collision with a tractor at NAS Cecil Field. Damaged beyond the repair capabilities of *Ark Royal*, the Buccaneer was transported back to Britain aboard RFA *Fort Grange*. After repair at Hawker Siddeley it joined the RAF in January 1979.

Bombing the *Torrey Canyon*

On 18 March 1967 the very large crude carrier *Torrey Canyon* was in transit past Pollards Rock, part of the Seven Sisters reef, located between the Scilly Isles and Lands End. Containing approximately 120,000gal (550,000ltr) of crude oil, the vessel experienced a problem with its automatic steering system that diverted the ship from its course, causing it to strike the reef some 16 miles (25km) from Lands End. As there was very little experience in dealing with such a disaster, very little was done initially and the oil began to leak out in considerable quantities to afflict the beaches of both Britain and France. The tanker being jammed solidly onto the rocks, tugs sent to recover it were unable to do so and the increasing pressure generated by the sea finally caused the vessel to break up into two sections. This massive breach allowed even more oil to escape, thereby increasing the scale of the disaster.

When it became obvious that the ship could not be recovered the decision was taken to move dispersant vessels into the area in order to control the spill. As this would take some time to organize properly, air power was seen as a short-term control option and Buccaneers drawn from 736 and 800 Squadrons at Lossiemouth were tasked to bomb the ship in an attempt to burn the oil off. Operations began on 28 March, the aircraft being armed with 1,000lb HE bombs. The lead aircraft was flown by the strike commander, also the commanding officer of 736 Squadron, Lt Cdr David Howard, who arrived over the target at 15.30hr to begin the attack. The selected profile was to approach the target at 500mph at an altitude of 2,500ft (750m). The first Buccaneer dropped two bombs, one of which failed to explode, the second aircraft dropped two bombs onto the rear section while a further six machines bombed the stricken tanker. Eventually forty-two bombs were dropped of which thirty hit the tanker, which ignited some of the oil sending smoke up to a height of 20,000ft (6,000m).

Supporting the Buccaneer strikes were the Hunters of 229 OCU from Chivenor, which attacked the tanker with drop tanks filled with a napalm mix. (This was the first time that the RAF had used napalm under operational conditions.) A reconnaissance flight the next day revealed that the tanker appeared to be untouched, while the fires of the previous day had been doused by the ever roughening seas. The next attack used eight Hunters from West Raynham and twenty-six from 229 OCU, which dispensed both 3in rockets and napalm tanks. Following the Hunters came eight Buccaneers from Lossiemouth, who again bombed the stricken tanker with 1,000lb bombs – at least one of these went down the funnel into the engine room. A second Buccaneer strike followed that day, the napalm being supplied by four Sea Vixens.

The next day the *Torrey Canyon* was surveyed again and the giant ship still appeared undamaged by the numerous air attacks. Further attacks were undertaken using six Sea Vixens and eight Buccaneers, all carrying 1,000lb bombs. The incendiary part of the attack was supplied by three Sea Vixens, thirty Hunters carrying drop tanks containing kerosene, and six Hunters carrying tanks containing specially filled petrol bombs, and rockets that were intended to ignite the mixture. This massive assault finally had the desired effect as by nightfall the wreck was barely above the waves and the oil leak had reduced to a trickle. During this aerial bombardment some 165 1,000lb bombs, 30,000gal (140,000ltr) of napalm and 10,000gal (45,000ltr) of aviation fuel were dropped on or around the stricken tanker. Although the initial air attacks were unsuccessful, the final conclusion meant that the environmental damage was kept to a minimum.

The Later S.2 Contracts

Following on from the ten aircraft purloined from the Buccaneer S.1 production line came further contracts. The first was for twenty aircraft commissioned under contract KC/2F/048/CB.9(a), dated 5 May 1964. The next, KC/2F/125/CB.58(a) of 25 October 1965, was for seventeen aircraft. Contract KC/2F/153/CB.58(a) covered thirty machines and was confirmed on 12 April 1966. KC/2F/179/CB.58(a), issued on 27 June 1967, covered the purchase of fifteen aircraft that were to be capable of carrying the Martel missile from the outset, the remainder of the fleet being brought up to this standard during maintenance or manufacturer's rework.

XT269–XT272

The first three aircraft from the batch XT269 to XT288 began their careers with 700B Squadron at Lossiemouth. XT269 first flew on 15 March 1965, followed by XT270 and XT271 on 4 and 21 April, respectively. Time with Blackburn was short for the first two machine as they arrived in Scotland after a few days of shakedown flying being coded 732/LM and 733/LM consecutively. 734/LM was applied to XT271 when it pitched up at the beginning of June. All three survived their sojourn with the IFTU to join 801 Squadron when it officially re-equipped with the Buccaneer S.2. All three were given tail codes that represented the HMS *Victorious* air wing, although the early months of 1966 were spent in training for this cruise. During the *Victorious* cruise XT269 was plagued by the usual range of defects, though none were serious enough to keep it grounded for any length of time, and it went to RNAY Sydenham for maintenance during June 1967 in company with XT270 and XT271.

During the work-up period the next aircraft from this batch arrived to join the squadron having made its maiden flight on 17 June 1965. However, XT272 left 801 Squadron before *Victorious* sailed, joining 809 Squadron on a temporary loan in July 1966. A move to 736 Squadron followed in October for training duties, this role continuing until May 1970 when 800 Squadron assumed ownership. The Buccaneer's naval career ended in August 1971 when it was selected for use in the test bed role. A trip to Marshalls of Cambridge was undertaken during 1973 for the installation of a modified nose assembly that was intended to house the various radar systems destined for the Panavia Tornado, the aircraft being flown by crews from BAe Warton and RAE Farnborough as required.

Of the first three machines XT269 remained with 801 Squadron, being recoded 233/H for a voyage aboard HMS *Hermes*. XT270 was also recoded for the *Hermes* trip, although it was the designated spare aircraft and was not required, so it was passed to 800 Squadron as 107/E

The code 650/LM shows that XT275 is being operated by 736 Squadron at Lossiemouth. By 1971 the Buccaneer was on the strength of 809 Squadron, remaining with them until the end of operations aboard HMS *Ark Royal*. BBA Collection

for a future deployment with HMS *Eagle*. A similar fate befell XT271, which joined 800 Squadron as 105/E. Both aircraft survived the deployment, although the crew of XT270 counted themselves lucky men when their machine was hit by a 1,000lb bomb dropped by XT278. Such was the damage inflicted upon the aircraft that it needed to be returned home as deck cargo, being taken by road to Hawker Siddeley for extensive repair work.

XT273 and XT274

From XT273 the remaining Buccaneer S.2s were delivered directly to the front-line units. XT273 first flew on 28 June 1965, arriving at Lossiemouth in February 1967 for 800 Squadron, with whom it was coded 113/E. This particular machine seemed to have problems when acting in the tanker role as events in March 1967 showed. During this trip the hose remained extended after dispensing fuel, forcing an emergency landing was needed at Lossiemouth. No sooner had this fault been rectified when, a few days later, incorrect fuel tank readings resulted in a single-engined landing as the onboard fuel was too low to keep both running. The next mishap occurred in August 1968 when the hose and drogue assembly was lost; this was followed by three undercarriage red warnings during the subsequent approach to the airfield at Thorney Island. The landing was aborted and the Buccaneer was ordered to return to Lossiemouth. Once in Scotland the undercarriage override was operated

and a safe landing made. A month later a fuel contents problem experienced during a tanker sortie from HMS *Eagle* resulted in the pod being jettisoned, this being followed by a safe carrier landing.

Having survived its series of mishaps with 800 Squadron, XT273 joined 809 Squadron as 025/R, via maintenance at RNAY Sydenham. The Buccaneer would survive its time aboard *Ark Royal*, being transferred to the RAF in 1973.

No.800 Squadron received XT274 in March 1967, it having been diverted via 'C' Squadron A&AEE for catapult trials. Coded 103/E, the aircraft was involved in working up for the unit's deployment aboard HMS *Eagle*. During this cruise the only persistent defect to plague this machine was bomb hang ups, which required some rectification. Leaving *Eagle*, XT274 was diverted to RNAY Sydenham for maintenance, which was completed in February 1970. Its new unit was 809 Squadron, who coded their new acquisition 026/R. The aircraft's career with 809 Squadron continued until May 1972 when the undercarriage collapsed on landing at Lossiemouth due to hydraulic system contamination. As the Buccaneer was due to leave naval service anyway, it was moved to Brough via sea and land for extensive repairs, after which XT274 joined the RAF.

XT275–XT278

No.801 Squadron would the recipient of the next four machines. XT275, XT276 and XT277 arrived in October 1965, being

Having first served with 809 Squadron, XT279 later served with 800 Squadron as 102/E, remaining with them until transferring to the RAF in 1972. Trevor Smith Collection

allocated the codes 241/V, 242/V and 243/V, respectively. After seven months with the unit the first two aircraft were transferred to 736 Squadron for training duties, while XT277 joined 809 Squadron in January 1966.

XT275 remained in the training role until May 1972 when, after maintenance at RNAY Sydenham, it joined 809 Squadron, being coded 021/R soon after arrival. By August 1973 the Buccaneer had left the Royal Navy to join the RAF. In contrast, XT276 stayed with 736 Squadron until transferred to 800 Squadron in May 1970. By April 1972 the aircraft had departed the Fleet Air Arm for continued service with the Royal Air Force. XT277 left 801 Squadron in January 1966 for service with 809 Squadron, being coded 320/H for a deployment aboard HMS *Hermes*. Although XT277 seemed to be plagued by engine problems and bird strikes it managed to complete its service with the FAA, departing to join the RAF in June 1972.

The next aircraft to join 801 Squadron was XT278, which joined in November 1965 although its sojourn there was short and 809 Squadron acquired the Buccaneer two months later, applying the code 321/H prior to a deployment aboard HMS *Hermes*. While the aircraft was subject to the usual range of operational defects, none were serious enough to ground the aircraft for any length of time and in March 1969 XT278 was handed over to 800 Squadron, who changed its coding to 104/E and applied the name 'Lady Penelope II' before the unit

departed for HMS *Eagle*. Near the end of this voyage the aircraft suffered major damage to the port wing fold mechanism. The damage being beyond the capabilities of the carriers articifers to repair, the damaged aircraft was shipped back to Britain aboard a Royal Fleet Auxiliary vessel for repair and maintenance. This was completed by April 1973 when 809 Squadron became the new owners, applying the code 033/R, although seven months later XT278 was at the manufacturers for preparation for RAF service.

XT279–XT282

The next four machines, XT279 to XT282, were delivered directly to 809 Squadron at Lossiemouth during January and February 1966 and were coded 322/H to 325/H. They were aboard *Hermes* while the carrier worked up in home waters, during which period a problem with stability during catapult launches came to the fore. Investigations were undertaken at A&AEE during October 1966 using XT280, the result being that instructions were issued to all operators concerning the setting-up of the tailplane control systems.

HMS *Hermes* then sailed with her air wing to the Middle East, where various exercises were carried out. Although the usual range of Buccaneer problems were encountered, it was during the Atlantic phase of the cruise that most of the excitement occurred. The American base at Wideawake airfield on Ascension Island (a tiny island in mid-Atlantic) was most

surprised to find two Buccaneers turning up in November 1967. The first was XT280, which landed with an engine fire warning indication. While that was being repaired by a team from the carrier, XT279 arrived after the starboard engine had flamed out on approach to HMS *Hermes*. XT279 returned without incident to *Hermes* while XT280 had to make an emergency return to Ascension Island after the port engine compressor failed. After replacement of the damaged powerplant XT280 returned to *Hermes* without further incident.

Not long after returning home XT279 suffered a double engine flame-out after flying through the blue dye stream that had just been released by the FAA air display team, 'Simon's Circus', in their Sea Vixens. Fortunately the port engine was quickly relit and the Buccaneer landed safely. No.800 Squadron assumed ownership of XT279 in June 1970, recoded 109/E, while XT280 joined 809 Squadron as 033/R during April and XT281 moved to the training unit, 736 Squadron, as 235/H. All three machines eventually joined the Royal Air Force, XT279 in May 1972, XT280 in October 1978 and XT281 in September 1971.

The fourth machine from this tranche, XT282, survived its detachment with 809 Squadron aboard *Hermes*, returning to Britain for in depth maintenance in October 1968. Once returned to flying 800 Squadron assumed ownership as 102/E, but its use by this unit was measured in days. On 31 August 1970 the Buccaneer experienced severe hydraulic problems during a bombing run over the Tain ranges. While the crew did everything possible to return the aircraft safely to the ground, the malfunctioning of the undercarriage, which required the use of the emergency hydraulic services, and the failure of the arrestor hook to lower fully meant that during the attempted landing at Lossiemouth the starboard wing tip struck the ground with great force, the impact also causing extensive damage to the undercarriage legs. The crew were left with no option but to eject. Both did so safely, while the stricken Buccaneer crashed into the surrounding countryside.

XT283–XT288

Of the remaining aircraft from this contract, XT283 joined 809 Squadron in February 1966, but remained without an identifier until joining 800 Squadron in January 1967 as 111/E, in preparation for a deployment aboard HMS *Eagle*. This machine was prone to hydraulic problems in its early years of service, the first being a pump failure in September 1967, followed two months later by a serious leak. It was not until October 1968 that the hydraulics – this time the air brakes – malfunctioned. After this hiccup the aircraft departed for the trip aboard *Eagle* which was completed with little incident, returning to Britain in December 1968. After in-depth maintenance XT283 joined 809 Squadron as 023/R, remaining as part of the *Ark Royal* air wing before joining the RAF in July 1974.

XT284 and XT285 were delivered directly to 736 Squadron for training duties. XT284 joined 809 Squadron in March 1966 while XT285 remained in the training role until flown to RNAY Sydenham for in-depth maintenance and modification work in February 1970. Upon completion of this work the Buccaneer was allocated to the RAE at West Freugh in November 1971, to undertake avionics test work for the forthcoming MRCA (Panavia Tornado). Having undertaken a few test flights, the Buccaneer was flown to Marshalls of Cambridge so that an extended, reprofiled nose could be installed. The purpose of this installation was to fully test the radar and avionics intended for the MRCA, a task it performed until being lost in a crash on 5 July 1978 whilst flying from West Freugh.

The next Buccaneer in the sequence, XT286, joined 800 Squadron in January 1967 as 112/E, remaining with them until joining 809 Squadron as 022/R. XT286 endured the usual range of defects, although the crew managed to frighten themselves when some rocket projectiles were inadvertently released in October 1970. This aircraft finally left the Fleet Air Arm in July 1973, arriving at St Athan for reworking to RAF standard.

XT287 made its first flight on 19 December 1965 although it was allocated to Lossiemouth Station Flight rather than to any particular unit. While awaiting allocation the Buccaneer was used for familiarization flights, during one of which a failure to raise the flaps before the limiting speed was reached caused damage to the flaps. After repair the aircraft was shipped aboard HMS *Victorious*, joining up with 801 Squadron in January 1967. The aircraft, as 230/H, embarked as part of the squadron aboard HMS *Hermes* in December for a cruise in the Far East. At the completion of this cruise XT287 flew to the manufacturers for modification and maintenance work, arriving at Brough in October 1970. After the work was completed the Buccaneer spent the period from March 1971 to August 1973 on RAF strength, although it then reverted to the FAA, joining 809 Squadron as 036/R. This return to its original masters ended in November 1978, the Royal Air Force adding XT287 to its inventory.

The final machine from this batch, XT288, joined 800 Squadron as 102/E in February 1967, remaining with them until 1969, its only claim to fame being a tendency for bombs to hang up. After a period for maintenance that lasted from January 1969 to April 1972 the Buccaneer was transferred permanently to the RAF.

XV152–XV168

The next batch of Buccaneers for the Fleet Air Arm was seventeen strong, all being delivered throughout 1966. XV152 joined 809 Squadron in May 1966 as 324/H for a cruise aboard HMS *Hermes*. The cruise took the carrier to both the Middle and Far East, XV152 suffering from the usual range of defects before flying off to Lossiemouth in December 1967. After the usual bout of maintenance and modification the Buccaneer was issued to 736 Squadron as 653/LM, with whom it stayed until joining 809 Squadron as 024/R in November

Having served aboard *Victorious* and *Hermes*, XT287 finished its Royal Navy career with 809 Squadron, with whom it was coded 033/R. Trevor Smith Collection

1969. Few major defects affected the aircraft, the major one being damage to starboard wing structure after the main undercarriage door broke off in flight. The aircraft was flown to Lossiemouth in May 1972 where it was repaired by a working party from No. 71 MU. At the completion of these repairs 809 Squadron resumed ownership before XV152 was transferred permanently to the RAF in October 1973.

An aircraft with a very short service history was XV153, which arrived at Lossiemouth to join 801 Squadron as 232/V in June 1966. For reasons best known to their Lordships of the Admiralty XV153 was launched from HMS *Victorious* on 26 October 1966 fitted with the same stores combination that had caused the loss of XN979. To the surprise of very few people the Buccaneer immediately pitched nose-up while the port wing

dropped, the aircraft stalling into the sea just off the Philippines. Fortunately the crew had their hands close by the ejection seat handles, and were well clear of the out-of-control aircraft before it crashed.

No. 800 Squadron received XV154, XV156, XV157, XV159, XV160, XV161 and XV163 during the last three months of 1966. All were given codes reflecting the forthcoming cruise aboard HMS *Eagle*: 106/E, 100/E, 107/E, 101/E, 105/E and 110/E. During their time with 800 Squadron these Buccaneers were involved with the bombing of the stricken tanker *Torrey Canyon*, although XV154 and XV156 suffered from one of the type's perennial earlier problems: their bombs hung up, though both eventually managed to jettison their uncooperative weapons. While all this excitement had been going on XV160 had been given the name 'Lady

Penelope', retaining this until flying to RNAY Sydenham for a much-needed overhaul and modification to RAF standard during 1969 to early 1970, after which the aircraft was transferred to the RAF that July.

In contrast XV154 transferred to 809 Squadron as 021/R in November 1969, remaining with the *Ark Royal* wing until joining the RAF in December 1973. No.809 Squadron was also the recipient of XV156 in September 1969 with whom it was coded 020/R. *Ark Royal* yielded XV156 to the RAF in October 1973.

XV157 also ended its days in RAF hands, though it had the odd adventure prior to getting there. The first occurred aboard HMS *Eagle* in June 1967 when the aircraft suffered a total hydraulic failure upon engine start-up, which resulted in the brakes losing their grip. As the

After being displayed at Biggin Hill XV153 was placed on the strength of 801 Squadron. It was lost while trialling a non-standard underwing load, which caused the nose to pitch up uncontrollably. The crew ejected safely while the aircraft crashed into the sea. Trevor Smith Collection

XV158 of 736 Squadron, sporting a full reconnaissance package mounted on the bomb bay door. This view also shows the extended wing tips that were fitted to the Buccaneer in its early days. Trevor Smith Collection

Quite often on detachment the Royal Navy Buccaneers would take an air-transportable starter unit, which made the aircraft independent of ground equipment at any base visited. BBA Collection

Buccaneer rolled towards the deck edge the handling crew scrambled hastily to place chocks behind the wheels; even so the crew jettisoned the canopy as a safety measure. At the completion of the *Eagle* cruise XV157 was flown off to Brough for maintenance and modification, joining the RAF in June 1970, although its RAF career was slightly interrupted in January 1971 when it was loaned to 736 Squadron.

XV161 left 800 Squadron in March 1969 when it arrived at RNAY Sydenham for an overhaul that was completed in October. Now coded 032/R, the Buccaneer was allocated to 809 Squadron for service aboard HMS *Ark Royal*, remaining with then until transferring to the RAF in October 1973.

Of the three remaining aircraft from this batch, XV158 joined 736 Squadron at Lossiemouth in July 1967, but on 20 May 1970 the crew ejected over the Moray Firth after the undercarriage failed to lower properly; both survived. XV159, whilst serving aboard HMS *Eagle* as 101/E, suffered the usual selection of problems associated with the type including bomb hang-ups over the *Torrey Canyon*, engine malfunctions and the failure of the port wing to spread correctly in August 1967. Repairs kept XV159 on the ground until September 1968, when 736 Squadron became its new operator. On 3 March 1969 XV159 collided with XN980 during air combat training, forcing the crew to eject.

XV162 first flew in August 1966 and was delivered to Fleetlands for overseas ship-ment. By January 1967 it had arrived aboard HMS *Victorious*, having been inspected at Changi prior to joining 801 Squadron. Although XV162 suffered the usual range of Buccaneer defects it survived its tour aboard *Victorious* and arrived at Belfast in July 1967 for repaint-ing and modification work. Once this was complete XV162 rejoined 801 Squadron aboard HMS *Hermes*. During this tour much effort was expended in training for the tanker role, both as dispenser and receiver. During these sorties various prob-lems were encountered including damage to the windscreen when withdrawing from the tanker and the failure of the hose to reel in when acting as a tanker. By mid-1968 HMS *Hermes* was in the Far East where the air wing undertook exercises with the various air forces in the area. During preparation for one of these sorties in December 1968 an aircraft fire system check resulted in the release of the prac-tice bomb carriers and the tandem bomb beam onto the deck; fortunately no-one was injured during this incident.

XV162's final misfortune in naval service occurred aboard *Hermes* in February 1970. During the investigation of an engine defect, full-power ground runs were required for which the aircraft was lashed securely to the deck. Even with full brake power XV162 pulled itself clear of its lashings and careered across the deck, striking two other aircraft before it was brought under control. After being moved ashore the Buccaneer was repaired at

Lossiemouth before departing to Belfast in December 1971 for a major overhaul. This was completed in May 1972 when XV162 was transferred to the RAF, becoming part of 12 Squadron. The aircraft's career with 12 Squadron was cut short on 13 June 1972 when it was lost in a crash off Bridlington, both crew being killed.

XV163 was another Buccaneer that seemed to have problems with bombs hanging up, which happened twice in 1967. Worse was to happen in September 1968 when the aircraft pitched down uncontrollably during a night flight. The pilot, unsure of whether the aircraft could be recovered, ordered the observer to eject through the canopy which he did success-fully. Much to the chagrin of the observer, the pilot regained control and successfully landed the aircraft at Lossiemouth; the unfortunate observer was later picked up by the rescue services.

Having survived this malfunction and the remainder of its time aboard HMS *Eagle*, XV163 was flown to RNAY Sydenham in April 1969 for maintenance and modifications. Having completed its overhaul the Buccaneer was returned to Lossiemouth to undertake pre-release flying prior to joining a unit. It was during one of these flights in August 1969 that the tail flaps failed during the approach, the result being a severe nose-down pitch-ing. Yet again the observer was requested to eject which he did while the pilot oper-ated the emergency hydraulic systems and recovered the aircraft safely back to

Lossiemouth. After repair the aircraft was allocated to 809 Squadron as 027/R in January 1970. Fortunately for the crews of 809 Squadron, XV163 did not repeat its tendency to pitch down, and survived to join the RAF in March 1974.

Having first flown on 6 May 1966, XV155 joined 801 Squadron as 233/V for service aboard HMS *Victorious* in July 1966. During the deployment with *Victorious* the aircraft was operating from Changi when the nose failed to lift on take-off, which left the Buccaneer crew no option but to engage the arrestor gear. During this deployment the aircraft also had problems with weapons release including bombs hanging up and rockets misfiring, followed by a problem with the refuel pod that required the crew to make an attempt to cut the hose: this was initially unsuccessful, the hose finally detaching when the aircraft touched down at Luqa, Malta. Having survived its time aboard *Victorious* XV155 was flown to RNAY Sydenham for an overhaul and modifications, arriving in June 1967.

Arriving back at Lossiemouth the Buccaneer was allocated to 801 Squadron as 233/V in July 1967 and had only been flying for seven days when the port engine seized. A successful single-engined landing was made and the aircraft entered the hanger for an engine change. The voyage for XV155 ended in February 1968 when a wing strop failed while the outer panel was being lowered manually. The impact damage severely damaged both parts of the airframe, so the Buccaneer was prepared for transport aboard RFA *Robert Dundas*, arriving at the manufacturers in March. Once repairs were completed in May 1969, the aircraft was transferred to the RAF.

Of the last five aircraft from this batch, two were immediately delivered to the MoA air fleet for trials purposes, these being XV164 and XV165 which both entered the inventory in September 1966. The purpose of their trials was the fitment of instrumentation for stability trials. Upon completion of the manufacturer's flight trials, both aircraft were handed over to A&AEE Boscombe Down, which put both machines through rigorous trials including launches from HMS *Hermes*.

At the completion of these flights XV164 was allocated to 801 Squadron as 235/V. While undertaking pre-deployment flying XV164 suffered a starboard engine flame-out as it disconnected from a Victor tanker, though the engine was later

relit without further trouble. The career of this aircraft ended on 16 September 1969 when all lateral control was lost, leaving the crew with no other option but to eject. Both escaped safely thanks to the newly fitted rocket ejection seats, this being the first time such a system had been used in anger.

After its spell at Boscombe Down, XV165 was allocated to 803 Squadron as 610/LM, with whom it remained except for short-term detachments with 800 and 809 Squadrons before entering an overhaul programme in April 1970. By July that year XV165 was officially on RAF charge.

The next machine down the line was XV166, which was allocated to 736 Squadron as 654/LM, arriving in June 1967. Except for the usual range of defects this aircraft remained in service with the Buccaneer training squadron until passing to the RAF in June 1971.

XV167 and XV168 both entered service with 801 Squadron at Lossiemouth in June 1967, coded 236/V and 231/V respectively. XV167 was an unlucky aircraft from the outset, as it seemed to have numerous problems with its weapons system: bomb hang-ups and uncommanded weapon releases were common, this being topped by the loss of a Bullpup missile that detached from its pylon whilst operating from HMS *Hermes*. The final straw occurred on 29 January 1970 when XV167 overrode the hold-back of the port catapult aboard *Hermes*. With both engines running at full power the Buccaneer accelerated, the crew sensibly electing to eject and the aircraft falling into the sea just forward of the carrier's bows. XV168 remained in service with 801 Squadron, finally leaving the Fleet Air Arm in November 1971 to join the Royal Air Force.

XV332–XV339

The next batch of Buccaneers, thirty strong, was serialled XV332 to XV361. The first two machines were allocated to 801 Squadron as 233/H and 234/H respectively. XV332 remained with 801 Squadron until transferring to 809 Squadron as 031/R having spent some time on detachment with the RAF for conversion training. By November 1978 the transfer to the RAF was made permanent.

XV333 seemed to be another aircraft that experienced problems with bombs

hanging up or releasing earlier than expected. Having survived its time aboard *Hermes* XV333 was temporarily transferred to 12 Squadron RAF in October 1971, although it had rejoined the FAA and 809 Squadron as 030/R by the end of that month. A final and complete transfer to RAF ownership occurred in November 1978.

Next off the production line was XV334, which first flew on 11 January 1967 and was allocated to A&AEE at Boscombe Down for trials work in July 1967. By August 1968 XV334 was with 736 Squadron at Lossiemouth for training purposes, remaining with them until January 1970 when 801 Squadron assumed ownership. This ended in December 1972 when the aircraft was transferred to the RAF.

The following machine, XV335, was delivered to 736 Squadron as 656/LM in September 1967. It was a crew from this unit that was flying the aircraft during an air combat sortie when it entered an uncontrollable spin, leaving the occupants with no option but to eject, which both did safely.

XV336 arrived at Lossiemouth in February 1967, being held in storage over the following twelve months before being allocated to 801 Squadron, with whom it remained until February 1969 when 800 Squadron assumed ownership. By April 1972 XV336 had been transferred permanently to the RAF.

XV337, which had entered service with 800 Squadron in August 1967 as 101/E, was destined to become a flying test bed. 809 Squadron assumed ownership of XV337 in July 1972 recoding it 026/R. Its time with the Royal Navy ended in September 1973 when the manufacturers accepted the aircraft for overhaul and modification work at Brough. Upon the completion of this work the Buccaneer was allocated to A&AEE in December 1974 for MRCA trials work, which continued until it was struck off charge for scrapping in December 1976.

XV338 was used first as a static display airframe at Lossiemouth for a visit by senior officers, this being followed by a similar usage in May 1967 at the Paris Air Show. From Paris XV338 was loaned to A&AEE, eventually joining a naval flying unit, 736 Squadron, in December 1967. The aircraft remained in the support role until February 1970 when 801 Squadron became its operator. By October 1971 the Royal Air Force had added XV338 to their inventory.

Buccaneer S.2 XV339 was accepted by 803 Squadron in October 1967, although one month later the Lossiemouth training unit, 736 Squadron, had assumed ownership. The aircraft's training role ended in April 1968 when 809 Squadron claimed the airframe as 326/LM. This sojourn, too, was short-lived, as it rejoined 736 Squadron in October 1968, remaining with them until dispatched to RNAY Sydenham for overhaul in May 1971. Having completed its maintenance, XV339 was subject to the usual round of flight testing. During one of these flights incorrect selections led to fuel starvation of the engines that resulted in the aircraft crashing, though both crew ejected safely. The aircraft was formally written off on 6 October 1972.

The Royal Navy were not great users of the underwing fuel tanks, preferring to fit pylons instead. This was especially useful for 736 Squadron where the crews spent part of their training time dropping smoke and flash bombs on the Tain Ranges. XV338 was part of 736 Squadron, coded 651/LM, before joining the RAF in 1971. Trevor Smith Collection

XV340–XV343

The following four machines would complete their period with the Fleet Air Arm to join the RAF. The first, XV340, joined 809 Squadron as 321/H in November 1967 prior to embarking aboard HMS *Hermes*. Having survived its time aboard the carrier XV340 the Buccaneer returned to shore-based, duties moving to 736 Squadron in September 1969 to undertake training duties. This was the aircraft's final FAA role before it joined the RAF in July 1973.

XV341 made its maiden flight on 11 April 1967 and joined 800 Squadron in December 1968, after a period undergoing modification work. The Buccaneer was named 'Melodie Angel', during its time aboard HMS Eagle from September 1969 to January 1970. Back on land, 800 Squadron retained ownership of the aircraft until it was flown to Honington to join 12 Squadron RAF in July 1973.

No.736 Squadron was also the main operator of XV342, who received it in November 1967. It remained in their care until transferred to 800 Squadron in April 1970. This period with the FAA ended in January 1973, when the RAF assumed ownership.

The next aircraft in the sequence, XV343, was not so lucky, being lost in a crash on 12 March 1973. Prior to that the Buccaneer had entered service with 800 Squadron as 111/E in December 1968. Although subject to the usual range of defects, XV343 survived its time aboard

XV340 of 736 Squadron approaches Lossiemouth for a landing. Trevor Smith Collection

Unusually XV343 is parked with its airbrakes closed and its flaps in the up position. It was while serving with 809 Squadron as 033/R that the aircraft was lost in a fatal crash on 12 March 1973, while approaching Honington to land. Trevor Smith Collection

Eagle and was transferred to 809 Squadron in May 1972. It was during a flight in 12 March that, as the aircraft entered the circuit at Honington, the aileron droop/tailplane flap system malfunctioned, causing the aircraft to become uncontrollable. Unfortunately, only the pilot ejected safely, the observer being killed.

XV344–XV361

As the Buccaneer squadrons were well established the remaining aircraft from this batch were delivered piecemeal to whichever unit needed a replacement, thus XV344 began its career with 809 Squadron, XV345, XV358, XV359 and XV361 with 800 Squadron, XV346 with 801 Squadron, XV349 with 736 Squadron, and XV354, XV355, XV357 and XV360 with 803 Squadron. It should be noted that not all of the last eighteen aircraft joined the FAA, as XV347, XV348 and XV350 were retained for trials purposes with both the manufacturers and the trials organizations before joining the RAF.

There was a slight hiccup in the Buccaneer delivery schedule that primarily affected XV351, XV352 and XV353. The cause was the Martel missile modification programme, which was finally catching up with the new-build aircraft.

This saw XV351 first flying in September 1967 and not being seen again until January 1969, as it was being modified for Martel carriage, followed by the inevitable trials work. During this period trials of the command ejection system were also carried out. XV351's first operator was 12 Squadron at Honington where it arrived in December 1969. During a detachment to Karup, Denmark, in May 1971 the aircraft burst a tyre on take-off, which resulted in the navigator ejecting just before the aircraft hit the barrier. After repairs XV351 returned to service, remaining with the RAF until joining 809 Squadron in March 1974. To confuse matters, it changed designation at the same time: having been converted to carry the Martel its RAF designation became S.2B, while with the navy it changed to S.2D (those aircraft that remained unconverted were designated S.2A/S.2C, respectively). Aboard *Ark Royal* XV351 was used for all-up weight trials during which the total weight was increased incrementally until the maximum was reached. On 11 November 1974 XV351 crashed into the mud flats at the Wainfleet bombing range; the navigator managed to eject but the pilot was killed.

By the time XV352 was rolling down to completion the Martel upgrade was being carried out at Brough as part of the

construction process. This delayed its first flight until 18 April 1968. By July XV352 was at RAE Bedford where the Martel system was put through its paces, while further trials involved the use of conventional weapons dropped from the Martel pylons. After RAE XV352 was transferred to A&AEE Boscombe Down in September, remaining with them for trials work until transferred to RAF charge in October 1972.

Although XV353 made its maiden flight in October 1967 it was engaged in modification work and subsequent trials until December 1968, when 800 Squadron assumed ownership. During its time with this unit XV353 suffered a major incident which in an older aircraft type would probably have resulted in its scrapping: while undertaking carrier practise landing aboard HMS *Eagle* on 25 April 1969 the Buccaneer caught the fourth arrestor wire, drifted across the deck and ended up the flight deck catwalk. Such was the extent of the damage that the Buccaneer was returned to Brough by road for rebuilding, which kept it on the ground until it was issued to 12 Squadron in January 1971. By December 1973 XV353 had rejoined the Fleet Air Arm, becoming part of 809 Squadron aboard *Ark Royal*.

XV344 remaining with 809 Squadron

XV358 near the end of its servicing cycle: it has been towed out of the hanger for engine runs. At this stage quite a lot of components were missing, such as the nose radome assembly and numerous access panels.
Trevor Smith Collection

XV354 was on the strength of 809 Squadron as 035/R when this portrait was taken. When *Ark Royal* was retired the Buccaneer was transferred to the RAF. Trevor Smith Collection

until 800 Squadron assumed ownership in October 1970, the aircraft having had an unremarkable career with its first operators. This tour ended in June 1972 when the aircraft was shipped to RNAY Sydenham for overhaul joining, 809 Squadron at the end of this work in August 1973. Coded 034/R, the Buccaneer continued in service with this its last unit until withdrawn in November 1978, its next port of call being the RAF.

The four aircraft that joined 800 Squadron were coded 103/E, 101/E, 100/E and 106/E, respectively, for the unit's tour aboard HMS *Eagle*. XV345 had an uneventful career with 800 Squadron, the only highlight being the inadvertent jettisoning of the wing tanks onto the carrier's deck in July 1969. By April 1972 the aircraft had left the Royal Navy to became part of the RAF's inventory.

Aircraft XV358 also embarked aboard HMS *Eagle*, although it soon found itself aboard another vessel and on its way back to Britain after making a heavy landing aboard the carrier, which caused the nose wheel to collapse. After repair XV358 resumed its career with 800 Squadron, but it soon required in-depth attention from the maintainers after suffering a bird strike while operating from Lossiemouth in November 1970. Such was the severity of the strike that the canopy disintegrated and communications were lost between the crew members. Unsure of the condi-

tion of the pilot, the observer ejected while the pilot returned the Buccaneer to base. After repairs 800 Squadron resumed ownership, although a move to 736 Squadron took place in January 1972. Twelve months later XV358 was in the colours of 809 Squadron, having passed through RNAY Sydenham for maintenance in the meantime. 809 Squadron used the aircraft until it flew off from *Ark Royal* to join the RAF.

XV359 was another Buccaneer that would join the RAF after its FAA service, having served with 800 Squadron until August 1973 when it moved to 809 Squadron via a maintenance period at RNAY Sydenham; 809 Squadron relinquished it in November 1978.

XV361 completed its tour aboard HMS *Eagle* without any major incidents and finally left 800 Squadron in March 1974 when it joined 809 Squadron, coded 027/R. XV361 remained with 809 Squadron operating from *Ark Royal* until transferred to the RAF in November 1978.

XV356 had undertaken its maiden flight in November 1967 but did not join 800 Squadron until January 1969, having been delayed due to extensive modification work. Whilst in FAA service XV356 suffered the usual range of defects before transferring to the RAF in March 1972.

Of this batch of machines only XV346 was allocated to 801 Squadron, as 239/H, in February 1968. Having survived its time

aboard *Hermes* XV346 then joined the Buccaneer training unit, 736 Squadron, in July 1968. During a training flight on 13 February 1969 the aircraft ran into a severe snowstorm at an altitude of 1,000ft (300m), which disorientated the crew so much so that the Buccaneer struck the sea. Both crew managed to eject safely from the aircraft, being picked up later by a rescue helicopter.

Replacing XV346 with 736 Squadron was XV349, which arrived at Lossiemouth in May 1969 having spent much of the previous two years on loan with the manufacturers for unspecified trials duties. By March 1971 this Buccaneer had left Lossiemouth for Honington where it became part of the RAF inventory.

The final four Buccaneers joined 803 Squadron at Lossiemouth during 1968, being coded 614/LM, 615/LM, 612/LM and 613/LM, respectively. XV354 completed its tour with 803 Squadron in May 1970, becoming part of 809 Squadron as 035/R. This tour was completed by January 1974 when the RAF assumed ownership. In contrast XV355 left 803 Squadron in July 1969, being transferred to 800 Squadron for a tour aboard HMS *Eagle*. 800 Squadron was the aircraft's last naval operator as a transfer to the RAF took place in March 1972. The next aircraft, XV357, was flown by 803 Squadron from June 1968 to May 1970 when it was transferred to 809 Squadron.

ABOVE: **Lossiemouth is the location for this portrait of XV864 of 809 Squadron. Visible just behind the Buccaneer is one of the F-4 Phantoms from *Ark Royal*'s air wing.** Trevor Smith Collection

LEFT: **XV865 of 809 Squadron parked on the flight line at Pensacola alongside a Grumman A-6 Intruder.** Trevor Smith Collection

This final period of naval operation ended in October 1973 when the Royal Air Force added the Buccaneer to its inventory. Except for the usual range of operational defects, XV361 completed its time with 803 Squadron without incident, moving to 800 Squadron as 105/E in December 1968 and staying on their charge until the RAF assumed ownership during April 1972.

XV863–XV869

The final contract for fifteen aircraft was trimmed down to just seven, the final eight being cancelled. All of these Buccaneers were built from the outset as Martel-capable aircraft. The first was XV863 which was retained by the manufacturers for trials before joining 809

Squadron in June 1969. After a spell with 736 Squadron from April 1970 to November 1973, it rejoined 809 Squadron. By November 1978 the RAF had added the aircraft to their inventory.

809 Squadron gained XV864 straight from the manufacturers in March 1969, the Buccaneer remaining with them until the training unit took it over in May 1970. A return to 809 Squadron took place in November 1973, and XV864 remained with them until the RAF assumed ownership in October 1978.

Another Buccaneer that joined the RAF after naval service was XV865, which entered the 736 Squadron inventory in May 1969, remaining with them until transferring to 809 Squadron in December 1973. Coded 022/R, the aircraft stayed with 809 Squadron until changing to RAF ownership in November 1978.

Also joining the RAF at the end of its naval career was XV866, which arrived at Lossiemouth in November 1968 and was held in storage until delivered to 809 Squadron in June 1969; it stayed with them until joining 736 Squadron in April 1970. At the completion of this phase of its naval service XV866 was utilized by the manufacturers and the A&AEE for Martel missile C(A) release. By September 1974 809 Squadron had resumed ownership of XV866, retaining it until transferring to the RAF in December 1978.

803 Squadron received XV867 in June 1969, applying the code 611/LM soon afterwards. 809 Squadron were the next operators of this Buccaneer from October 1973, coding it 024/R in the process. By November 1978 XV867 had finished with the FAA, joining the RAF after reworking at St Athan.

The following aircraft, XV868, had its entry into naval service delayed until May 1969 as it had first been used by the Lossiemouth Station Flight before being loaned to MinTech for arrester barrier trials. 809 Squadron loaned the Buccaneer to the manufacturers for Martel fitment trials, retaining the aircraft for the Paris Air Show. Having rejoined 809 Squadron, XV868 was then transferred to 736 Squadron as 656/LM, with whom it remained until rejoining 809 Squadron in October 1973. At the completion of its time with 809 Squadron XV868 was transferred to the RAF, flying to St Athan in November 1978.

The last Buccaneer delivered to the Fleet Air Arm was XV869, which was delivered to 736 Squadron in May 1969, being coded 641/LM in the process. A diversion to A&AEE for Martel trials began in April 1972, the aircraft transferring to the manufacturers for maintenance work eight months later. A&AEE resumed control of XV869 in April 1974, taking the aircraft to sea aboard *Ark Royal* for shock trials upon the Martel missile, these flights being completed by September 1974 when 809 Squadron assumed ownership. With the code 023/R applied XV869 remained with 809 Squadron until joining the RAF in December 1978, thus bringing to an end the Buccaneer's service with the Royal Navy.

XV868 was initially allocated to 736 Squadron, but joined 809 Squadron in 1973 before transferring to the RAF in 1978. Trevor Smith Collection

With power supplies and an air starter hose plugged in, XV869 of 809 Squadron has its crew strapped in by the ground crew. Trevor Smith Collection

XV339 of 736 Squadron sporting rocket pods on the inner pylons and basic CBLS carriers on the outers. Although training was carried out using the rocket pods, only the SAAF used them in anger. BBA Collection

Ark Royal and the Buccaneer

The aircraft carrier HMS *Ark Royal* first operated the Blackburn Buccaneer during the vessel's fourth commission, which took place between 1961 and 1964. In February 1963 aircraft from 801 Squadron were temporarily assigned to the carrier, their commanding officer being Cdr E. R. Anson, who commanded *Ark Royal* in 1976.

It was, however, the carrier's sixth commission, between 1970 and 1973, when the Buccaneer became a permanent fixture aboard the carrier. Prior to this *Ark Royal* had undergone a major rebuild in Devonport Dockyard, where preparation for the Phantom was the central theme. This 'Phantomization' of the carrier came as a surprise to many within the Admiralty who thought HMS *Eagle* a far better candidate for this reconstruction, it being in better condition overall. Suffice it to say the choice of *Ark Royal* was not a naval decision, but a political one.

Changes incorporated in *Ark Royal* as part of this £32 million refit included a flight deck with increased surface area and an angled deck of 8.5 degrees; included in this new deck was a waist catapult in place of the starboard bow catapult, the port bow catapult being retained and upgraded. The radar systems and electronic surveillance measures equipment were improved, much of it being fitted to a new 'lattice' mast mounted on the enlarged island superstructure. As the new flight deck impinged on the space occupied by the ship's anti-aircraft guns, they were completely removed and replaced by four Seacat surface-to-air missile launchers. Preliminary sea trials were carried out around Christmas 1969, *Ark Royal* being cleared for service use early in the New Year.

On 24 February 1970 HM the Queen Mother was at the recommissioning ceremony at Devonport Dockyard, after which the carrier was assigned to the fleet's Western Station. The air wing for this commission comprised of 809 Squadron with Buccaneer S.2s, 892 Squadron with Phantom FG.1s, 824 Squadron with Sea Kings and 849B Squadron with Gannet AEW.3s and a single Gannet COD.4 for general duties use. Work-up trials with the air wing were undertaken in June in the Moray Firth. During September *Ark Royal* was one of the carriers involved in the major NATO exercise *Northern Wedding*. Following on from this multinational exercise came *Lime Jug 70*,

which was more famous for a collision between *Ark Royal* and a Soviet Kotlin-class destroyer than anything else. Having sailed in the Atlantic and the Mediterranean, the carrier next went to the West Indies to use the Atlantic Fleet Weapons Range during June 1971, this being followed by visits to various American ports.

Some excitement was then provided by the Guatemalan government, which began to make threatening noises towards British Honduras (now Belize) at the beginning of 1972. The answer was to launch a pair of Buccaneers to make thunderous flypasts over Belize City, which convinced the Guatemalans to desist. The return trip was supported by other Buccaneers of 809 Squadron, which supplied in-flight refuelling with of the buddy refuelling pods; during the final leg home the aircraft were buzzed by USAF F-106 fighters, which had not been informed of the Buccaneers' presence.

1972 was also the year in which HMS *Eagle* was decommissioned for good and *Hermes* was converted into an anti-submarine/commando carrier, leaving *Ark Royal* as the only such strike carrier available to the Royal Navy. By February *Ark Royal* was off the coast of Puerto Rico to undertake Exercise *Landtreadex* in concert with the USS *Franklin D Roosevelt*. During this operation eight Buccaneers undertook a strike on the hulked USS *Connelly*, sinking it with ten iron bombs – this slightly miffed the USN, as they had wanted first crack at the target!

By the middle of the year *Ark Royal* was at Portsmouth, departing from there in September to take part in Exercise *Strong Express*, this being followed in November by *Exercise Corsica 72* in the Mediterranean Sea before returning to Devonport for Christmas. 1973 saw *Ark Royal* engaged in a series of exercises, the first being *Medtrain 73* in February after which the ship transited to the Azores for Exercise *Ruler*. At the completion of this deployment the carrier sailed to the United States for exercises in conjunction with its old sparring partner, USS *Franklin D Roosevelt*. These exercises were concluded in July ,the carrier returning home that same month. By 26 July HMS *Ark Royal* was Devonport for in-depth maintenance, which marked the end of that commission.

The ship's overhaul was deemed complete in 1974 and she was rededicated on 24

Sailing under full power, HMS *Ark Royal* is preparing to recover aircraft; this kind of performance was also required to launch aircraft. Visible on the deck are a Buccaneer, two Phantoms, a Sea King, a Wessex and a Gannet.
BBA Collection

April at Plymouth. After shakedown trials and the subsequent rectification work, the ship returned to sea with only a part air wing, as the ship's Buccaneers were employed in development flying of the Martel air-to-surface strike missile from the carrier. By 12 July *Ark Royal* had received her full air wing, although they soon became one Buccaneer short when one nose-dived into the deck on landing. Exercise *Northern Merger* – a major NATO exercise during which the carrier operated in concert with USS *America* – kept the ship and its crew occupied during September 1974. At the conclusion of this exercise the carrier deployed to Malta where the air wing decamped to Luqa, from where it continued flying operations.

Brasex 75 saw *Ark Royal* in company with other ships undertaking exercises with the Brazilian Navy during May, this being followed by a period tied up in Gibraltar for a much-needed rest. *Westaxe* followed in early July 1975, while the major NATO exercise *Ocean Safari* kept the carrier employed throughout the remainder of the autumn.

In 1976 HMS *Ark Royal* became a film star during the making of the BBC series *Sailor*. Although the BBC was aboard, the military work of the vessel continued and in February Exercise *Springtrain* was undertaken. September saw Exercise *Teamwork 76* as the centre of attention, and in this month the vessel's final commander, Captain Anson, took over the reins. The new boss had only been aboard a few days when *Ark Royal* became engaged in Exercise *Display Determination*, this being completed by 12 October. This was the carrier's final deployment for this commission, the ship returning to Britain in time for Christmas.

By now *Ark Royal* was becoming tired and the supply of spares from HMS *Eagle* was in danger of drying up, so it was fairly obvious that crunch time had come for the ship. Prior to any decision being made over its future HMS *Ark Royal* recommissioned in time for the Silver Jubilee Review at Spithead in May 1977. At the completion of the review the ship's crew undertook a pre-voyage work-up that was followed by a rectification period in Devonport. The vessel finally sailed for operations on 1 September, collecting its air wing along the way. After the usual air wing work-up period, the ship was involved in *Ocean Safari 1977*, this being followed by a trip to Gibraltar in November. Departing from Gibraltar toward home, the air wing left for Lossiemouth while the carrier arrived at Plymouth for Christmas.

On 5 April 1978 HMS *Ark Royal* departed on her last deployment, the venue being the eastern seaboard of the United States. In May the carrier undertook a mock battle with USS *John F Kennedy* under the title of *Solid Shield*. After a sojourn in port at Maryport, the ship took part in a reinforcement exercise called *Common Effort*. Straight after this *Ark Royal* took part in that year's *Northern Wedding*. The ship then sailed for the Mediterranean to participate in Exercise *Display Determination*, which ended when the carrier tied up in Malta for a last visit in November. Heading for home, the air wing departed: the last steam-launched aircraft was Phantom 012/R. On 4 December HMS *Ark Royal* sailed into Devonport for the last time after twenty-three years of service, having steamed some 900,000 miles (1,450,000km) in this period.

In this view of a Buccaneer on the catapult, the attachment of the launch bridle can clearly be seen, as can the angle of the aircraft and the steam being generated by the catapult. BBA Collection

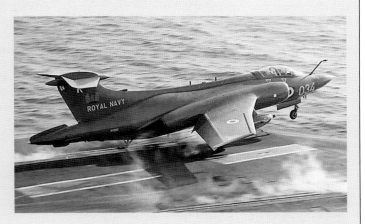

A Buccaneer of 809 Squadron caught at the moment of departure from *Ark Royal*. After its last refit the catapults were fitted with bridle catchers, which reduced the cost of each launch and reduced the clutter on the ocean floor. BBA Collection

HMS *Ark Royal* proceeds at speed away from the camera with many of its aircraft on the flight deck. BBA Collection

CHAPTER EIGHT

The Buccaneer with the Royal Air Force

The TSR2/F-111 Debacle

The story of the Buccaneer in Royal Air Force service is one of indecision, government interference and official indifference. The saga began on 6 April 1965 when the new Labour Government cancelled the proposed replacement for the RAF's Canberra light bombers, the BAC TSR2. This was a particular blow to both the British Aircraft Corporation and Rolls-Royce, as both had worked hard to develop this most advanced of strike aircraft. The TSR2 had never been popular with the Labour Party, who justified its cancellation on cost grounds, a decision that remains controversial to this day. There was also a suspicion that American pressure was being brought to bear especially in the field of exports, and that some form of behind-the-scenes trade-off was negotiated.

The replacement for the TSR2 was to be the General Dynamics F-111K swing-wing strike aircraft – this was a version of the USAF's F-111A with British avionics. However the F-111 was going through a sticky patch in its development at the time, with aircraft crashing for no apparent reason. Eventually all the problems with this aircraft were ironed out and the F-111 went on to serve the USAF faithfully for many years, but the UK order was cancelled before the first F-111K had even flown. Having dumped the TSR2 and the F-111, after spending large amounts of money on both projects, the government then decided to purchase the McDonnell Douglas F-4 Phantom. Even here interference was experienced, as there was an insistence upon installing British engines and avionics. While the latter were integrated without too much trouble, the choice of the larger Spey engine in place of the standard General Electric J79 powerplant resulted in a Phantom that was slower and more fuel-hungry that its J79-powered counterparts.

Early Opposition to the Buccaneer

All these shenanigans meant that the venerable Canberra B(I)8s had to soldier on in service while a replacement was sought. An indication of the MoD's thinking came from Denis Healey, Defence Secretary in the Labour government at the time, who commented that the role of the TSR2 could be carried out by either land- or ship-based Buccaneers. The Buccaneer had first come to the notice of the Royal Air Force in 1957 when Brough had put forward a version of the Buccaneer in answer to requirement OR.339 – the Canberra replacement that was originally filled by the TSR2. In this proposal Blackburn had proposed to develop a de-navalized version of the aircraft, which had been stretched to increase its attractiveness to the RAF. However, with the RAF's heart set upon an aircraft developed specially for their needs, the Blackburn idea was formally rejected. On a more personal note, intense rivalry between the RAF and Royal Navy also played a part in this decision: the junior service had always refused to even consider purchasing aircraft designed for the Navy, this harking back to the 1930s when the Air Ministry controlled aircraft purchases for both organizations.

Blackburn continued to offer new versions of the Buccaneer to the MoA and the RAF. The first was the Mk 2*, which featured more powerful Spey engines and many of the avionics that had been developed for the TSR2. Also intended for this version was landing gear capable of operating from soft-field surfaces, a demountable gun pack and a Spectre rocket engine to boost take-off performance. A second improved specification added even more TSR2 avionics to the design. Making the transition towards a

TSR2-based Buccaneer was quite an easy step as Buccaneers had already been involved in the development of the TSR2. Fitted with a TSR2 avionics suite, the development aircraft had operated from Turnhouse, Edinburgh, achieving consistent speeds of 500kt at an altitude of 100ft (30m). By now part of the Hawker Siddeley group, Blackburn were not undaunted by yet another government rejection despite the upgraded Buccaneer offering great cost savings for a slight reduction in capabilities. A second attempt by Hawker Siddeley saw them offer the Buccaneer S.2**, a supersonic version of the previous design that was nearly as capable as the F-111.

Buccaneers Are Ordered

By January 1968 the F-111 deal was dead and, in a complete turnaround in attitude, the government ditched nearly a dozen years of opposition to the Buccaneer, announcing on 10 July that the Buccaneer was purchased to replace the cancelled F-111s. The first contract, KC/2F/258, was issued to Brough in January 1969 covering twenty-six aircraft. A further seventeen machines were ordered under contract K58A/316, which was issued in 1974. A final small batch of three aircraft intended as attrition replacements was ordered under contract K/A6a/362. The decision to run down the Fleet Air Arm would allow a further sixty-four aircraft to join the RAF inventory. A further three aircraft, not intended for service usage, were ordered for the development organizations under contract K58a/316, for use by the A&AEE, RAE or DARA as required.

The Royal Air Force received two different versions of the Buccaneer, the S2A and the S2B. The former was not capable of carrying the Martel missile while the second could, and the BLC pipework carried in the inner wing sections of the 'A' version was a far simpler version to install. While the 'B' version was a far more capable machine, its BLC pipework required much controlled violence with 'egg' poles to push into position, and from an observational point of view the pylons were slightly further outboard to accommodate the Martel, and later the Sea Eagle, fit.

Luqa airport on Malta, and it's hot as the pilot of a 15 Squadron Buccaneer waits for access ladders to exit his aircraft. Once the chocks are in and the crew are clear, the ground crew will begin the aircraft's recovery. BBA Collection

Buccaneers Join the RAF

The first RAF unit to equip with the Buccaneer was 12 Squadron based at Honington which, having previously operated the Avro Vulcan B.2, had reformed on 1 October 1969. The first machine delivered to the RAF was XV350 which was officially handed over just after its first flight on 11 February, having been reworked by Brough to the standard required by the RAF. As this was a period of transition there was a frequent interchange of aircraft between the services and 809 Squadron, which used Honington as its home base while ashore from *Ark Royal*, was allocated to the Buccaneer maritime strike force when so based. In these early days the 12 Squadron Buccaneers were finished in a gloss scheme of two greys and green overlaid with red, white and blue national markings. Defining the aircraft's operator was the fox head badge carried on the engine nacelles,

which represented the unit's time operating the Fairey Fox high-speed day bomber. Careful examination of these badges will reveal that each aircraft's badges had different expressions: some will be smiling, others will look left or right, and there was even a pair with eye patches.

Soon after formation, the 12 Squadron Buccaneers were involved in developing the tactics applicable to an aircraft that was intended to act in the maritime strike, nuclear attack and conventional bomber roles. Supporting the Buccaneer squadrons was 237 OCU, which came into existence in 1971 and would replace 736 Squadron as the naval training organization when the latter unit disbanded at Lossiemouth in February 1972.

XW525–XW528

While the initial deliveries made to the RAF were refurbished naval aircraft, the first new Buccaneer delivered to the service was XW525, which made its initial flight on 8 January 1970, this being followed the formation of the first RAF Germany unit, 15 Squadron, on 1 October 1970. Destined to serve its time at RAF Laarbruch, this unit was later joined by 16 Squadron in 16 January 1973. 208 Squadron, once mounted on the Hawker Hunter, re-formed with the Buccaneer on 1 July 1974 at Honington. A final unit, 216 Squadron formed on the type on 1 July 1979 and was intended to use refurbished aircraft that had been relinquished by 809

Although XV350 was ostensibly delivered to the RAF it spent its time with the manufacturers and various trials organizations, developing weapons, systems and tactics for the Buccaneer force. BBA Collection

Seen from underneath, careful observation of the wings will reveal some light-coloured strips leading out towards the wing tips. These areas are in fact unpainted and were left as such so that the non-destructive teams could carry out their work without hindrance. Trevor Smith Collection

Squadron. However, the crash of an aircraft during a *Red Flag* exercise over the Nevada desert would put paid to this unit gaining more machines, so 216 Squadron lost its handful of Buccaneers and re-equipped with the much larger Lockheed Tristar instead.

Whether it was because the RAF Buccaneers were purely land-based or because there had been subtle changes in crew training methods, their losses were less than those of their naval counterparts. What also kept the losses to a manageable level was the period that had elapsed between the introduction of the Buccaneer S.2 and its acceptance by the RAF, by which time many of the faults and defects had been ironed out.

Of the new-build machines, XW525 was retained until 1974 by Hawker Siddeley for C(A) clearance flying before joining 237 OCU by November 1974. A transfer to 12 Squadron had been effected by May 1976, although the Buccaneer was being flown by 208 Squadron when it crashed into Claerwen reservoir, near Rhayader in Wales, on 4 April 1977. The loss was attributed to the failure of the tailplane mounts while the crew were undertaking collision avoidance manoeuvres with two RAF Hunters. Fortunately both crew

ejected and survived. The second aircraft, XW526, served with 15 Squadron in Germany from April 1970 to November 1976 when it moved to its sister unit, 16 Squadron. This Buccaneer was lost in a crash on 12 July 1979 when a wing detached during manoeuvres at near Osnabruck. In this case one of the crew ejected to safety but the other was killed.

More lucky was XW527, which joined 15 Squadron in July 1970 and remained with them until 16 Squadron assumed ownership in April 1973. A transfer to Britain and 208 Squadron took place in July 1977, although by February 1978 12 Squadron had assumed control. XW527 alternate between both the Honington-, later Lossiemouth-based, units before the aircraft was withdrawn from service during the type's rundown in 1994. While the majority of its siblings were completely reduced to scrap, the nose of this aircraft still survives.

Another aircraft that was delivered to 15 Squadron was XW528, which arrived in Germany in August 1970. 15 Squadron was the aircraft's only operator, XV528 staying with them until the Buccaneer fleet was grounded in 1980 after the crash in Nevada. In order to return as many of the Buccaneers to service as possible, a full

inspection of each airframe was undertaken and it was during this process that evidence of fatigue failure in the vicinity of Rib 60 was discovered. Moved by road to the maintenance base at St Athan during August 1980, XW528 was inspected further and placed on a possible repair list. Once the entire fleet had been inspected the decision was taken to declare some of the airframes as beyond economic repair, allowing some of the aircraft in store at St Athan to be used as donor aircraft. This was the fate of XW528, which was stripped of all usable spare parts before being transferred to Coningsby for battle damage repair training as 8861M.

XW529–XW533

The following five aircraft, XW529 to XW533, were also delivered directly to 15 Squadron in Germany. The first three arrived in September, October and November 1970 while the other two arrived in January and March 1971. XW529 departed from Germany for MOD(PE) use with by A&AEE and the manufacturers, arriving in July 1974. It primary purpose was for weapons development with the AV/AVQ-23E *Pave Spike* laser designator pod, and the associated 1,000lb Paveway guided bomb. Having completed these trials, the Buccaneer was allocated to trials of the Sea Eagle missile and then the ASR 1012 avionics package, which was fully explored aboard this aircraft. After a full life as a test bed, XW529 was finally scrapped in October 1992.

XW530 had a far more exciting life. After its time with 15 Squadron it was transferred to 16 Squadron in February 1973, remaining there until November 1979 when 216 Squadron at Honington became the aircraft's short-term owners. In February 1980 XW530, in common with the remainder of the Buccaneer fleet, was grounded after the crash of XV345 during *Red Flag*. By September 1980 XW530 had been cleared to resume flying, but now with 208 Squadron as 216 Squadron had been disbanded. In June 1961 XW530 transferred to 12 Squadron, wearing its last three serial digits as a tailcode.

When Operation *Pulsator* was put into action in September 1983 XW530, along with XV359, XV361, XX885, XX901 and XZ430, flew combat support patrols from

ABOVE: **XW527 wears the full 16 Squadron markings – very reminiscent of those sported by the unit's earlier Canberras. Both types were allocated to one task: to provide SACEUR with a tactical nuclear strike option.** Adrian Balch

RIGHT: **Originally operated by 15 Squadron, XW529 was later transferred to the test and trials organizations for use in weapons development.** Trevor Smith Collection

BELOW: **XW529 on display at Waddington complete with a polar bear badge on the fin. Being a trials aircraft, XW529 was not repainted in the matt finish applied to front-line aircraft. During its life the aircraft was used for ASR 1012, Sea Eagle, Pave Spike and Laser Guided Bombs.** BBA Collection

Akrotiri, Cyprus, in support of the British Army over the Lebanon, the army contingent being part of a UN peacekeeping force. To emphasize the message that the Buccaneer was still a potent machine it was not unusual for a sortie to depart from Akrotiri and carry out high-speed, low-level passes over known trouble spots. After returning to Britain XW530 joined 12 Squadron at Lossiemouth in November 1984.

In early 1990 the Martel missile was withdrawn from service use, being replaced by the far more capable Sea Eagle. Both 12 and 208 Squadrons was equipped with this weapon for anti-shipping use.

When Saddam Hussein unleashed the Iraqi armed forces upon the almost defenceless Kuwait in August 1990, the response of the west was to reinforce the Saudi armed forces. For the Buccaneer

fleet the orders were to prepare certain aircraft to take part in Operation *Granby*, these modifications including chaff and flare dispensers and a coat of Alkali Removable Temporary Finish, better known as Magnolia. Coded 'E',XW530 plus XX899 'P', XX892 'I', XW547 'R', XW533 'A' and XX889 'T' were flown to the ex-RAF base at Muharraq, using tanker support for refuelling and navigation assistance. Initially XW530 carried no nose art although as the campaign progressed the name 'Glenmorangie' was applied, this being complemented by twelve bombing mission symbols on the starboard side of the nose.

At the completion of hostilities XW530 returned to Lossiemouth, arriving on 17 March 1991. 12 Squadron resumed ownership of the aircraft until the unit disbanded in October 1993, the Buccaneer joining

208 Squadron. In February 1994 208 Squadron disbanded, which resulted in the grounding of the remaining Buccaneers. XW530 is currently on display at the Buccaneer service station in Elgin.

In contrast to XW530 the next Buccaneer, XW531, which had served with 15 Squadron in Germany, returned to Britain and 12 Squadron at Honington in January 1971. This sojourn was short as 237 OCU took over the aircraft three months later for use in the training role. A return to Germany followed some weeks later, the Buccaneer resuming its career with 15 Squadron. By November 1974 XW531 had returned to Honington and 12 Squadron, with whom it was flying when the pilot lost control while operating near Bodö, Norway, the aircraft crashing on 29 October 1976. A Buccaneer with an even shorter life was

LEFT: **Buccaneer S.2 XW987 looking decidedly scruffy. It sports the basic 'raspberry ripple' trials scheme with acamouflaged fins and rudder, plus an intake sporting the desert scheme.** BBA Collection

BELOW: **Hawker Siddeley used every opportunity to display the Buccaneer at trade shows such as Farnborough. Here, one of the prototypes sports triple mounts of 500lb bombs on each pylon, not a load actually carried in service.** Trevor Smith Collection

After service in Germany with 16 Squadron XW533 returned to Britain to join 208 Squadron. Not long after returning the Buccaneer underwent Sea Eagle upgrading, this later being followed by the ASR1012 upgrade programme. Trevor Smith Collection

XW532, which had joined 15 Squadron in January 1971. On 25 March the aircraft crashed near Laarbruch during a low-level transit flight.

A longer-lasting airframe was XW533 which joined 16 Squadron in March 1973, passing to 12 Squadron in February 1978. By July 1979 the short-lived 216 Squadron had taken on XW533, although this period ended in 1980 after the Nevada crash. When the Buccaneer fleet resumed operations XW533 was on the strength of 12 Squadron, remaining with them until January 1981 when 237 OCU acquired the aircraft for crew training duties. During 1982 and 1983 the Buccaneer was back in Germany serving with both the Laarbruch squadrons, though this ended in November 1983 when training duties at Honington called once again. By 1985 the Buccaneer was at Brough for the installation of the ASR 1012 avionics suite. In April 208 Squadron was operating the aircraft, although this ended in February 1989 when 237 OCU added it to their inventory.

The start of Operation *Granby* saw XW533 being given its coat of magnolia and the 'A' tailcode. In company with the remainder of the detachment, XW533 returned to Lossiemouth and further service with the Operational Conversion Unit in March 1991. By September 1992 this veteran of many years' service had been done to destruction in an Elgin scrapyard.

XW534–XW538

Deliveries having begun with the strike squadrons in Germany, 237 OCU was next on the delivery list, gaining five Buccaneers straight from the manufacturers: XW534, XW535, XW536, XW537 and XW538. Departing from Honington, XW534 flew to Germany for 15 Squadron, arriving in October 1972. Except for a short loan to 16 Squadron during July and August 1978 XW534 continued with 15 Squadron until it was grounded in 1980 for in depth wing spar inspections. Cleared to resume flying, XW534 was on the strength of 16 Squadron by March 1981, although it had returned to its former owners by June 1982. By September 1982 the Buccaneer had been flown to St Athan for temporary storage where it remained until

---

Operation *Pulsator*

Bringing into sharp focus the problems that have beset the Middle East were the years of conflict that ravaged the Lebanon. Britain's last foray into that benighted country began on 16 September 1983 when the British Forces Lebanon, BRITFORLEB, in the shape of the Queen's Dragoon Guards, arrived to take up peace-keeping duties in the south east quadrant of Beirut. During this period the British soldiers were subjected to many attacks by various Arab factions, who frequently took potshots at the British positions when conflict amongst themselves waned.

Air support initially took the form of supply flights provided by Lockheed C-130 Hercules for the heavy items, these being deposited at Beirut airport while distribution was by Boeing Vertol Chinooks, both types having their camouflage highlighted by prominently displayed Union Jacks. Bedecking everything in sight with British flags acted as no guarantee to the safety of the troops and their air support, however, so some airborne metal of a more lethal intent was called for.

The answer was to dispatch a force of six Buccaneers, crews and ground crews to RAF Akrotiri in Cyprus as Operation *Pulsator*. The six aircraft – XV359, XV361, XW530 from 12 Squadron, and XX885, XX901 and XZ430 from 208 Squadron – were in place by September. Once established at Akrotiri one of their first actions was to dispatch a pair of Buccaneers to Beirut to fly low and fast over the area of the city being patrolled by the British contingent. Given the low altitude and the thunderous noise generated, these over-flights had the desired effect as the assaults upon the British positions reduced considerably.

While the flights had obviously impressed the locals the detachment remained on full alert, so at least four of the serviceable aircraft were kept fully fuelled and armed, ready to go within minutes, in effect a mini-QRA. In order to familiarize themselves with the local area and the war zone, the remaining aircraft, if fit to fly, were utilized for training duties, all six being rotated in and out of the QRA role as required. By April 1984 all six Buccaneers and personnel had returned to Britain. This looked to be the end of the more warlike part of the aircraft's career however in 1991 this would all change.

The ASR 1012 Programme

While the navigation and avionics suite fitted the Buccaneer fleet had undergone some revision, by the early 1980s it was felt that the whole system needed a major overhaul, especially with the advent of the Sea Eagle 'fire and forget' anti-ship missile, which would be hampered by the antiquity of the aircraft's systems. The result was Air Staff Requirement 1012 (ASR 1012). As always with such things the defining factor was the amount of money available, so the total number of Buccaneers to be upgraded was limited to forty-two. To select the airframes to be modified the fatigue life of the active RAF fleet was analysed, as was their actual serviceability state and the amount of time left prior to the next major servicing.

The design stage for the programme began in February 1985 with the first aircraft arriving at Woodford in early 1986. The ASR 1012 package included: the Ferranti FIN 1063 INS; refinement of the *Blue Parrot* radar system; a new Plessey ASR 899 radio, modernization of the ARI 18228 ECM/ESM; Sky Guardian 200 Radar Warning Receiver; the Sea Eagle system; equipment to support Sidewinder models AIM-9G and -9L; and Tracor AN/ALE-40 chaff and flare dispensers to improve the type's self-defence capability. Also included was the ability to operate in a Nuclear, Biological and Chemical (NBC) environment, with alterations to the cockpit that allowed the aircrew to gain the full benefit of the AR5 flight suits. The installation of the Sky Guardian system saw the wing leading edge pods reinstated, although these too were reworked to house the E/J Band receivers in place of the earlier S/X Type.

The ASR 1012 programme was carried out on small batches of Buccaneers, the final machine returning to Lossiemouth in 1989. As each batch returned to Scotland an equal number of aircraft was released to undergo the process. 208 Squadron complete the process first, followed by 12 Squadron and finally 237 OCU.

Serial number	ASR 1012 set number	Remarks
XW529	Prototype	Retained standard wing tips
XV865	Set No.01	Fitted with extended wing tips
XX900	Set No.02	Fitted with extended wing tips
XV353	Set No.03	Fitted with extended wing tips
XZ431	Set No.04	Fitted with extended wing tips
XV867	Set No.05	Fitted with extended wing tips
XT279	Set No.06	Retained standard wing tips
XV342	Set No.07	Fitted with extended wing tips
XT286	Set No.08	Retained standard wing tips
XV161	Set No.09	Retained standard wing tips
XN976	Set No.10	Fitted with extended wing tips
XW530	Set No.11	Fitted with extended wing tips
XX901	Set No.12	Fitted with extended wing tips
XV352	Set No.13	Fitted with extended wing tips
XW547	Set No.14	Retained standard wing tips
XX895	Set No.15	Fitted with extended wing tips
XV864	Set No.16	Fitted with extended wing tips
XV869	Set No.17	Retained standard wing tips
XN981	Set No.18	Fitted with extended wing tips
XW543	Set No.19	Fitted with extended wing tips
XW527	Set No.20	Fitted with extended wing tips
XW546	Set No.21	Retained standard wing tips
XX893	Set No.22	Fitted with extended wing tips
XZ432	Set No.23	Retained standard wing tips
XX899	Set No.24	Fitted with extended wing tips
XV332	Set No.25	Fitted with extended wing tips
XV333	Set No.26	Fitted with extended wing tips
XN983	Set No.27	Retained standard wing tips
XV165	Set No.28	Retained standard wing tips
XV863	Set No.29	Fitted with extended wing tips
XT280	Set No.30	Fitted with extended wing tips
XX892	Set No.31	Fitted with extended wing tips
XV162	Set No.32	Retained standard wing tips
XW534	Set No.33	Retained standard wing tips
XX894	Set No.34	Fitted with extended wing tips
XW533	Set No.35	Fitted with extended wing tips
XW542	Set No.36	Fitted with extended wing tips
XV359	Set No.37	Fitted with extended wing tips
XT287	Set No.38	Retained standard wing tips
XT288	Set No.39	Retained standard wing tips
XX889	Set No.40	Fitted with extended wing tips
XV361	Set No.41	Fitted with extended wing tips
XX885	Set No.42	Fitted with extended wing tips

moved to Woodford for the application of the ASR 1012 avionics update, which added Sea Eagle capability to the type's inventory. At the completion of this upgrade XW534 was utilized by A&AEE for ASR 1012 clearance, this being completed by October 1989 when it was delivered to 12 Squadron. No.27 MU at Shawbury was the aircraft's next destination, where it was stored prior to being scrapped in October 1992.

January 1973 was a bad year for XW535 as it crashed near Minden, some 11 miles from Gutersloh, the pilot having lost control while avoiding another aircraft. Prior to being reduced to scrap metal XW535 had departed from 237 OCU to join 16 Squadron arriving in October 1972. A transfer to 15 Squadron took place on 8 January 1973 the Buccaneer crashing sixteen days later.

Another unfortunate to be lost in a crash was XW536 which had left 237 OCU in November 1972 15 Squadron at Laarbruch. A transfer to the other Laarbruch unit, 16 Squadron, took place in January 1973, although by April 1975 15 Squadron had resumed ownership. On 16 June 1975 XW536 and XW528 was undertaking a practice sortie over the North Sea when both aircraft collided. After the collision XW528 struggled back to base while the crew of XW536 had to eject.

XW537 moved from the OCU to 15 Squadron in January 1973. By May 1977 16 Squadron was crewing the aircraft, which remained with them until the Buccaneer fleet was grounded in 1980. When the surviving Buccaneers were cleared to resume flying XW537 joined 237 OCU, remaining with them until it crashed on approach to Wattisham on 23 September 1981.

The last of this group was XW538 which left 237 OCU in May 1973 to join 16 Squadron staying with them until the 1980 grounding. In contrast to many of the other grounded Buccaneers, XW538 was one of the detachment taking part in *Red Flag* when the accident happened, so its investigation was carried out at Nellis AFB. At the completion of this work XW538 was considered unsafe to fly back to Germany so arrangements were made to ship the aircraft home. XW538 arrived at Hull docks in February 1980 and was moved by road to Brough. After further assessment the Buccaneer was declared beyond economic repair and so moved by road to Abingdon in August 1980 for battle damage repair training. By September 1981 the battered remains of XW538 were on the fire dump at Lossiemouth, being finally cleared by December 1985.

XW539–XW550

The record for the shortest Buccaneer service life is probably held by XW539, which was delivered to 12 Squadron on 19 October 1971 and was lost in a crash on 4 January 1972, when it flew into the sea while flying at low level over the Irish Sea near the Isle of Man.

A slightly longer-lived machine was XW540, which was delivered to 15 Squadron along with the next nine aircraft, XW541 to XW548. MoD(PE) operated XW540 on a short-term loan before it joined 15 Squadron in May 1972 with whom it stayed until July 1979 before moving to Honington to join 216 Squadron. By 1980 this aircraft alongside the rest of the fleet was grounded after the *Red Flag* crash. By August 1980 XW540 had resumed flying with 12 Squadron, staying with them until July 1983 at Honington. When the Buccaneer units moved north to Lossiemouth XW540 joined 208 Squadron in July 1983. A move round the perimeter track to 12 Squadron occurred in August, XW540 remaining

with them until 237 OCU became its operator. In August 1986 it returned to 12 Squadron, with whom it was flying when it crashed on 22 April 1987 while flying over the sea near Duncansby Head, at the northern tip of Scotland.

Of the next nine machines, XW541 joined 15 Squadron in December 1971 while the remainder were delivered throughout 1972. A short period with 16 Squadron was followed by a return to Britain and 12 Squadron in November 1978. Grounded alongside the remainder of the Buccaneer fleet, XW541 was retained at St Athan for spares recovery. Four years later the Buccaneer was at Honington for use as a weapons loading trainer, this ending in early 1991 when P&EE Foulness acquired it for their nefarious purposes.

XW542 remained with 15 Squadron in Germany until returning to Britain to join the nascent 216 Squadron in July 1979. Grounded in 1980, XW542 was moved to St Athan for inner wing rebuilding, this being completed by May 1981 when 12 Squadron at Lossiemouth became the new owners. 208 Squadron took over XW542 in July 1983. From Lossiemouth MoD(PE) acquired the aircraft for trials purposes prior to its entering Brough for the installation of the ASR 1012 avionics package. By May 1985 XW542 was back in regular service with 12 Squadron, remaining with them for five months before 237 OCU

took the aircraft on. By October 1989 XW542 was with 208 Squadron, its final operator with whom it remained until withdrawal.

Germany was the home for XW543 until it was grounded in February 1980, being transported to St Athan for an inner wing transplant. Upon completion XW543 was reissued to RAFG, joining 16 Squadron in January 1982. A move to Honington for training duties took place in November 1983, although this ended in April 1984 when it was placed in store at St Athan. 12 Squadron, by now at Lossiemouth, received XW543 in January 1987 and it remained with them until 14 May 1992 when it landed at St Mawgan after suffering a hydraulic failure. As this was close to the end of the Buccaneer's career, the decision was taken to scrap the aircraft.

An aircraft with a shortened service life was XW544, which remained in Germany until being grounded in 1980. Resuming flying, XW544 returned to Germany although it left in July 1983 for storage at 27 MU, Shawbury. It next role was for training at No. 2 School of Technical Training, Cosford, who accepted it in February 1984. After the machinations of various novice engineering tradesmen, the Buccaneer was withdrawn from use in 1985.

Another Buccaneer that ceased flying after the grounding of 1980 was XW545,

Having served with 16 Squadron until 1979, XW549 returned to Britain and 12 Squadron, with whom it operated until the Buccaneer fleet was grounded after the crash of February 1980; it was then stripped for spares. Adrian Balch

which spent its entire life with the Germany wing until 1979. After a short period with the manufacturers the aircraft was dispatched to St Athan for storage. By 1986 XW545 had been stripped of all usable spares and so was dispatched to Pendine ranges for use as a target.

The next airframe, XW546, continued flying after its wing transplant at Bitteswell. This had taken place during 1980, after which XW546 rejoined the Germany Buccaneer wing from July 1983; five months later 237 OCU acquired this aircraft for use at Honington. In September 1985 the aircraft was at Woodford for the installation of the ASR 1012 avionics suite, returning to Lossiemouth after completion. In April 1994 XW546 was withdrawn from use, being scrapped shortly afterwards.

Buccaneer XW547 moved from unit to unit a very regular intervals. After 15 Squadron, XW547 joined 16 Squadron in 1974. Two years later it was with the OCU, although this sojourn only lasted until mid-1979 when the newly formed 216 Squadron took it over. After the 1980 grounding and a wing transplant at Bitteswell, the Buccaneer was delivered to 12 Squadron at Honington in April 1981, remaining there until 208 Squadron gained its services. When 208 Squadron relocated to Lossiemouth XW547 went with them, spending short periods with both 12 Squadron and 237 OCU before being prepared for Operation *Granby* in January 1991. In concert with the other aircraft from the detachment, 'Guinness Girl' with its eleven mission markings returned to Lossiemouth in March 1991, rejoining 12 Squadron soon afterwards. By

1993 XW547 had ceased flying, being allocated to the Cosford museum for display purposes, though it currently resides at RAF Museum, Hendon.

Destined to stay with the Germany wing, XW548 joined 15 Squadron in January 1973 and moved to 16 Squadron twelve months later. While flying near Volkel on 3 February 1977 XW548 suffered a severe engine fire that left the crew with no other option but to eject, which both did safely.

XW549 remained in Germany with 15 and 16 Squadrons before returning to Britain in December 1979, when 12 Squadron at Honington took charge. When the Buccaneer fleet was grounded in February 1980 XW549 was moved to St Athan for spares recovery, spending its final days in store. Eventually the remains were transferred to Kinloss for training purposes. It should be noted that these airframes were missing their engines, outer wings, air brake assemblies and many other parts, including the inner wing BLC ducting when they were finally disposed of.

A similar story surrounded XW550, which spent its entire life in Germany until it was withdrawn from service in February 1980 for use as a donor airframe for other aircraft. Eventually the remains were scrapped, although the nose was later saved.

XX885–XX901

Of the next seventeen airframes, one was delivered to the RAE while the remainder were delivered directly to the RAF. Ten of these aircraft, XX885 to XX894, were delivered to the Germany-based Buccaneer squadrons.

XX885 remained in Germany until February 1972 when 12 Squadron assumed ownership, although this was short-lived as 216 Squadron then acquired the aircraft. After the 1980 grounding XX885 was returned to St Athan for replacement of its inner wing assembly, rejoining the service and 208 Squadron at Lossiemouth in July 1983. When Operation *Pulsator* began this Buccaneer was detached to Cyprus in support of British forces acting on behalf of the UN in Lebanon. By May 1984 XX885 had returned to Lossiemouth and 12 Squadron, although 208 Squadron resumed ownership in June 1988. A short period in storage ended in January 1991 when 208 Squadron assumed ownership once more, the Buccaneer being prepared for Operation *Granby*. 'Hello Sailor', complete with seven mission symbols, returned home to Lossiemouth, rejoining 208 Squadron in March 1991. Thirteen months later 12 Squadron acquired the Buccaneer, by which time it was wearing a light grey overall finish. In October 1993 this Buccaneer was retired from active service.

XX885's intended role as a training airframe meant that it was kept under cover, so when put up for auction in 2000 it was in excellent condition. The successful purchasers on 16 March were Hawker Hunter Aviation based at RAF Scampton. A complicated journey by road and sea finally saw XX885 arrive at its new Lincolnshire home. HHA were determined to get the most from their new purchase, so inquires were made to the CAA concerning about getting XX885 – later to be registered G-HHAA – flying again. One of the obstacles that faces anyone trying to fly an ex-military jet of any complexity in UK

XX885 was one of the late-build machines that survived the post-crash inspections, going on to serve successfully during the Gulf War of 1990–91. Trevor Smith Collection

skies is the wariness of the CAA over the engineering support required for such a machine. Luckily HHA were able to gain a BCAR A8-20 classification for XX885 in the complex aircraft category – this effort alone required some 2,750 man hours by HHA staff to achieve. This was not the end of the story as HHA embarked upon the process of gaining flight certification for their Buccaneer, which required input from outside contractors amounting to another 3,250 paid-for man hours. All this effort finally paid off when G-HHAA was cleared for flight in the complex category by the CAA on 9 December 2005. HHA have begun a full overhaul of the Buccaneer and have estimated a return to flight date some time in 2006.

XX886 was another aircraft that was withdrawn from use after the 1980 fleet grounding; prior to that the aircraft had remained in Germany until joining 216 Squadron in May 1979. Withdrawn from use, the aircraft was transferred for use as a weapons load trainer at Honington, where it was finally scrapped. A similar history exists for XX887 which remained at Laarbruch for weapons load training, this ending in February 1984 for spares recovery and storage. Eventually the remains were transferred to Shawbury where they were scrapped in October 1991.

It would appear that the later-build Buccaneers represented by this batch were favourites for spares recovery after the 1980 grounding, as this was the fate that befell XX888 which spent its entire flying career with the RAFG Buccaneer wing. After a period at St Athan, the remains were transferred to Shawbury where everything but the nose was scrapped.

The next six machines also went to the Germany squadrons, the first being XX889 which remained with 16 Squadron from February 1975 until June 1977 when 15 Squadron assumed ownership. Two years later 16 Squadron had regained XX889 and continued to operate it until the entire fleet was grounded after the 1980 crash. After being cleared to resume flying, the Buccaneer returned to flying with 12 Squadron in March 1982 although it had transferred to the other Lossiemouth strike unit, 208 Squadron, by October 1983. A short period with the OCU took place between December 1986 and May 1987. XX889 was one of the machines that took part in Operation *Granby*, being coded 'T' in the process. Eventually the name 'Longmorn' and fourteen bomb

15 Squadron's XX888 banks away from the camera assigned to RAFG. This was one of the Buccaneers that was stripped for spares after the February 1980 crash. Trevor Smith Collection

mission symbols were applied to the starboard side of the nose, these being on display when the Buccaneer returned to Lossiemouth in March 1991.

A short period with 12 Squadron ended in October 1991 when 208 Squadron took XX889 onto their inventory until January 1992, when 12 Squadron applied its Fox head badge to the aircraft. In October 1993 the aircraft's final transfer took place, to 208 Squadron with whom it remained until flown to St Athan for disposal in April 1994. Since that date the Buccaneer has entered preservation, being first shown at the Jet Age museum.

XX890 also served with 15 Squadron, but its service life was short as it was badly damaged when landing at Laarbruch on 18 August 1977. Another Germany-based Buccaneer that ended its life prematurely was XX891, which served with 15 Squadron between July 1975 to 1980 when the fleet was grounded. XX891 resumed flying once the grounding order had been lifted, continuing with 15 Squadron until it joined 16 Squadron in August 1983. Eight days after changing owners XX891 stalled on approach to Laarbruch, killing one crew member in the process.

No.16 Squadron received XX892 in August 1975, retaining ownership until at least 1982. A return to Britain and 237 OCU took place in March 1984, this being followed in 1986 by a move to British Aerospace where the aircraft underwent the ASR 1012 modification programme. That completed in August 1986, the Buccaneer was issued to 208 Squadron and was in their care when orders came to prepare XX892 for

Operation *Granby*. In its new paint scheme and coded 'I', the aircraft gained the name 'Glen Lossie' and eight bomb symbols on the starboard nose. Returning to Britain, XX892 remained with 208 Squadron until withdrawn from use in 1984. The airframe was sold for scrap, although the nose was saved.

Buccaneer XX893 spent much of its life with the Germany wing until it joined 208 Squadron at Lossiemouth in November 1983. XX893 was prepared for Operation *Granby* although it was always intended that it would remain as one of the spare aircraft and it was never deployed to the Middle East. XX893 remained with 208 Squadron until withdrawn from use in early 1994, after which it was scrapped.

Issued to 16 Squadron in December 1975, XX894 had joined 15 Squadron by February 1976 and was being flown by them in Nevada on *Red Flag 80* when XV345 crashed. After the crash the entire detachment was grounded, XX894 being cleared to return home and going to Boscombe Down for use as the fleet investigation aircraft. By September 1981 the Buccaneer was issued to 12 Squadron, staying with them until July 1983 when 208 Squadron assumed ownership. By October 1989 12 Squadron had acquired XX894, and it was still the owner when the aircraft was prepared for use during Operation *Granby*. Coded 'O', the Buccaneer soon gained the name 'Aberlour' and seven mission symbols below the starboard cockpit. Upon returning to Britain the aircraft rejoined 12 Squadron, remaining with them until October 1983 when 208 Squadron took

237 OCU was operating XX893 when this portrait was taken. This aircraft was one of those modified to ASR 1012 standard. Trevor Smith Collection

charge. After withdrawal the Buccaneer was flown to St Athan for disposal, arriving in April 1994. Since that date the now-privately owned aircraft has spent time at Kemble and Farnborough before ending up at Bruntingthorpe in September 2003.

XX895 was another Buccaneer that went on Operation *Granby*, but prior to its Middle East adventure it would served with 12 Squadron at Honington from 1976 until September 1980, having undergone a

major servicing and a clearance to fly after the fleet grounding. By now in Germany with 15 Squadron the Buccaneer remained on the continent until August 1984 when 237 OCU assumed ownership. A move to Lossiemouth and 12 Squadron took place during May 1988. During Operation *Granby* XX895 was detached from 208 Squadron, with whom it remained until withdrawn from use in March 1994, after which it was flown to St Athan for disposal.

In contrast to the above machines, XX896 was only used by the RAF for a short period. The only unit to fly the aircraft was 12 Squadron based at Honington, with whom it served from January 1976 until grounded after the crash in Nevada in 1980. Instead of being returned to flying the Buccaneer was sent to St Athan for use as a donor machine, after which the remains were sent to Shawbury for long-term storage, being scrapped there in September 1991. The only operator of XX898 was 12 Squadron, who used the Buccaneer from June 1976 until it was lost in a crash on approach to Lossiemouth on 17 June 1982, both crew ejecting successfully.

A far luckier machine was XX899, which joined 12 Squadron at Honington in September 1976, remaining with them until transferring to 208 Squadron in August 1980, having been cleared to resume flying after the fleet grounding. This sojourn at Honington lasted only a month as XX899 soon returned to Germany and 15 Squadron, remaining on inventory until July 1983 when 16 Squadron assumed ownership. A return to

Remaining in service after the February 1980 crash, XX895 underwent the ASR 1012 programme and served through the Gulf War. In this view it wears the badge of 237 OCU and carries CBLS carriers on the outer pylons. Trevor Smith Collection

Britain and 237 OCU occurred in March 1984, the aircraft still being on charge when the Honington wing relocated to Lossiemouth in October. Six years later 12 Squadron had assumed ownership of XX899 when it took part in Operation *Granby*. Coded 'P' the Buccaneer soon gained the name 'Laser Lips Laura', although it did not gain any mission symbols. Upon returning to Britain 12 Squadron resumed ownership, although for its final few months of use the Buccaneer was operated by 208 Squadron. Upon withdrawal XX899 was scrapped, although the nose was rescued and is currently with the Midland Air Museum.

In early 1977 XX900 was cleared by the manufacturers for use by the RAF, the first unit being 208 Squadron. In August the aircraft was allocated to the first RAF detachment to *Red Flag*, for which purpose a wraparound desert scheme was applied to the forward part of the aircraft. Having completed its trip to Nevada XX900 returned to Britain, moving on to 208 Squadron in May 1979. A short time with 216 Squadron began in July, the *Red Flag* crash in 1980 ending this association. In August 1980 the Buccaneer joined 12 Squadron and was on their inventory when deployed to Akrotiri for use in Operation *Pulsator*. Having supported the British contingent of the UN trying to keep the peace in the Lebanon, XX900

was transferred to 208 Squadron at Lossiemouth in March 1984. XX900 was one of the aircraft selected to undergo the ASR 1012 rework by the manufacturers, rejoining 208 Squadron in October 1990. Short term usages by the OCU and 12 Squadron concluded the aircraft's career, which ended in April 1994 when XX900 landed at St Athan at the completion of its final flight. Avoiding the scrapman, the Buccaneer now resides at Bruntingthorpe.

The final machine from this batch, XX901, joined 208 Squadron in January 1977. This was another Buccaneer that took part in *Red Flag '77*, and it remained with 208 Squadron through the various trials and tribulations that afflicted the Buccaneer fleet in 1980, transferring to 237 OCU in March 1984. In September 1986 XX901 underwent the ASR 1012 update, rejoining 208 Squadron in March 1987. By May the OCU were flying the aircraft, a situation that continued until March 1990 when 208 Squadron resumed ownership. In January 1991 XX901 was prepared for Operation *Granby*, being coded 'N. Named the 'Flying Mermaid' amongst others, the Buccaneer also acquired nine mission symbols, which it still bore when it returned home in March. XX901 remained in service until 31 March 1994, after which it was flown to St Athan for disposal. Fortunately this aircraft also escaped the scrapman, being currently on display at Elvington.

XZ430–XZ432

The final three Buccaneers delivered to the RAF were serialled XZ430 to XZ432, and all started their careers with 208 Squadron. XZ430 served with that unit from May 1977 until February 1981, joining the OCU from that date. A return to 208 Squadron followed a month later, the Buccaneer remaining with them until it crashed on 20 May 1984, both the crew being killed when the aircraft impacted the sea.

The second machine XZ431 remained on the strength of 208 Squadron until August 1980 when 12 Squadron assumed ownership. By June 1983 XX431 had rejoined 208 Squadron, departing for ASR 1012 conversion work during 1987. Once this work had been completed XX431 returned to 208 Squadron in September 1987. A transfer to 12 Squadron occurred in January 1990, with whom it remained until June 1993 when 208 Squadron resumed ownership. By March 1994 the Buccaneer had been withdrawn from use, flying later to Manston for crash rescue training.

The last Buccaneer constructed, XZ432, remained with 208 Squadron from October 1977 until moving to 15 Squadron later that month. XZ432 remained with the RAFG Buccaneer wing until February 1979, when 12 Squadron at Honington assumed ownership. This

XX901 rolls down the perimeter track wearing the intake badge of 216 Squadron. This was a short-term allocation as the Nevada desert crash put paid to this unit, which reformed in November 1984 with Tristars.
Trevor Smith Collection

ABOVE: **XZ431 spent its entire service life with the UK Buccaneer force before being transferred to Manston for fire training practice.** Trevor Smith Collection

LEFT: **Coded K, XZ432 of 15 Squadron returned to Britain in February 1979, having served in Germany from 1977 to 1979. This was the last Buccaneer constructed.** Trevor Smith Collection

BELOW: **With an ECM pod under the port outer pylon, Buccaneer XZ432 was on the strength of 12 Squadron when this photo was taken. The other wing could carry a Sidewinder missile on the outer pylon.** BBA Collection

continued until March 1979 when a short sojourn with 216 Squadron was ordered. This period ended when the fleet was grounded in 1980. By August 208 Squadron were flying XZ432, a situation that continued until June 1985 when the OCU assumed control. Except for a short period with 12 Squadron the Buccaneer remained with the OCU until withdrawn in October 1992, being scrapped soon afterwards.

The Ex-FAA Buccaneers

The Royal Air Force also acquired Buccaneers from the Fleet Air Arm as the fleet carriers of the Royal Navy were retired. Eventually fifty-seven of the original seventy-five machines were available for re-use. The first transfers involved four aircraft – XV155, XV347, XV348 and XV349 – that changed inventory in 1969, all being allotted to 12 Squadron based at Honington.

Of these aircraft XV155 spent part of 1973 and the early months of 1974 with 237 OCU for initial crew training before returning to the manufacturers for upgrading to S.2B standard. The aircraft's career with the RAF resumed in May 1976 with 12 Squadron although this terminated in March 1979 when XV155 was allocated to the Strike and Fighter Test Squadron at Boscombe Down for trials purposes. This change in role ended in February 1980 after the *Red Flag* crash, the Buccaneer

---

Hunters for the Pirates

The Hawker Hunter had a long association with the Buccaneer, as no dual-control version of the Buccaneer was built. The pilot's instrument panel in the Buccaneer was dotted with many tiny gauges and a series of strip gauges: to simulate this layout, a number of Hunters were modified with the port (pupil's) side of the instrument panel fitted with Buccaneer instrumentation (the instructor's side remained unchanged). A TACAN system was included, and in this condition with the OR946 IFIS installed the type was designated Hunter T.7A.

To operate these aircraft 237 OCU was formed at Honington on 1 March 1971, replacing 736 Squadron which disbanded on 25 February 1972. Alongside the Hunters at the OCU was a selection of Buccaneers, many of which were of a lower modification standard than the front-line machines as their only purpose was to be flying airframes.

When XV345 crashed in the Nevada Desert in February 1980 and the entire Buccaneer fleet was grounded, arrangements had to made for the crews to continue regular flying. To that end the Hunter two-seaters of the OCU were joined by a further six machines drawn from storage at 5 MU, Kemble. Eventually a total of thirty-four Hunter trainers was issued to the active squadrons. (The two Germany-based squadrons quickly cleared two Buccaneers each so that a strike QRA could be maintained.) As more and more Buccaneers became available for flying duties, so the on-loan Hunters were either returned to their original operators or to store.

Once the Buccaneer force had been rationalized the number of Hunters available was reduced to ten airframes, most of which were allocated to 237 OCU while single examples were allocated to each operational unit. When the Buccaneer force began its rundown many of these venerable machines were sold to private owners.

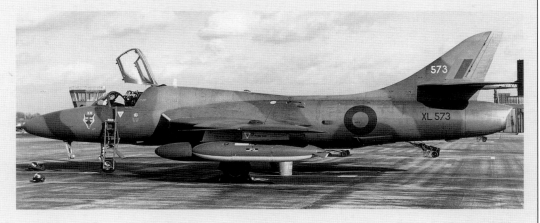

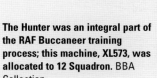
The Hunter was an integral part of the RAF Buccaneer training process; this machine, XL573, was allocated to 12 Squadron. BBA Collection

The OCU also used the Hunter for training duties, this example being the IFIS-equipped WV322. Trevor Smith Collection

Seen here parked outside the hangar at Honington, Buccaneer S.2 XV155 would soon sport the badge of 12 Squadron. Trevor Smith Collection

moving to St Athan for use in the inner wing donor role. After a full spares recovery the remains of XV155 were transferred to Brough for static testing in 1981. At the completion of these tests XV155 was scrapped.

The career of XV347 in RAF service was very short as its time with 12 Squadron ended on 9 December 1971 when the port

Parked on Honington flight line, this Buccaneer S.2 has only just been delivered to the RAF as its gloss finish and lack of squadron marks shows. BBA Collection

engine disintegrated while the Buccaneer taxied, setting the aircraft alight. XV348 had a slightly longer time with its new masters, serving with 12 Squadron from 1970 until returning to the manufacturers for upgrading to S.2B standard in 1972. At the completion of this work XV348 was issued to 15 Squadron as part of the RAFG Buccaneer Wing, arriving in July 1973.

The aircraft returned to Britain and 12 Squadron in August 1975, remaining in their care for two years until 237 OCU assumed ownership. By 31 October 1977 XV348 had been written off in a crash after striking power lines near Glom Fjord, Norway. Unfortunately one of the crew members lost his life in the crash, while the other ejected to safety.

XV349 was issued to 12 Squadron, passing on to 237 OCU in May 1973 after a major overhaul. Its time with the OCU lasted only a month for post-maintenance test flying, before the aircraft flew to RAFG and 15 Squadron. By 1974 XV349 had returned to the manufacturers for S.2B upgrading, this being completed by December 1975 when 12 Squadron assumed ownership. Until 1980 when the fleet was grounded, the aircraft alternated between 12 Squadron and the OCU. This was another machine that ended up at St Athan for spares recovery before its remains were transferred to 27 MU, Shawbury, for long-term storage in 1983 – it remained thus until scrapped in October 1991.

Only two Buccaneers were transferred from the Royal Navy in 1970, these being XV160 and XV165. XV160 spent its first three years in storage at Honington as a 'hanger queen' before being issued to 237 OCU in March 1973, remaining with

ABOVE: **Buccaneer S.2 XV348 of 12 Squadron carrying three Martel training rounds and a data link pod. This aircraft was lost in a crash in Norway on 31 October 1977.** BBA Collection

them until February 1976 when 208 Squadron assumed ownership. By August 1977 the aircraft was participating in *Red Flag '77* at Nellis AFB, Nevada. XV160 remained with 208 Squadron until November 1979 when it joined 12 Squadron. After the fleet grounding in 1980 XV160 was in storage at St Athan before being prepared for further service with 16 Squadron; it arrived at Laarbruch in August 1981. The aircraft's service life ended on 20 September 1982 while the squadron was detached at Decimomannu, Sardinia, for weapons training. During an attack manoeuvre the aircraft entered an uncommanded spin, which in turn caused a structural failure that forced the crew to eject.

One of the first early-build Buccaneers to resume flying after the fleet grounding was XV165, which had transferred to the RAF and 12 Squadron in July 1970. XV165 rejoined 12 Squadron, remaining with them until March 1988 when 237 OCU took on the aircraft for training duties. By February 1994 the aircraft had been scrapped at Shawbury, with the nose going to Farnborough for display.

Six Buccaneers were transferred from the Royal Navy in 1971: XT270, XT281,

This view of XV349 shows the Martel missile on its special pylon. After service with 12 Squadron XV349 was used by 15 Squadron in Germany for a short period before rejoining 12 Squadron. Trevor Smith Collection

XV165 spent much of its time operating with 12 Squadron, whose badge is on the intake flank. It is obviously waiting its next crew as the air starter hose is already plugged in. Trevor Smith Collection

XT287, XV166, XV168 and XV333. XT270 was issued to 12 Squadron in February 1971, remaining on their charge until May 1973 when the OCU assumed ownership. A move to the manufacturers for S.2B upgrading took place in February 1974, the Buccaneer returning to Honington in June 1976. After the 1980 crash, XT270 ended up at St Athan for spares recovery before moving to Shawbury for deep storage, which ended in October 1991 when the remains were scrapped.

XT281 and XT287 were both issued to 237 OCU in late 1971, returning to the manufacturers for upgrading to S.2B during 1972 and 1973. After the upgrade was complete XT281 was issued to 12 Squadron and was operated from Cold Lake CFB for cold weather trials. When XV345 crashed in Nevada XV281 was immediately grounded, finally returned to

Britain aboard ship. It would never fly again, being used as a weapons loading trainer until October 1992, when the aircraft was scrapped. In contrast XT287 rejoined the FAA after its conversion, remaining on their charge until the RAF assumed ownership again in August 1980. After a major servicing XT287 was issued to 15 Squadron where it was coded 'F' and named 'MacRoberts Reply'. After a short sojourn with 16 Squadron, the Buccaneer returned to the manufacturers for the incorporation of ASR 1012 during 1984. When ready for reissue XT287 joined 12 Squadron and spent the remainder of its life at Lossiemouth, spending time with all the based units until May 1992 when it was withdrawn and scrapped.

XV166 spent its RAF career with the RAFG squadrons until crashing on approach to Honington on 4 March 1976. XV168 was far luckier as it was initially

issued to 12 Squadron in October 1971 and rejoined the same unit after the fleet grounding in 1980. By October 1993 XV166 had been transferred to Brough for use as a gate guardian.

XV333 was issued to 12 Squadron and alternated between the OCU and 12 Squadron before joining 16 Squadron in Germany during February 1974. Only a month later the FAA reclaimed XV333 for use by 809 Squadron aboard *Ark Royal*, which continued until December 1978 when the naval wing disbanded. By early 1979 the Buccaneer had returned to RAF charge, although it underwent the S.2B upgrade programme before being issued to 15 Squadron in September 1979. By September XV333 was at St Athan awaiting inspection and clearance checks, which were completed by October 1981 when 12 Squadron assumed ownership. In November 1985 XV333 was undergoing ASR 1012 upgrading, returning to Lossiemouth and 208 Squadron in May 1986. By November 1993 the aircraft was being held in reserve, this ending in March 1994 when it was transferred to RNAS Yeovilton for preservation.

In 1972 one of the largest transfers of naval Buccaneers took place, most of these coming from the recently disbanded 800 Squadron. A total of eleven machines was involved: XT276, XT279, XT288, XV157, XV162, XV334, XV335, XV336, XV338, XV356 and XV360. Between 1972 and 1980 all of these aircraft except XT279 arrived at Honington for 12 Squadron, and alternated between this unit, 208 Squadron and 237 OCU before all were grounded in 1980.

Of these ten machines XV157, XV334, XV336, XV338 and XV356 were used for spares recovery and as inner wing spar donors before being scrapped. Of the others, XV162 had the shortest RAF career, lasting with 12 Squadron from May 1972 until 13 June 1972 when it crashed in the North Sea near Bridlington; unfortunately both crew lost their lives. A similar fate befell XV360 which was on the strength of 237 OCU when it crashed on 29 July 1975 into the sea off the coast of Norfolk.

The remaining three aircraft continued in RAF service, XT276 joining the RAFG wing in August 1980. This ended in January 1982 when the Buccaneer was damaged in a landing accident. Periods in storage at St Athan and Shawbury ended in June 1986 when the fire crews at

XT281 of 12 Squadron surrounded by ground equipment; it does not yet have the details painted on its Fox head badge. Note that the bomb door is fully rolled open. Trevor Smith Collection

XT287 pictured early in its RAF career, resplendent in the original gloss finish. As this aircraft was allocated to 237 OCU, it sports the early twin cutlass badge of that organization on the intake flanks. Adrian Balch

On tow, XT271 of 237 OCU sports a CBLS under the port wing. As was regular RAF practice, the airbrakes are open and the flaps are down. BBA Collection

Catterick were given the remains to play with. Another Buccaneer which resumed flying after 1980 was XT288 which was utilized by the manufacturers during 1980 for Sea Eagle integration trials after it had undergone a full spar inspection. Periods spent with A&AEE ended in August 1987 when 12 Squadron assumed ownership, which continued until May 1994 when the aircraft was withdrawn from service. XV355 also ended up at Lossiemouth in 1982, being used by all the based units until withdrawal from service in 1980, being scrapped soon afterwards.

The final aircraft in this group, XT279, joined 237 OCU in November 1972 and remained with them until the fleet grounding in 1980. After repair XT279 was issued to 15 Squadron, remaining with them until transferring to 16 Squadron in August 1983. In March 1984 XT279 was at St Athan for a major servicing and modifications work, which was completed in October 1986. From that date until May 1992 XT279 was on the strength of 208 Squadron; it was then withdrawn and scrapped.

Another large batch of ex-naval Buccaneers would join the RAF in 1973: XT271, XT277, XV152, XV154, XV156, XV340, XV341, XV342 and the ill-fated XV345. Of these nine aircraft, five were issued to 12 Squadron based at Honington, all arriving during the first six months of that year.

XT271 was utilized by all the Honington-based units before it was trans-ferred to RAFG in February 1978, although eleven months later 237 OCU was operating XT271. After being cleared after the 1980 grounding this Buccaneer resumed flying with the OCU at Lossiemouth, arriving in Scotland during May 1987. Alternating between the OCU and 12 Squadron, XT271 was finally with-drawn from use in 1993 its fate being to meet the scrapman. XT277 was not quite so lucky as it was withdrawn from service after the fleet grounding in 1980, having spent its entire working life with units at Honington.

Another aircraft that spent the time until 1980 doing the rounds of the Honington units was XV341, which was transferred to RAFG in October 1981. By November 1983 the Buccaneer was being employed by MOD(PE) for various flight trials before rejoining 12 Squadron in April 1985. Four months later XV341 was damaged beyond economic repair during a hard landing at Lossiemouth.

Between 1973 and 1980 XV342 was being utilized by the various units at Honington before the 1980 grounding. By September the Buccaneer had resumed flying duties, although by this time 16 Squadron of RAFG were flying the aircraft. Four years later XV342 was in store at St Athan, remaining there until October 1988 when 208 Squadron acquired it. When 208 Squadron disbanded XV342 was put up for disposal, later being scrapped.

The final machine delivered to 12 Squadron was the ill-fated XV345 which was operated by the Honington-based units until transferring in March 1979 to 16 Squadron at Laarbruch. Four months later the aircraft had moved to 15 Squadron and was one of those deployed to Nellis AFB, Nevada, for *Red Flag '80*. On 7 February 1980 XV345 was operating over the Nellis ranges when the starboard wing structure failed during a violent manoeu-vre, both crew being killed. Investigation of the wreckage and of surviving aircraft revealed that the forward ring spar assem-blies on many aircraft had cracks of various lengths around the bolt holes.

The initial course of action adopted by RAF Strike Command was to ground the entire Buccaneer fleet while a programme of repair was planned. Areas that required further investigation centred around the remaining fatigue life of each aircraft. Some of those aircraft that had less time left were in fact the newest machines, which had been flown more extensively than their older siblings in an attempt to equalize the fatigue lives. Another factor was the extent of the damage to each wing spar, but as some machines had both cracked spars while others had one, it was decided that those aircraft with the lowest fatigue lives would be repaired; thus the oldest and some of the youngest Buccaneers would find themselves being used as donor machines to rebuild the remainder of the fleet. During these

XV357 of 208 Squadron just prior to the application of the tone-down colour scheme. Clearly visible in this view is the bulged shape of the bomb bay fuel tank. Trevor Smith Collection

rebuilds a great deal of structural work was undertaken that in many ways re-lifed the selected aircraft. Not all the damaged aircraft required a full rebuild, as some of the wing spar cracks could be polished out using – of all things – dental burrs and mild grinding paste, this being achieved through access holes cut into the wing skins.

Of the remaining four aircraft transferred to the RAF in 1973 two, XV152 and XV156, joined 208 Squadron at Honington alternating with 237 OCU until the fleet was grounded in 1980 after the Nellis crash. Both aircraft were declared surplus and moved to St Athan by road where they underwent spares recovery; eventually both would fall to the scrapman's axe. XV154 was the only ex-naval aircraft delivered to the OCU and was in their care until grounded in 1980. XV154 was cleared to resume flying in June 1982, although this ended in June 1984. After time spent as a repair airframe, the Buccaneer was sold for scrap.

The final machine from 1973's transfers, XV340, was allocated to 16 Squadron at Laarbruch, although this ended in March 1975 when 12 Squadron added XV340 to their inventory. After a short period with 208 Squadron the Buccaneer returned to Germany and 15 Squadron. As with all of the fleet it was grounded in 198, this being the end of its service life. Periods spent engaged in battle damage repair finally ended in 1991 when the Pendine Ranges became its last home.

1974 saw the pace of transfers slowing as only seven Buccaneers joined the RAF that year. The recipient of many of these aircraft was 208 Squadron, who gained XT275, XT278, XV161 and XV357. All four arrived in the early months of the year, although XT275 would transfer to 15 Squadron in September 1978 after conversion to S.2B standard at Bitteswell. When the fleet was grounded in 1980 XT275 was withdrawn from use as its wing spar structure was found to be extensively cracked; eventually the airframe was scrapped at Shawbury in 1993.

Another aircraft that alternated between Honington and Laarbruch was XT278 which was also eventually scrapped, in this case at Catterick. XV161 survived the 1980 grounding order to end its days at Lossiemouth with 12 Squadron, having spent its entire time with the British-based squadrons. Buccaneer XV357 also spent its entire service life based in Britain although it did survive the fleet grounding, ending its days with P&EE at Foulness.

XT274 and XT286 were the only two aircraft from the 1974 batch assigned to 12 Squadron, both alternating around the Honington-based units. After the 1980 grounding XT274 ended its days with 237 OCU, finally being withdrawn in May 1985 for use as a target on the Pendine Ranges. XT286 ended its time at Honington in January 1978 to go to Bitteswell for S.2B modification work. At

the completion of the modifications 16 Squadron assumed ownership of the aircraft in January 1980. When the Buccaneer fleet was grounded XT286 was placed in storage at St Athan, finally being issued from there to 208 Squadron at Lossiemouth in October 1983. The ASR 1012 modifications were embodied on this machine throughout most of 1987, the aircraft rejoining 208 Squadron once this was complete. When 208 Squadron disbanded XT286 spent some time at Abingdon for repair training before being scrapped at Shawbury in 1993.

The last Buccaneer transferred in 1974 was XV163, which alternated between the OCU and 208 Squadron on either side of the fleet grounding in 1980; by February 1992 the aircraft was in store at Shawbury where it was scrapped in 1994.

By 1975 the rate of transfers had to slowed, just four aircraft being delivered, of which XT283, XT284 and XV354 went to 208 Squadron. All three alternated between the Honington based units, but only XT283 survived the fleet grounding, being returned to 237 OCU with whom it continued in service until moving to Boscombe Down for use as a trials aircraft. Of the other two, XT284 was used in the BDRT role before being scrapped while the other went to Manston for fire-fighting training. No.237 OCU received the last machine transferred in 1975, this being XT273. During its entire service life the Buccaneer remained with the British-

ABOVE: In this shot the airbrakes are partially open and the hook is down, as are the flaps and ailerons.
Bob Archer

RIGHT: XT283 spent much of its RAF career with the OCU although it was loaned to A&AEE on occasion as the badge of 'A' Squadron carried on the fin reveals.
Trevor Smith Collection

A pair of Buccaneers, with XV354 of 208 Squadron nearest, streak out to sea. Under wartime conditions both would be carrying Martel missiles, later to be replaced by the Sea Eagle. Trevor Smith Collection

Desperately looking around for the ground crew are the crew of XT273 of 12 Squadron, who are waiting for the ladders to exit their machine. Unusually this aircraft sports a reconnaissance package mounted on the bomb door. Trevor Smith Collection

Practice bombing is obviously the order of the day for XV352 of the OCU, as the selection of CBLS carriers under the wings reveals. Note the lack of ESM pods on the wing outer panels. Trevor Smith Collection

based units, finally retiring for scrapping in 1992.

No Buccaneers were transferred to the RAF in 1976 and only one, XV352, changed ownership in 1977. Joining 208 Squadron in mid-1977, the aircraft stayed with them even after the 1980 grounding. For three years from 1986 to 1989 the OCU operated XV352. From this date 208 Squadron used the Buccaneer, taking it to war coded 'U' in 1991. By the end of Operation *Granby* XV352 had been named 'Tamdhu' and was wearing ten mission symbols upon its return to Britain. During the aircraft's final days XV352 remained with 208 Squadron, before being withdrawn and placed in store during April 1994.

In 1978 809 Squadron and HMS *Ark Royal* had a clear-out of their Buccaneers, transferring eight aircraft (XV358 and XV863 to XV869) to the RAF. XV863 remained with 16 Squadron after the fleet grounding, before returning to

Coded KF in the 12 Squadron sequence, XV864 of 12 Squadron taxies out to undertake a training mission.
Trevor Smith Collection

Having served with 809 Squadron XV868 joined 12 Squadron when the *Ark Royal* air wing disbanded. During its time with 12 Squadron this Buccaneer spent some time on the Falklands Islands with XV353 in early 1983. Trevor Smith Collection

Buccaneer XV869 pictured at the Canberra 30th birthday party. It was allocated to 12 Squadron, with whom it spent most of its career. BBA Collection

Initially delivered to 216 Squadron, XV865 is seen here in the colours of 208 Squadron, by which time it was Sea Eagle-capable. Trevor Smith Collection

Lossiemouth in April 1984. Periods were spent with 208 Squadron, though the aircraft was with the OCU when it was called up for Operation *Granby*. Coded 'U' and wearing the name 'Sea Witch', the Buccaneer wore six strike symbols when it returned to Lossiemouth. XV863 rejoined the OCU, remaining on their charge until disbandment, when it was became the Lossiemouth gate guardian.

XV864 was one of the 16 Squadron machines that was stranded at Nellis after the crash of XV345; it was returned to Britain for investigation and repair. Once cleared to resume flying the Buccaneer rejoined 16 Squadron in July 1982, although it had returned to Britain for use by the units at Honington by November 1983, remaining with the wing after transfer to Lossiemouth. When the Buccaneer officially retired in March 1994 XV864 was moved to Manston for fire training duties.

In contrast to its siblings XV866 served 16 Squadron until 1980 when it was withdrawn and placed in storage, first at St Athan, then at Shawbury, until scrapping took place in 1991.

12 Squadron was the recipient of XV868, with whom it remained until 1985 when 208 Squadron operated the Buccaneer for the following three years. From 1988 to late 1991 the aircraft served with 12 Squadron until withdrawal, XV868 being scrapped in 1992.

Although it was allocated to the RAF in November 1978 it was not until September 1979 that XV869 was issued to 208 Squadron, remaining with them after the 1980 fleet grounding was lifted. When the Buccaneer units moved to Lossiemouth XV869 was utilized by all of them, remaining in use until withdrawn in March 1990 for storage at Shawbury, where it scrapped in 1994.

The short-lived 216 Squadron gained XV865 in January 1980, the aircraft having been in storage and undergoing modification work up to that point. Cleared after the fleet grounding, XV865 was utilized by the Lossiemouth Buccaneer units before being withdrawn from service when the Buccaneer retired. It currently resides at the Imperial War Museum at Duxford.

XV867 spent its entire career with the British-based units, finally ending its days with 208 Squadron. The aircraft was finally withdrawn from service on 10 September 1993 when the undercarriage collapsed on landing at Leeming; the aircraft was later scrapped, being beyond economic repair.

The last aircraft from this group, XV358, never served with an operational unit, being held in storage from 1978 until being declared withdrawn as a result of the 1980 fleet grounding. Eventually XV358 was transported to Brüggen for BDRT training where was eventually scrapped.

Only one transfer took place in 1979, this being XV332 which had spent a short period with RAF during 1969 to 1974 before rejoining 809 Squadron. When finally reallocated to the RAF the short-lived 216 Squadron assumed ownership, although this ended after just four months in February 1980. Cleared to resume flying, XV332 joined 12 Squadron and alternated between the British-based units both at Honington and Lossiemouth. In January 1991 the aircraft was prepared as an Operation *Granby* reserve. At the completion of hostilities XV332 resumed its flying career with the Lossiemouth units before retiring in 1994. After periods at Cottesmore and Marham the bulk of the aircraft was scrapped, the nose being saved for preservation.

Only two machines were transferred in 1980, these being XV353 and XV359, which both went to 12 Squadron at Honington. After the fleet was cleared to resume flying both aircraft were used by the Lossiemouth units. XV353 was scrapped at Lossiemouth in 1994 while XV359 ended its days as a fireman's plaything at Culdrose.

Sporting the chevron of 208 Squadron on the nose, the winged eye badge on the fin plus the MS coding, XT280 trundles past the camera complete with CBLS carriers under the wings. Trevor Smith Collection

During March 1983 XV353 and XV868 were detached to the Falkland Islands from Lossiemouth. Flying with tanker support to Ascension Island, the two bombers continued on their journey after a night stop. When they arrived at RAF Stanley the landing must have been similar to that of an aircraft carrier as it included the use of arrestor gear. The detachment, sent as a warning to Argentina and to confirm the Buccaneer's suitability for such operations, ended in July when both aircraft returned to Lossiemouth.

In 1981 XT280 was the only machine transferred to the RAF, although it had to undergo a full inspection after the 1980 crash before moving to 12 Squadron in March 1984. Ten years later the Buccaneer was scrapped at Lossiemouth.

The final Buccaneer transferred to the RAF was XV361, which was initially assigned to 15 Squadron before moving to 12 Squadron in July 1983. This was one of the Buccaneers assigned to Operation *Pulsator* duties. By September 1986 XV361 had moved to 208 Squadron, remaining with them until flying to Aldergrove in April 1994 for preservation by the Ulster Aviation Society.

Wearing the badge of 12 Squadron on its flanks, XV361 is fitted with underwing fuel tanks, and CBLS carriers on the outer pylons. Trevor Smith Collection

Buccaneer Development Aircraft

While the Buccaneer was primarily employed as a front-line Navy and RAF strike aircraft, some were diverted to cater for the needs of the development organizations. During their time in the ranks of the development organizations the Buccaneers were based at the RAE bases at Farnborough, Bedford and West Freugh, while A&AEE Boscombe Down also operated various aircraft when needed.

Throughout its time with the trials fleets the Buccaneers were allocated mainly to weapons and delivery systems development. One of these programmes involved clearing the Matra Martel missile system for naval use, for which purpose the Buccaneer S.2 prototype XK527 was used. During these flights up to four missiles were fitted to the aircraft, which was launched and recovered from HMS *Ark Royal* without incident. Ironically, given all the work involved in its development, the Martel system, jointly developed by the Dynamics Group of British Aerospace and Engins Matra of France,

was not fully deployed until 12 Squadron formed to operate the Buccaneer.

Another weapon cleared for the Buccaneer was the Matra rocket pod, these requiring the use of XV350 that was operated by 'A' Squadron at Boscombe Down. This machine was later deployed for trials of Sea Eagle and the *Pave Spike* laser targeting system. To assist in clearing the latter system, XV350 was detached to Edwards AFB, California, and Eglin AFB, Florida during July 1973 and October 1980, respectively. Also involved in the *Pave Spike* trials was Buccaneer XW529, which had been purloined from 15 Squadron in 1971. Operating alongside XV350 during the Sea Eagle trials was XT288, which was on the strength of 'A' Squadron, A&AEE, although it was bailed to British Aerospace during this period. At the completion of the Sea Eagle trials XT288 remained with British Aerospace, as it was slated to be the first aircraft to receive the ASR 1012 avionics suite update.

By the time this portrait was taken XW987 was a mish mash of components: it sports the fin and rudder assembly from a camouflaged aircraft and an intake assembly still painted magnolia. The mounting on the wing tip carries the cameras required for recording purposes. This aircraft is still flying at Thunder City in South Africa. BBA Collection

Currently flying with Thunder City at Cape Town, XW987 was one a small batch of Buccaneers constructed purely for testing purposes. Real Wings Collection

While the earlier trials fleet were acquired in a piecemeal manner, it was decided in 1973 to purchase a small batch of Buccaneers to be dedicated purely to trials work. Serialled XW986 to XW988, these three aircraft would also give benefits to other aircraft types that required a platform for systems and weapons developments. All three aircraft were manufactured between late 1973 and early 1974 and delivered to 'C' Flight at RAE Farnborough between January and June 1974. To emphasize their status as development machines and to create a distinctive, camera-friendly pattern each Buccaneer was delivered in a green, yellow and white scheme, although this was subsequently replaced by a variation on the standard RAE red and white 'raspberry ripple' finish. Each was fitted with thirty-one camera mounting positions, although it was the norm for only ten to be used at any one time, their purpose being to record weapons separation from the aircraft. When the Buccaneers were being used for weapons drops they were based at West Freugh in Scotland.

The Buccaneer trials fleet was also heavily involved in the development of radar and avionics systems. The first aircraft involved was one of the Mk 2 prototypes, XK526, which was allocated to the Royal Radar Establishment at Pershore. When the

RRE was absorbed into the RAE, XK526 was bailed to Marshalls of Cambridge before moving to RAE Thurleigh in 1977. However by 1983 XK526 was on the gate at Honington where it replaced S.1 XK531. Two of the other Buccaneers assigned to this role were XT272 and XT285, both of which was allocated to the Tornado development programme. To that end both were delivered to Marshalls where modified nose sections were installed that could house the Tornado scanner and avionics boxes. XT285 crashed near West Freugh on 5 July 1978; XT272 continued to act as a test bed with RAE Farnborough until retirement.

Other Buccaneers involved in avionics development work included XX897, XW526 and XN975, although the latter was lost in a crash in West Germany on 14 June 1978. Sub-contract research work also involved the Buccaneer, examples being XV359 and XT287 engaged in communications systems development and XV344, which was loaned to the Cranfield Institute of Technology between 1979 and 1982. When the Royal Air Force retired its Buccaneers those of the trials organizations continued for a little longer, finally touching down for the last time in 1994.

CHAPTER NINE

The Buccaneer with the SAAF

Foreign Sales Problems

In July 1958 the British Minister of Supply, Aubrey Jones, announced in the House of Commons that Blackburn Aircraft Company had been given permission to make a presentation to the United States Navy in an attempt to sell them the Buccaneer. Unfortunately for both Britain and the manufacturers, the officials chosen to make this pitch to the Americans were ill-prepared for such a task. Not only was this team under-briefed concerning the Blackburn machine, they had a very sketchy knowledge of the Grumman A2F, later the A-6 Intruder family, being developed for exactly the same role. Another factor that proved negative to this team's attempts was the lack of qualified engineers to explain the finer technical points of the aircraft. This approach seemed to be symptomatic of the day, as many excellent British aircraft projects failed to find overseas buyers as they were up against American teams that were far more capable of presentation and marketing, and far more knowledgeable about the all-important engineering details.

Into this post-war sales cauldron the British team stepped badly briefed about their own product and woefully lacking in information concerning the Grumman machine. Given these failings it should come as no surprise to find that the British efforts failed completely and that Grumman's A2F eventually entered USN and USMC service as the A-6 Intruder.

While America has always been regarded as the most difficult market to crack, others have proven more receptive to the British approach. One such potential purchaser was quickly identified as Germany, which was looking for a land-based aircraft configured for maritime strike over the Baltic Sea to replace the ageing Hawker Sea Hawks currently equipping the Kriegsmarine. The West German government had originally spotted the Buccaneer on display at Farnborough and had been immediately impressed by its capabilities, especially as it was being sold as a naval strike aircraft.

Having made their interest known, various officers from the Kriegsmarine spent time as observers aboard the carriers *Ark Royal*, *Eagle* and *Victorious*, where they were struck by the enthusiasm of the Buccaneer crews even though the S.1 was underpowered. The impressions were later gathered together with whatever hard information was made available, and presented in a report to the Admiral who headed the Kriegsmarine. His reaction was to contact the Ministry of Supply and Blackburn to garner more solid information in the form of brochures, so that a final decision could be made.

With such an order almost in the bag, the various officials involved promptly set about killing the deal through a mixture of incompetence and lethargy. To clear these classified brochures for movement to another country, a whole raft of pointless red tape was put in place. First, these brochures had to travel by diplomatic bag to the British Embassy in Bonn, having been cleared for export by the Ministry of Aviation.

After arriving at the Embassy in Germany, the paperwork languished in various in-trays while the Kriegsmarine Chief of Staff fumed in Kiel waiting for an official to deliver the paperwork. After some weeks the Embassy decided that the only course of action was to return them to Britain as no-one seemed to have any idea of who or what they were for. A few days later the brochures arrived back at the Ministry of Aviation, where they were booked into the registry without fanfare. Having not heard anything from Germany, Blackburn was undoubtedly concerned about the lack of response. Contacting Bonn and Kiel, the manufac-

G-2-1 eventually became 411 of the South African Air Force. Of note are the enlarged underwing fuel tanks tested on this version. BBA Collection

162

G-2-2, the second machine for the SAAF, rolls out to undertake a test flight. In the aircraft's early days in South Africa they sported enlarged markings, and a dark grey and PRU-blue finish. BBA Collection

turers discovered that their carefully crafted brochures had never been delivered due to official ineptitude, thus the deal died. Instead, the Kriegsmarine was equipped with the far less capable Lockheed F-104 Starfighter. The repercussions from this potential sale falling through were widespread: its failure nearly killed the entire Buccaneer programme, which was only saved by the development of the Spey engine that improved the aircraft's performance significantly.

The South African Contract

Fortunately Hawker Siddeley, having absorbed Blackburn, decided that a very good aircraft like the Buccaneer S.2 was deserved of another chance on the world stage. The chance occurred in January 1963 when Hawker Siddeley signed a contract with the Republic of South Africa for sixteen aircraft. Although trumpeted as a great deal for Britain, it was part of a political deal that had resulted in the Simonstown Agreement, which granted South Africa access to modern weapons in exchange for use of the Simonstown base near Cape Town. With the supply of the Buccaneer and access to the port of Simonstown, both Britain and South Africa were able to undertake patrols and defence of the sea lanes round the tip of Africa; these sea routes had gained increased significance to both America and Europe with the closure of the Suez Canal in 1956.

Although outside the agreement, the SAAF had already replaced its elderly Short Sunderland with the far more capable Avro Shackleton MR.3 for long-range patrol, while Douglas C-47s replaced the earlier Lockheed Venturas for inshore coverage. The weaponry supplied under Simonstown also included three Whitby class frigates, ten Westland Wasp anti-submarine helicopters, plus the Buccaneers. Even if the Simonstown Agreement had not figured in this sale, the South African Air Force were already convinced that the Buccaneer was the ideal machine for their Strike Command, as it had the long range they required, was could carry a heavy load and was capable of using weaponry that could be used over both land and sea.

The Buccaneer S.50

Designated the Buccaneer S.50, the South African version was very similar to its Royal Navy counterpart, the Buccaneer S.2. One of the most obvious differences was the provision for a pair of Bristol Siddeley BS605 single-chamber rocket motors to boost the aircraft's take-off capability under 'hot and high' conditions. This motor utilized the smaller chamber of the proven Stentor rocket motor as its core, the fuel being a mix of High Test Peroxide and kerosene. They could generate 8,000lb (35.6kN) of thrust for a short period to literally blast the Buccaneer into the sky, and could be retracted into the rear fuselage when not in use. The S.50 retained the arrestor hook for use with airfield arrestor systems; the hydraulic wing fold mechanism was deleted, although the wings could still be folded manually.

The inclusion of the rocket pack eventually ended up being a waste of time as it was only used a handful of times throughout the aircraft's long career in South Africa. Militating against its use were the intensive logistics required to support the system and the long turn-round times required to replenish the system. Eventually the rocket packages were removed, the space later being utilized for the chaff and flare defensive system.

The first Buccaneer S.50 undertook its maiden flight on 9 January 1965, both the aircraft and its rocket installation performing satisfactorily. Having completed the flight tests without incident, the first aircraft was then employed on Nord AS.30 missile trials.

The unit selected to operate the Buccaneer S.50 was 24 Squadron based at Waterkloof air base, south of Pretoria; it was the altitude of Waterkloof at 4,941ft (1,506m) that had brought up the requirement for the rocket booster package, even though it had a longer than average – 6,000ft (1,800m) – runway. No.24 Squadron initially reformed in May 1965 at Lossiemouth, where the crews trained on Buccaneer S.1s operated by 736 Squadron. Once the first S.50s became available they were delivered to Lossiemouth where they replaced the FAA aircraft in the crews' syllabus.

Into Service

While the military side was progressing without too much incident, the political side of the deal was anything but calm. While the situation had been stable when the contract was signed, the election of a Labour government in 1964 with Premier Harold Wilson in charge had altered Britain's outlook towards South Africa: the UK now intended enforce the United Nations arms embargo against South Africa. This placed the Buccaneer order in jeopardy as none had been delivered and the United Nations and the new Labour Government had strong objections to delivering aircraft to a regime that might use them to enforce the policy of apartheid. As the aircraft had already been manufactured, approaches were made to the Indian government to sell the SAAF Buccaneers to them. In the end, however, the South African government successfully put pressure on Britain to deliver the sixteen aircraft, although the British cancelled an option on twenty more.

Having secured the sixteen Buccaneers, South Africa wasted no time in getting them out of Britain. On 27 October 1965 two flights of four aircraft set off for South Africa. After a staging stop for refuelling on the Canary Islands, the first aircraft touched down at its new base in the after-noon of 3 November. Unfortunately one of the Buccaneers, serial number 417, crashed into the sea after suffering a double engine flame-out and a stall en route, requiring all of the resources of the SAAF and the South African Navy to rescue the crew, both of whom had ejected safely. Under other circumstances the aircraft lost in the transit crash would have been replaced, but due to the embargo this did not occur.

Not wishing to lose another aircraft, the SAAF decided that the remainder of the Buccaneers were to be transported by sea. The first four were cocooned and moved to Hull docks, where they were loaded aboard the SA *Van Der Stel*. This batch arrived in Cape Town on 5 August 1966, while the other four arrived on 17 October aboard the SA *Langkloof*. After the aircraft had arrived in South Africa they were moved to Waterkloof, where 24 Squadron resumed their training regime. During their early years the Buccaneers of 24 Squadron were involved in joint exercises with the Fleet Air Arm, as well as taking part in missions to sink two tankers in South African waters.

Sinking the *Wafra*

The first mission involved the tanker *Wafra*, which was en route to Cape Town laden with 60,000 tons of crude oil. On 27 February 1971 the vessel sent a Mayday message reporting that the engine room was flooded and the ship was not under full control. The Soviet tanker *Gdynia* took the stricken ship under tow in an attempt

LEFT: **When the Buccaneers arrived at Waterkloof AB the national markings were reduced slightly, in size while the badge of 24 Squadron was applied to the flanks of the engine nacelles.** BBA Collection

BELOW: **As the Buccaneers became more involved in the border wars over Angola, the earlier colour scheme was replaced by a coat of overall grey while the national markings were removed.** BBA Collection

Aircraft 414 was one of the SAAF Buccaneers that would survive; it is currently preserved at Swartkop.
Trevor Smith Collection

to save it and drop anchor in Mossel Bay. Unfortunately the tow line snapped, although the freighter *Pongola* managed to place a line aboard and later resume the tow. While the small freighter attempted to keep the tanker clear of the South African coast, the increasingly heavy seas were pushing the tanker inexorably coastwards. In a last, desperate attempt to stop the ship grounding the anchors were dropped, but even this last desperate effort was in vain as the anchors dragged and the ship was driven towards the shore. Eventually the inevitable happened and the *Wafra* struck the shore stern first, the resultant impact straining the hull plating. The crew quickly abandoned ship while the ruptured oil bunker tanks began to dump their load into the sea.

The initial reaction by the South African authorities was to attempt to tow the *Wafra* clear of the shore using the ocean-going tug *Oceanic*, so that the remaining oil could be transferred to a waiting vessel. Eventually, after numerous attempts the tug finally pulled the ship off the shore on 8 March. However by this time the vessel's owners, Getty Oil, had decided to write it off as it was considered that the transfer of the cargo was far too dangerous; therefore the decision was taken to tow the tanker out to deep waters and sink her. By this time the *Wafra* was 90

miles from the coast, but she was down by the stern and becoming difficult to steer; also, the weather was deteriorating and this, coupled with an increasing sea state, raised fears of the ship breaking up and spilling its complete cargo. To counteract this possibility it was decided to sink the vessel as quickly as possible, and the assistance of the SAAF was requested.

Two Buccaneers were sent to carry out the attack; on 10 March the aircraft departed Waterkloof for Langebaanweg AB near Cape Town, support equipment and ground crews going aboard a Transall C-160 transport aircraft. The detachment established itself quickly, so by that evening the two aircraft were on their way to the *Wafra* which was adrift some 150 miles offshore. Circling the tanker at a safe height was a SAAF Vickers Viscount with the South African Minister of Defence, P.W. Botha, and other officials aboard. Supporting the Viscount and Buccaneers were a pair of Shackletons, which also acted as mounts for a gaggle of journalists. The mission briefing for the Buccaneers was to sink the ship without causing the contents to explode and so increasing the risk of pollution. Therefore the intended strike point was the 98ft ballast tank amidships, which was filled with compressed air and a hit on which should allow the vessel to sink slowly. A secondary targeting point

was the extreme bow section, which would also assist the vessel to sink.

The weapon chosen was the Nord AS.30, the use of which was considered to be good training. The attack profile required the Buccaneers to approach at an altitude of 3,000ft and 450kt. The launch point was to be 4 miles from the target, which was now being driven by a wind that was gusting up to 50mph while the ship itself only stood 15ft above the water at its highest point. The first missile, launched by Major S. Van Garderen, was aimed slightly high: it skimmed over the ballast tank to explode in the sea some 60ft from the ship. The second launch had to be steered clear as one of the observation aircraft had intruded upon the target zone. A third missile hit the ship, blowing a 15ft hole in its side, but this was insufficient to sink the vessel. The fourth missile, aimed at the bow, missed its target. Having launched all the available missiles, the disconsolate crews flew their Buccaneers home. A further missile strike was undertaken by the Buccaneers, although yet again further AS.30 hits failed to sink the tanker.

On 11 March Shackletons from 35 Squadron SAAF dropped depth charges alongside the ship, which caused further damage, but left it afloat. A final attack in the early hours of the following day saw six depth charges dropped on one side of the

Buccaneer 416 is currently preserved at Ysterplaat and wears the intermediate finish; this was the original, minus national markings, although the 24 Squadron badge still remains. Trevor Smith Collection

ship while a further three were released on a second pass. The concussive and explosive effects successfully set fire to the *Wafra* which sank some forty minutes later. During this attack twelve AS.30 missiles and nine depth charges had been expended in sinking this vessel.

Sinking the *Silver Castle*

The South African Air Force and its Buccaneers were in action again in 1972. On 20 April the Liberian-registered tanker *Silver Castle*, laden with 18,000 tons of crude oil, collided with the South African cargo vessel SA *Pioneer* in thick fog close by the mouth of Bushmans River. Such was the force of the collision that the tanker's stern section was severely damaged, bursting into flames soon afterwards. The fire was left to burn itself out after which the recoverable oil from sixteen of the twenty-two tanks was pumped into another vessel. As the *Silver Castle* was beyond economic repair it was decided to scuttle the ship. All the usual methods were tried, but tankers are tough ships and hard to sink, so the help of the SAAF was again requested. By this time

the stricken ship was adrift 170 miles south-east of Cape St Blaize.

Six aircraft were chosen for the attack under the command of Commandant P. Gouws, all of which departed Waterkloof on 15 May for the Flying Training School airfield at Langebaanweg. Five of the six aircraft were launched early the following morning, each armed with 1,000lb bombs; once the five attack aircraft had departed safely, the sixth took off to act as a tanker for the them on the homeward leg. The attack on the *Silver Castle* lasted only ten minutes, during which twenty-seven bombs were dropped of which nineteen were seen to strike the ship. A follow-up flight by an Avro Shackleton of 35 Squadron revealed that only a small oil slick remained on the surface.

Peacetime Service

In between all this excitement the SAAF Buccaneers managed to set a few records. The first of these flights was undertaken on 13 December 1966 when one of 24 Squadron aircraft, crewed by Commandant A. M. Muller and Major T. J. de Munnink covered a distance of 6,000

miles (9,650km) in nine hours and five minutes, utilizing its flight refuelling capability in the process. In 1970 the Buccaneers were involved in another unusual exercise, this being the Argus 'Tip to Top' race held on 28 May. Starting at the Brixton Tower in Johannesburg and ending at Table Top mountain in Cape Town, the Buccaneer crew had to transit from Johannesburg to Jan Smuts airfield, start the aircraft and take off, then land at D. F. Malan airport, travelling from there to the top of the mountain. Also taking part in this race were a Canberra crew and a Mirage III pilot. The Buccaneer crew completed the race in two hours and nineteen minutes, the Mirage pilot completed the course as the winner in two hours sixteen minutes while the Canberra crew came in third a few minutes after the others.

The Buccaneer crews of 24 Squadron worked hard to increase their aircraft's capabilities, one of the first being in-flight refuelling. Although the 430gal slipper tanks mounted under the inner wings helped extend the aircraft's range, this was quickly increased by the use of buddy refuelling pods, and later by bomb bay tanks as installed on the RAF Buccaneer S.2. The modified bomb bay tanks were supplied by British Aerospace: even though there was supposedly an arms embargo in force, the British company had continued to supply spares and components to the SAAF Buccaneer force. This the author can verify, as he once saw a set of Buccaneer air brakes covered in SAAF serials and part numbers, and resplendent in the SAAF's unique grey and PRU blue scheme, delivered to St Athan for installation into an RAF aircraft. With its increased fuel capacity the Buccaneers could also act as tankers for the SAAF's Mirage IIIs and Mirage F.1s, as well as each other. For many years this was the SAAF's only in-flight refuelling capability, though dedicated tankers were eventually acquired.

In a similar manner to both the Fleet Air Arm and the Royal Air Force SAAF flew its Buccaneers low and hard. However, this had adverse side effects such as an attrition rate that saw the fleet decrease to nine by April 1978, at least two having been lost in a mid-air collision.

Operation *Reindeer*

Although South Africa was becoming more isolated from the world community

due to its apartheid policy, and was beset by internal troubles due to the African National Congress, it was to its borders that it soon turned its attention. The end of Portuguese rule in Angola during November 1975, after a long and bitter conflict, meant that Angola could now act as a base for the South West Africa People's Organization (SWAPO) guerrillas fighting for the independence from South Africa of what is now Namibia. Laying down a warning against making incursions across the border, South Africa launched Operation *Savanah*, which saw

ground forces backed by a full range of air cover travel deep into Angola, only stopping within artillery range of the capital, Luanda. Having made what they thought was their point the South African forces withdrew over their own border.

The Angolans continued to make numerous incursions across the border, so the South African authorities decided that a positive statement had to be made. The chosen place was Cassinga, a small Angolan mining town that was home to a large SWAPO brigade. The cue for the South African attack was an incursion by

The South African Nuclear Bomb

Although they were never used in anger, information released after the change of government from the white-only administration to one formed by members of the ANC revealed that South Africa was well on the way to completing the manufacture of half a dozen air-droppable nuclear weapons. It was reported that Israel was heavily involved with developing these bombs, basing the carriage and delivery systems on those developed for the Israeli Air Force. Production of weapons-grade plutonium was undertaken in South Africa while the whole programme was under the control of the South African arms manufacturer ARMSCOR.

While it was never confirmed, strong rumours circulated that South Africa dropped a low-yield device into the Indian Ocean using a Buccaneer as a carrier aircraft. The only evidence forthcoming about this event was supplied by the Americans, one of whose spy satellites picked up a signal that matched that generated by a low-yield weapon. While India and Pakistan were also heavily engaged in developing nuclear warheads, the intelligence services were well aware that neither programme was advanced enough for such a device to be exploded.

When the ANC came to power they followed one of their political tenets which stated that under no circumstances would they condone the development and deployment of such weapons. To verify this, nuclear inspectors were allowed into the country and they confirmed that the entire programme had been disbanded

Just cleaning up after landing – the airbrakes are closing and the flaps are retracting – Buccaneer 418 returns to the Waterkloof pan after a training flight. BBA Collection

Buccaneer 421 waiting its turn for refurbishment at SAAF Museum at Swartkop. These aircraft gave a good account of themselves throughout their service in the sun. Trevor Smith Collection

SAAF Buccaneer 421 looking the worse for wear; of note are the chaff and flare dispensers under the rear fuselage. It is currently preserved at Swartkop. Trevor Smith Collection

an eighty-strong force of SWAPO fighters, who crossed the border on 27 October 1977 to attack the South African security forces. The resultant battle saw most of the guerrillas killed during the firefight, while the remainder were tracked back to their base. In response, the South Africans planned Operation *Reindeer*, set for 4 May 1978.

The attack plan was one that would become familiar over the following years. First, a wave of Canberras carried out lay-down attacks at low level using anti-personnel weapons. These were followed by the Buccaneers, each of which dropped a full load of eight 1,000lb bombs armed alternately with delay and impact fuses. Having delivered their weapons, the Buccaneers returned to base while a large force of paratroopers was dropped onto Cassinga.

After returning to base one of the Buccaneer crews was briefed to attack insurgent bases at Chetequara, but en route to the target the crew was rebriefed by the Tactical Headquarters at Ondangwa about an armoured column of SWAPO forces heading for the town. Initial attacks were carried out by a pair of Mirages on combat air patrol, though their 30mm cannon shells only caused slight panic in the column. As the South African paratroopers were still awaiting helicopter pick-up it was imperative that further air support be supplied.

When the Buccaneer arrived it was cleared from its original flight plan by TAC HQ, being allocated to defence of Cassinga in company with the Mirages, who switched their attention to the personnel carriers while the Buccaneer took on the tanks. Unlike the earlier mission the Buccaneer was armed with rockets, some of which were launched towards the lead tank which exploded in a spectacular fashion, the destruction being accelerated by the inclusion of armour piercing rockets at every third round. The Mirages were having similar success against the personnel carriers while the Buccaneer used its rockets to destroy a second tank. After this pass the Mirages pulled out as their fuel was running low, leaving the Buccaneer patrol with the remainder of the force to deal with. This consisted of the two remaining tanks and a handful of armoured attack vehicles, one of which was firing at the Buccaneer. Further rockets were launched at the armoured attack vehicles, destroying two,

although the two remaining tanks managed to escape into the bush.

While the tanks were escaping, an anti-aircraft gun site took fired on the Buccaneer, which responded by blowing it up. At the end of the engagement two tanks, sixteen personnel carriers and most of the armoured vehicles had been destroyed, and the remaining troops dispersed. While this ground–air battle was going on, the SAAF helicopters had landed to pick up the troops; the two surviving tanks that had entered the bush reappeared and attempted to shell the helicopters and the troops. The Buccaneer swung round to attack the tanks, selecting half of its remaining rockets for the first vehicle. Unfortunately the firing system failed and the rockets stayed in their pods. The only option was to buzz the two tanks at speeds up to Mach 1, at the lowest possible altitude. After repeated high speed over-flights, the tanks turned away from the battle and retreated.

When the aircraft and its exhausted crew finally landed at Grootfontein, the after-flight inspection revealed a total of seventeen hits, the biggest of which was a 67mm shell that had gone through one of the wings. In addition, the port inner flap had been penetrated by a 37mm shell, 14.5 mm shells had hit the engines and windshield, and other small arm strikes had hit other parts of the airframe. For their heroic efforts the crew were awarded the Honoris Crux (Silver) and Commendation Medal by the Chief of the Defence Staff.

Further strikes against Cassinga were mounted from Waterkloof, for which they were armed with 1,000lb bombs. The first leg required ninety minutes of flying time and 150 miles, while the return leg ended at Grootfontein where the aircraft landed for refuelling before returning home. During these raids aircraft 412 and 416 were struck by 45mm ground fire, although both got home safely.

The Border Wars Continue

Soon after the Cassinga mission the SAAF Buccaneers turned their attention to targets in Zambia, where dive attacks using 1,000lb bombs were undertaken, each mission taking three and a quarter hours to complete.

Having undertaken a full range of daylight operations, the Buccaneers next turned their attentions to attacking targets

under the cover of darkness. The first such mission was undertaken at the beginning of March 1979, against SWAPO camps in Angola. Four Buccaneers were allocated to each attack, the aircraft flying in a trail formation separated in altitude by 500ft gaps. The first mission involved aircraft 413, 414, 416 and 422, each armed with eight 1,000lb bombs. Although the target was obscured by clouds, the location had already been plotted by ground radar which allowed the aircraft to bomb 'blind', and despite the cloud twenty-two of the thirty-two bombs landed within the target area.

A second four-aircraft night mission was launched on 14 March, though in the event only three took off as the fourth went unserviceable during crew-in. As this was a well-defended target, the attack was preceded out by Canberras of 12 Squadron dropping anti-personnel bombs in an attempt to suppress anti-aircraft fire. The strike force itself was faced by bad weather, which forced the three aircraft to fly at no more than 100ft to keep contact with a ground. A second full-strength mission was launched later that day, but during the Canberra softening-up attack one of the aircraft was shot down. Such losses had to be taken seriously, so to prevent it happening again the Canberra component was deleted from these attacks, while the Buccaneers would deliver their bombs by the act of toss bombing instead of level bombing.

Having decided to make this change to the method of delivery, the Buccaneer crews spent the next few weeks perfecting the art of toss bomb delivery. The SAAF decided to practise delivering their bombs in parallel tracks inside a box that was theoretically 800yd long by 500yd wide, this frequently giving an accuracy of 100yd. This training period ended on 5 July 1979 when a strike package was dispatched to a target in Angola, although only two of the four Buccaneers took off as the others became unserviceable. Supporting the Buccaneers was a flight of Mirage F.1 fighter-bombers, although these were lightly loaded in comparison with the Buccaneers.

As 1979 progressed the SWAPO and Angolan UNITA guerrillas began to receive better anti-aircraft missiles from their Cuban backers. It was during this period that the CIA began to increase its support to the SAAF, their reasoning being that although apartheid was reprehensible it was acceptable in the face of stopping the spread of Communism throughout Africa. The aid supplied by the Americans was welcome, as the radar-guided weapons now available to the guerrillas were proving troublesome. While the improved defensive measures were quickly incorporated into the Buccaneer fleet, that too was facing problems as only six aircraft were now available: 423 and 42 had been lost in separate crashes in July 1978, and 424 had crashed on a night training flight on 7 May 1979 near Roedtron. The six survivors were 412, 413, 414, 416, 421 and 422. Of these, four were flyable, one was undergoing deep maintenance while the other was held as a flyable reserve. As each Buccaneer in the shrinking SAAF fleet exhibited minor differences in handling each machine had its own specific crew assigned who would become used to the idiosyncrasies of each machine.

While the situation for 24 Squadron's inventory was perilous, they continued to develop tactics that would get the most from the Buccaneers. To keep the pilots current and to conserve the fatigue life of the remaining aircraft, a handful of Atlas Impala light trainer/attack jets was delivered to Waterkloof AB. The new tactics for night attacks revolved around the use of 6,000,000cd (candle power) flares. Using this source of illumination required one aircraft to run in at high speed and low level to release the flare, pulling up into a half loop to escape. After release the flare's parachute deployed and it illuminated the target. The three other Buccaneers would follow the first, coming in at low level and pulling up just before the target to release their bombs. By this time the fourth would have completed its escape and tucked in behind the other three, also releasing its bombs. This technique was first used on 24 May 1980, and was successful.

The next bomb run into Angola was directed at a major SWAPO base and required the services of sixteen Mirages plus the four flyable Buccaneers. As they approached the target the Mirages were met by a hail of SAM-2 and SAM-3 missiles that damaged two of them, although both did make it back to base. It was decided to abort the attack in order to preserve the dwindling Buccaneer fleet. As the war increased in sophistication the SAAF crews were forced to adopt a more stand-off approach to bombing. This approach was adopted against those targets that could not be identified precisely and so required the strike force to drop their bombs from higher altitudes onto the target zone. Such an attack was led by a Canberra with Mirages and Buccaneers making up a sixteen-aircraft package. The Buccaneers carried their usual load of 1,000lb bombs while the Mirages carried 500lb bombs. The Canberra carried a mix of 2,000lb and 500lb bombs. Pre- and post-strike reconnaissance was carried out by the Canberras, though their lack of sophisticated ECM meant that they had a Buccaneer escort to provide the electronic back-up.

It was during this period of the war that the Nord AS.30 missile finally came into its own. Having failed dismally in the sinking of a heavily laden oil tanker, the missile was found to be ideal for striking pinpoint targets. To use this weapon the aircraft entered a 30-degree dive, launching the missile from a range of 8 miles. At a distance of 3 miles the Buccaneer would pull up from its approach, continuing to guide the missile via a radio link. The

The intermediate scheme applied to the SAAF Buccaneers used the same colours as the first finish, though in this version they were matted, while the national markings were reduced in size. In this picture 416 also lacks fin flashes. Trevor Smith Collection

weapon was travelling at Mach 2 when it hit its target, arriving with the force of a 1,000lb bomb. During one of these attacks the four Buccaneers would attack in trail, each launching their four missiles. Eventually a total of thirty-two weapons was fired during these missions, of which two missed the target. To get the maximum usage out of these attacks the Buccaneers would also fly with a bomb load in the bomb bay.

Throughout the 1980s the Buccaneers of 24 Squadron continued to carry out attacks against targets in Angola using both iron bombs and Nord missiles. Another role was added to the inventory of the Buccaneers when the defunct reconnaissance capability was restored. The aircraft had originally been delivered with a small quantity of reconnaissance crates, but these had been destroyed when their carrier aircraft were lost in crashes. The SAAF developed their own bomb bay recce crate, which was built around a long-range oblique camera. Use of this system required the aircraft to approach the target at low altitude at a speed of 500kt. As the camera had an effective range of 6 miles, this was the point where the Buccaneer would enter a climb up to 20,000ft, all the while recording the scenes below. At the highest point of the climb the crew would half loop their aircraft, roll the right way up and descend rapidly down to low level for a high-speed transit back to base. Managing this system required the installation of a sighting system based on that fitted to the SAAF Mirages, which was modified to fit into the Buccaneer.

As the Buccaneer was by now operating

The SAAF Buccaneers		
Serial	Status	Fate
411	Crashed	Stalled during flight refuelling 04/01/73
412	Waterkloof AFB	Gate guard
413	Crashed	Hydraulic systems failure causing loss of control, 30/08/83
414	SAAF Museum	Preserved at Swartkop
415	Crashed	Crew disorientated during night navigation over the sea, 16/10/69
416	SAAF Museum	Preserved at Ysterplaat
417	Crashed	Crashed on delivery flight after double flame-out, 31/10/65
418	Crashed	Damaged during dropping of retarded bomb, 14/10/70
419	Crashed	Collided with 419, 24/11/72
420	Crashed	Collided with 420, 24/11/72
421	SAAF Museum	Preserved at Swartkop
422	Johannesburg	Preserved at the National Museum of Military History
423	Crashed	Double flame-out during night flight, 03/07/78
424	Crashed	Night exercise – crew disorientated, 07/05/79
425	Crashed	Stalled on approach to Waterkloof, 18/07/78
426	Crashed	Collided with another aircraft, 29/12/75

in high-threat areas, extra protective methods were required. These took the form of threat warning radar detectors under the nose, while at the rear of the fuselage chaff and flare dispensers, similar to those fitted to RAF machines, were installed.

Withdrawal From Service

Fortunately for the Buccaneer fleet talks were being held to end the conflict between South Africa and Angola, especially since the latter was ringing all of its primary targets with increasingly sophisticated air-defence systems, these being of Soviet origin but delivered via the Cuban advisors. The final Buccaneer mission undertaken by 24 Squadron over Angola took place on 6 February 1988; peace talks began in May and were successfully completed on 22 December. Similar events were happening in Zambia, Zimbabwe, Botswana and Mozambique, as all these countries had been badly disrupted during their entanglements with South Africa. On 10 April 1991 the Buccaneers of the SAAF ended their flying career when aircraft 416 was delivered to the SAAF museum at Ysterplaat, 24 Squadron having formally disbanded in March. Although the Buccaneer had given sterling service to the SAAF the fact that only four were now flyable and spares were becoming increasingly difficult to source meant that the type had to be retired.

CHAPTER TEN

The Gulf War and Withdrawal

Saddam Hussein came to power in Iraq in 1979, ruthlessly suppressed all opposition and took Iraq into a costly, but inconclusive, war against Iran between 1980 and 1988. In 1990 he resurrected Iraq's claim to ownership of neighbouring Kuwait, which had once been a province of Iraq. Bringing the whole situation to a head was a claim that since 1980 Kuwait had been stealing oil from Iraq, as both countries shared the Rumaylah oil field. Also bringing down Iraq's ire was the fact that Kuwait, in conjunction with other Arab oil-producing states, was over-producing oil and this high production was holding down the overall cost per barrel. In its war with Iran, Iraq had run up external debts of $40 billion, which accrued interest of $3 billion per year. While Iraq should have been able to pay its debts under normal circumstances, its spending on civil imports and military equipment exceeded its annual income. To alleviate this debt Saudi Arabia agreed to write off its share of the war loans, but Kuwait decided otherwise.

Added to the foregoing was Iraq's desire to secure safer access to the port of Umm Qasr, which would have required an invasion of the Kuwaiti islands of Warbah and Bubiyan. The final consideration must be the ego of Saddam Hussein: he had frequently portrayed himself as the leader of the Arab world, but his reputation had been dented by the inconclusive outcome of the war with Iran, so a short, sharp invasion of such a country as Kuwait could be seen as a re-statement of Iraqi dominance.

The Invasion and Diplomatic Response

In the early hours of the morning on 2 August 1990, Iraqi forces crossed the Kuwait border, even though they had been warned to remain where they were once the build-up had been observed. As the timing of the invasion had caught everyone, not least the Kuwaiti armed forces, off guard it was completed in a short space of time with little resistance being encountered in the process. When the news broke worldwide of the invasion most people were just getting to grips with the day (although the author was actually at 30,000ft between Ascension Island and the airport at Mount Pleasant, Falkland Islands!).

While the world's media concentrated upon the diplomatic efforts being made to oust the Iraqi invaders, others of a more sober disposition were preparing to use military force to return the status quo. During this period the Iraqi government was giving off mixed signals, one on hand Saddam Hussein was ranting about the 'mother of all battles' should anyone try to invade while his deputy, Tariq Aziz, was putting forward a more sober view. However, both politicians had a consensus: that Iraq would not pull out of Kuwait. With hindsight this was possibly the biggest mistake by Iraq, as control of the oil fields in the region by an unfriendly power would put oil supplies to the West at risk. Allied to the threat to the oil supplies already under Iraqi control was

Tango and Echo, XX889 and XW530, respectively, streak across the desert on a training mission. Bob Archer Collection

Buccaneer XW533 is seen from the starboard side, which reveals the range of nose art applied to this machine. Bob Archer Collection

the strong possibility that further invasions, principally against Saudi Arabia, could be undertaken should the Kuwait occupation be allowed to continue without any response.

The initial response driven by the United States and a – at the time – reluctant Britain, was to put a series of resolutions through the United Nations Security Council that called for Iraq to remove its troops, for the restoration of the Kuwaiti Royal Family to power and, more crucially, for the use of armed force to remove the invaders if required. The first of these was Resolution 660 which condemned the invasion, this being backed by the Arab League. Resolution 661 was issued on 6 August and put in place economic sanctions. On 25 August Resolution 665 put in place a maritime embargo, while an air blockade was confirmed on 25 September by Resolution 670. Resolution 678, issued on 25 November, allowed for the use of force should Iraq not remove its forces from Kuwaiti territory by 15 January: after that date member states were authorized to use all necessary means to achieve this.

The UN resolution passed with the only real dissent coming from Russia, who regarded Iraq as a good customer for weapons, amongst other goods. In response Tariq Aziz was sent to New York where he addressed the United Nations. His statement on behalf of the Iraqi government basically was that the regime would under no circumstances withdraw from Kuwait unless massive concessions were made by the West.

The Iraqi stance was obviously unacceptable, so Operation *Desert Shield* was put into action. This phase covered the massive deployment of allied troops to other countries in the Middle East, the principal destination being Saudi Arabia, which was seen as the next likely target for Iraq. The build-up saw massive amounts of military hardware, aircraft assets and naval support dispatched to the region. As well as the obvious hardware, incredible amounts of support material was also delivered to bases in the region, supplies of ammunition, fuel, food and sundry other items being housed in large makeshift depots.

The Military Response

While the diplomatic dance continued, either as a smokescreen for the build-up or as a last-ditch attempt to avoid conflict, plans were laid for the invasion and relief of Kuwait, this being run in parallel with another invasion plan that involved attacking Iraq in force. Throughout this period the Iraqi government continued to pour out more strident propaganda, much of which was greeted by laughter by the recipients. There was a more serious side to this period, as Iraq began to fire surface-to-surface missiles into Israel, causing casualties amongst the population.

The Royal Air Force deployment to the Gulf states began soon after the invasion, the principal strike aircraft involved being the Sepecat Jaguar and the Panavia Tornado. Providing support to these were the various squadrons that covered tanking and logistics, while a detachment of McDonnell Douglas F-4 Phantoms from RAFG were deployed to Akrotiri, Cyprus, as a precautionary measure, should any Iraqi Air Force aircraft evade the air umbrella slowly spreading over their country's skies. When the air war finally kicked off in the early hours of 16 January 1991, the strikes on Baghdad were only a precursor of the steel whirlwind that followed. During the following days the aircraft of the RAF undertook their fair share of attacks upon the Iraqi ground forces. The Tornados initially attacked primarily with the JP233

ABOVE: **XW533 'A' waiting for its crew on the Muharraq flight line. Visible in this view are the AIM-9 Sidewinder and** *Pave Spike* **pod under the port wing; the starboard would be carrying an LGB and an ECM pod.** Bob Archer Collection

LEFT: **One of the second batch of Buccaneers sent to the Gulf to reinforce the initial six aircraft. This is XV863, coded 'O', which wears seven mission marks on the nose plus the name 'Aberlour'. Currently this machine is preserved at Bruntingthorpe.** Trevor Smith Collection

BELOW: **Buccaneer XV352 – another arrival from the second batch of aircraft – at Muharraq. The nose sports the name 'Tamdhu' and ten mission marks.** Bob Archer Collection

anti-runway munitions dispenser package, but soon a change of emphasis saw them switching their attacks to the infrastructure of the country and its airfields.

A change of emphasis saw the Tornadoes' targets switching to the infrastructure of the country and its airfields. The preferred weapons for striking such targets was the laser-guided bomb, but this brought with it problem that TIALD laser targeting pod intended for the Tornado was still undergoing development and would not be ready for some weeks. The answer lay in the Buccaneer, which by now was quietly heading for retirement but which was wired to carry the Westinghouse AN/AVQ-23E *Pave Spike* laser guidance pod, which had come into service in January 1978 with the short-lived 216 Squadron.

Buccaneers are Deployed

While most other RAF squadrons were preparing to head out to the Gulf, 12 Squadron was in Gibraltar helping the Royal Navy to work up their ships prior to deploying into theatre, while 208 Squadron was at St Mawgan participating in NATO maritime exercises. Getting enough airframes together plus crews, engineers and their support equipment was a mammoth task, which required great diligence by all those selected to deploy to the Gulf and those involved in supporting them. The scheduled deployment date for

Seen from above, this Buccaneer sports a well-worn coat of magnolia. One bonus of this particular finish is that the airflow generated by the vortex generators is clearly seen moving aft over the wing. BBA Collection

the first six Buccaneers was between 26–29 January, the chosen base being Muharraq. When the advance party arrived at this ex-RAF base they found that a state of controlled chaos was in action, though they soon settled.

While the Buccaneer was elderly it was fully equipped with the latest gadgetry such as the *Have Quick II* secure radios, Mk XII Mode 4 IFF, an updated Marconi Guardian RWR and an AN/ALE-40 chaff and flare dispensing system under the rear fuselage. Also installed on the Buccaneer was the fitments for the AIM-9L

Down and dirty at low level, Buccaneer XX899 'P' streaks across the desert with an ECM pod under the wing. In action the Buccaneers bombed and target-marked from higher altitudes. Bob Archer Collection

Sidewinder missile, while those aircraft that had their TV tab display units missing had them refitted for use with *Pave Spike*.

On 26 January a Lockheed C-130 Hercules arrived at Muharraq to disgorge the first load of Buccaneer personnel and equipment. This first flight was to be followed by fourteen more, which delivered 170 personnel and almost 500,000lb (227,000kg) of freight. Later that day the first of the Buccaneers arrived; the last arrived in the early hours of the following morning. Showing how quickly the squadron support system was able to generate aircraft, the first four training sorties were undertaken on 28 January. A further six sorties were flown the following day while on 30 January the Buccaneer detachment began training with Tornado GR1s. The Buccaneers continued their training missions over the next few days, these including trips with available Tornados.

The Buccaneer Goes to War

On 2 February the Buccaneers finally entered the war, laser designating the Al Samawah road bridge on the outskirts of Baghdad, the bridge being destroyed as a result and all aircraft returning to base unscathed. At this point the total of Buccaneer sorties stood at eight. Three days later the combined Buccaneer/Tornado strike force was again attacking bridges with some success. Further similar sorties were flown the following day, though on this occasion surface-to-air missile activity caused some disruption. Three further Buccaneers flew into theatre that day with Tristar tanker support; eventually twelve aircraft were in theatre, with eighteen crews.

On 8 February the combined attack force again concentrated upon destroying bridges: four were later confirmed as destroyed while another was heavily damaged. The missions planned for 9 February was cancelled as the weather that day obscured the targets from the laser designators. Delays and switching of targets was the order of the day for 10 February as the initially intended targets had become obscured by smoke – probably a decoy measure – so the new targets were pontoon bridges erected to replace those already bombed out of existence. After one of these attacks a pontoon bridge was last seen floating away down the river it had recently crossed. A change of emphasis took place on 11 February when hardened aircraft shelters on an IAF airfield were attacked, at least five being destroyed. The irony of these attacks was that most of the HASs had been constructed by British contractors (although they were not invited back after the war was ended to repair them!). At the conclusion of this day's flying the Buccaneers had completed sixty sorties without loss.

Over the following days the Buccaneer/Tornado combination continued to attack road and rail bridges, and airfield facilities such as HASs. On 15 February the combined missions were programmed for an early departure, their intended targets being the main airfields within Iraq. One strike package hit its target although one aircraft had to bring its bombs back to base as it could not release them, while the other package aborted its attack as intensive anti-aircraft fire met the aircraft. The follow-up report mentioned that four HASs had been destroyed, as had an aircraft on the ground.

The missions planned for 17 February were badly disrupted by bad weather, although the Buccaneer/Tornado package did successfully attack and destroy some protected POL dispersals. Further weather problems caused disruption on 18 February, but at the second target the bombs were dropped unguided as there was no chance of collateral damage or civilian

XV530 sits on the Muharraq ramp waiting its next mission. Coded E, the Buccaneer sports an ECM pod under the starboard wing, while the port wing will later be armed with a Sidewinder. Bob Archer Collection

Surrounded by ground equipment and with ground crew in attendance, Buccaneer XX889 'T' sports a pirate flag on the nose plus a *Pave Spike* pod under the wing. Eventually named 'Longmorn' and sporting fourteen mission marks, this aircraft is currently with the Jet Age Museum. Bob Archer Collection

All three tanker types (Victors, Tristars and VC10s) performed well during the conflict, with the Tristars acting in the transit role and as refuel points for inbound and outbound mission aircraft. BBA Collection

Pictured at Upper Heyford, Buccaneer XV863 'S' sports six mission symbols plus 'Sea Witch' on the nose and the names 'Debbie' and 'Tamnavoulin'. This aircraft is currently acting as the gate guard at Lossiemouth. BBA Collection

casualties. Three sorties were planned for 19 February, although two were aborted due to bad weather while the third successfully destroyed various facilities on an airfield. Over the following two days no missions were flown by the Buccaneers as the weather had deteriorated even further.

The missions on the 21st were unsuccessful as some bombs fell short of the target, one failed to explode and another failed to release. A second sortie that same day was far more successful, the target airfield being hit successfully. By this date the Buccaneer sortie total stood at 148 with no losses. On 22 February further missions were flown by the combined packages; by this time the Buccaneers were carrying LGBs themselves, and the old problem of bombs hanging up resurfaced, though overall the strikes were successful. A more explosive day followed the next day when airfields were again attacked, resulting in a series of large explosions. A further attack that day on the same airfield saw nine LGBs hitting their targets, three falling short and one hanging up. Over the next four days the Buccaneer/Tornado combinations continued to attack their designated airfield targets, none being affected by the drifting smoke being generated by the burning oil wells.

By this time the ground offensive had got underway, and such was the ferocity of

this assault that the Iraqi forces fled in disarray, many surrendering as soon as the allied forces appeared. During the mission launched on 27 February Buccaneer XX885 managed to destroy an Antonov An-12 transport while undertaking an LGB attack on Shayka Mayher Air Base. The air war continued until 03.00hr on 28 February 1991, when operations were cancelled as the Iraqi leadership had sued for a ceasefire; nonetheless, the crews were held on two hours' readiness in case hostilities should have to resume. At the conclusion of the air war the Buccaneer force had flown 212 sorties without loss. The combined 12/208 Squadron detachment and its twelve aircraft returned to Lossiemouth in the early days of March. During their deployment the Buccaneers dropped 169 LGBs, destroying or badly damaging twenty-four bridges and fifteen airfields, including Shuaba, Basra and Artawi in the south, and Al Rashid and Habin near Baghdad. This had taken 218 missions to achieve and a total of 678.5 flying hours.

The Final Three Years

Having returned to Britain the Buccaneers, still in their tatty Gulf War finish, were very much in demand for air

displays complete with a spread of weapons to the fore. While the twelve Gulf Buccaneers were receiving much deserved plaudits, the remainder of the fleet had continued their normal roles. Both operational units, 12 and 208 Squadrons, were primarily involved with anti-shipping operations that were mainly concentrated around the Greenland–Iceland Gap, their principle weapon being the Sea Eagle missile, which had replaced the earlier Martel.

While the Buccaneer had proven its worth in combat its age militated against its remaining in service, so under the 'Options for Change' defence review the services of the aircraft were to be dispensed with. The first unit to go was 237 OCU, which disbanded on 1 October 1991. This disbandment meant that the remaining aircraft at Lossiemouth were reshuffled, so by September 1992 12 Squadron was operating XN981, XV332, XV353, XV864, XW527, XW530, XX889, XX894, XX899, XX900 and XZ431, while 208 Squadron was flying XT280, XV333, XV352, XV359, XV361, XV867, XW542, XX892, XX893, XX895 and XX901. Removals from service during this period included XT279, XT287, XV355, XV868, all of which were broken up for scrap, while XT283, XV342, XW529, XW546 and XZ432 were undergoing spares recovery prior to scrapping. During this period 208 Squadron lost one of its aircraft, the specially marked XN976 which crashed into the North Sea some 50 miles from Leuchars, killing both crew members. Although the OCU had disbanded a handful of Hunter two-seaters remained in service, these being WV318, XF967, XF995, XL568, XL614 and XL616.

While the Buccaneer force continued to shrink, training for their various roles continued. This included exchange visits, one of which was undertaken by 12 Squadron during late July 1993 when the 36th TFW at Bitburg AFB in Germany were their hosts. Six aircraft flew from Lossiemouth to Germany while a seventh, XV359, arrived from Fairford where it had been on display at the Royal International Air Tattoo. Aircraft now in service with 12 Squadron included XN981, XT280, XV332, XV359, XW527, XW530, XX885, XX889, XX894, XX899 and XX900 while 208 Squadron had XV168, XV333, XV352, XV361, XV864, XV865, XV867, XX892, XX895, XX901 and XZ431 on inventory. No. 12 Squadron disbanded on

ABOVE: Sporting a Sea Eagle missile under the wing is XV333, which had undergone the ASR 1012 upgrade process. After withdrawal the aircraft was transferred to the Fleet Air Arm Museum at Yeovilton for eventual display. Trevor Smith Collection

RIGHT: The final colour scheme applied to the Buccaneer was an overall light grey scheme, as applied to XX889 which is seen here being pulled out of its HAS. Trevor Smith Collection

BELOW: A moment of celebration and sadness as this line-up of Buccaneers at Lossiemouth held in March 1994 was the last time that so many would be seen together. The remainder of the fleet was withdrawn at the end of the month. Trevor Smith Collection

XX893 had been prepared for Operation *Granby* use although it was not deployed. After hostilities had ceased the Buccaneer resumed its full time career with 237 OCU although its fate was to meet the scrapman in 1994. Trevor Smith Collection

1 October 1993, most of its aircraft going into short-term storage while decisions were made concerning their future.

All of the remaining aircraft underwent a thorough investigation that revealed which machines were worth retaining in service. Factors considered were the remaining fatigue life, out-standing defects and the time to the next major servicing. The small Hunter fleet also reduced in size, with three going into store at Lossiemouth to await their fate. By January 1994 208 Squadron was operating Buccaneers XV332, XV352, XV361, XV864, XV865, XW527, XW530, XX889, XX894, XX895, XX899, XX900 and XZ431, and Hunters XF995 and XL614. Outside of the mainstream, some Buccaneers were still being used by the trials organizations: XW987 and XW988 were with the A&AEE at Boscombe Down while the Defence Research Agency at Farnborough continued to operate XW986 and XV344.

Prior to the Buccaneer ending its service, a photocall was held at Lossiemouth on 5 March 1994 during which some of the remaining aircraft were painted in the marks of previous operators. Therefore the line-up included: XV352, 237 OCU; XV361, 15 Squadron; XW527, 16 Squadron; XX900, 12 Squadron; XX901, 216 Squadron; XX894, 809 Squadron; and XX899, 208 Squadron.

On 31 March 1994 No. 208 Squadron disbanded at Lossiemouth, bringing to an end the military service of the Blackburn Buccaneer. Loved by the crews of the Fleet Air Arm, the aircraft was not originally favoured by the Royal Air Force, yet they soon came to appreciate its fine qualities, deciding that the only real replacement for the Buccaneer was another Buccaneer. Not a bad epithet.

Buccaneer Units

Fleet Air Arm

700Z Squadron, Lossiemouth
Buccaneer S.1, August 1961 to December 1962

700B Squadron, Lossiemouth
Buccaneer S.2, April 1965 to September 1965

736 Squadron, Lossiemouth
Buccaneer S.1, March 1965 to December 1970
Buccaneer S.2, May 1966 to February 1972
Buccaneer S.2B, January 1971 to March 1971

800 Squadron, Lossiemouth
Buccaneer S.1, March 1964 to November 1966
Buccaneer S.2, June 1966 to February 1972

801 Squadron, Lossiemouth
Buccaneer S.1, July 1962 to July 1965
Buccaneer S.2, October 1965 to July 1970

803 Squadron, Lossiemouth
Buccaneer S.1, July 1967 to August 1968
Buccaneer S.2, January 1968 to December 1969

809 Squadron, Lossiemouth
Buccaneer S.1, January 1963 to March 1965
Buccaneer S.2, January 1966 to December 1973
Buccaneer S.2C, July 1973 to December 1978
Buccaneer S.2D, October 1973 to December 1978

Royal Air Force

12 Squadron
October 1969 to August 1980, Honington
August 1980 to September 1993, Lossiemouth

15 Squadron
October 1970 to January 1971, Honington
January 1971 to July 1983, Laarbruch

16 Squadron
January 1973 to February 1984, Laarbruch

208 Squadron
October 1974 to July 1983, Honington

216 Squadron
July 1979 to July 1980, Honington
July 1980 to August 1980, Lossiemouth

237 OCU
February 1971 to October 1991

South African Air Force

24 Squadron
May 1965 to 3 November 1965, Lossiemouth
November 1965 to March 1991, Waterkloof AB

Buccaneer Crashes

Date	Model	Reg.	Operator	Details
12/10/59	NA.39	XK490	A&AEE	Stalled
05/10/60	NA.39	XK486	Blackburn	Instrument failure – crashed
13/05/65	NA.39	XK524	Blackburn	Tailplane stall
25/03/66	Buccaneer S.1	XN970	800 Sqn	Operating from HMS *Eagle*
28/03/66	Buccaneer S.1	XN950	736 Sqn	Overshooting Lossiemouth
09/06/66	Buccaneer S.2	XN979	801 Sqn	Operating from *Victorious*
30/06/66	Buccaneer S.1	XK528	RAE	Exploded in mid-air
08/08/66	Buccaneer S.1	XN949	736 Sqn	Crashed into sea
20/05/68	Buccaneer S.2	XV158	736 Sqn	Crashed into sea
01/07/68	Buccaneer S.2	XV335	736 Sqn	Crashed into sea
13/02/69	Buccaneer S.2	XV346	736 Sqn	Crashed into sea
03/03/69	Buccaneer S.2	XN980	736 Sqn	Mid-air collision
03/03/69	Buccaneer S.2	XV159	736 Sqn	Mid-air collision
16/09/69	Buccaneer S.2	XV164	801 Sqn	Crashed into sea
29/01/70	Buccaneer S.2	XV167	801 Sqn	Crashed on HMS *Hermes*
31/08/70	Buccaneer S.2	XT282	800 Sqn	Abandoned – hydraulic failure
08/12/70	Buccaneer S.1	XN968	736 Sqn	Crashed on approach
25/03/71	Buccaneer S.2	XW532	12 Sqn	Crashed low-level flight
05/06/71	Buccaneer S.2	XN978	12 Sqn	Loss of control
09/12/71	Buccaneer S.2	XV347	12 Sqn	Fire on take-off
04/01/72	Buccaneer S.2	XW539	12 Sqn	Crashed into the sea
15/02/72	Buccaneer S.2	XT269	809 Sqn	Rolled off carrier into sea
13/06/72	Buccaneer S.2	XV162	12 Sqn	Flew into sea
06/10/72	Buccaneer S.2	XV339	Sydenham	Crashed on test flight
24/01/73	Buccaneer S.2	XW535	16 Sqn	Loss of control
12/04/73	Buccaneer S.2	XV343	809 Sqn	Crashed on approach
11/1174	Buccaneer S.2	XV351	809 Sqn	Crashed into sea
16/07/75	Buccaneer S.2	XW536	15 Sqn	Mid-air collision
29/07/75	Buccaneer S.2	XV360	237 OCU	Loss of control
03/03/76	Buccaneer S.2	XV166	15 Sqn	Crashed on approach
29/10/76	Buccaneer S.2	XW531	12 Sqn	Loss of control
03/02/77	Buccaneer S.2	XW548	16 Sqn	Engine fire caused crash
04/04/77	Buccaneer S.2	XW525	208 Sqn	Lost tailplane – crashed
18/08/77	Buccaneer S.2	XX890	15 Sqn	Crashed on approach
31/10/77	Buccaneer S.2	XV348	237 OCU	Crashed after wirestrike
14/06/78	Buccaneer S.2	XN975	RAE	Loss of control
05/07/78	Buccaneer S.2	XT285	RAE	Crashed on take-off
12/07/79	Buccaneer S.2	XW526	16 Sqn	Wing failed on take-off
07/02/80	Buccaneer S.2	XV345	15 Sqn	Wing broke off – crashed
23/09/81	Buccaneer S.2	XW537	237 OCU	Stalled on approach
08/03/82	Buccaneer S.2	XN977	15 Sqn	Crashed on landing
17/06/82	Buccaneer S.2	XX898	12 Sqn	Loss of control
20/09/82	Buccaneer S.2	XV160	16 Sqn	Crashed after spin
11/08/83	Buccaneer S.2	XX891	16 Sqn	Stalled on approach
20/05/84	Buccaneer S.2	XZ430	208 Sqn	Flew into sea
14/06/85	Buccaneer S.2	XV341	12 Sqn	Tailplane failed – crashed
22/04/87	Buccaneer S.2	XW540	12 Sqn	Flew into sea
09/07/92	Buccaneer S.2	XN976	208 Sqn	Loss of control

NB: For details of SAAF crashes, refer to the table on page 171.

Buccaneer Production

Contract 6/acft/11790/CB.9(a), issued 2 June 1955 for six aircraft to Operational Requirement NA.39. XK486 to XK491.

Contract 6/acft/11790/CB.9(a), issued 2 June 1966 for fourteen aircraft to Operational Requirement OR.39. XK523 to XK536. (XK526/527 became Buccaneer S.2 prototypes.)

Contract KC/2F/05/CB9(a), issued 25 September 1959 for forty Buccaneer S.1. XN922 to XN935 and XN948 to XN973.

Contract KC/2F/05/CB9(a), issued 25 September 1959 for ten Buccaneer S.1, changed to Buccaneer S.2 in May 1961. XN974 to XN983.

Contract KC/2F/048/CB9(a), issued 5 May 1964 for twenty-nine Buccaneer S.2. XT269 to XT288.

Contract KC/2F/125/CB.58(a), issued 25 October 1965 for seventeen Buccaneer S.2. XV152 to XV168.

Contract KC/2F/153/CB.58(a), issued 12 April 1966 for thirty Buccaneer S.2. XV332 to XV361.

Contract KC/2F/179/CB.58(a), issued 27 June 1967 for fifteen Buccaneer S.2, Martel-capable. XV863 to XV877. (XV870 to XV877later cancelled.)

Contract KC/2F/258/CB.58(a), issued June 1969 for twenty-six Buccaneer S.2. XW525 to XW550.

Contract KC/2F/316/CB.58(a), for four Buccaneer S.2. XW986 to XW989. (XW989 later cancelled.)

Contract KC/2F/316/CB.58(a), issued August 1973 for seventeen Buccaneer S.2. XX885 to XX901.

Contract KC/A6a/362/CB.58(a), issued February 1977 for three Buccaneer S.2. XZ430 to XZ432.

Preserved Buccaneers

Complete Aircraft

NA.39

XK488 Fleet Air Arm Museum, RNAS Yeovilton, Somerset

Buccaneer S.1

XK532 Highland Aircraft Museum, Inverness, Scotland
XN923 Gatwick Aviation Museum, Charlwood, Surrey
XN953 Fleet Air Arm Fire School, Predannack Airfield, Cornwall
XN957 Fleet Air Arm Museum, RNAS Yeovilton, Somerset
XN964 Newark Air Museum, Winthorpe Show Ground, Nottinghamshire

Buccaneer S.2

XK526 RAF Honington (gate guard), Thetford, Suffolk
XN974 Yorkshire Air Museum, Elvington, North Yorkshire
XV361 Ulster Aviation Society, Langford Lodge Airfield, Co. Antrim

Buccaneer S.2B

XT288 National Museum of Flight, East Fortune, Lothian
XV168 BAe Brough (gate guard), near Hull, East Yorkshire

XV333 Fleet Air Arm Museum, RNAS Yeovilton, Somerset
XV350 East Midlands Aeropark, Nottingham East Midlands Airport, Leicestershire
XV359 Andrew Landon, Exeter, Devon
XV863 ('Debbie, Sea Witch') (stored) RAF Lossiemouth, Grampian
XV864 Defence Fire Services Central Training Establishment, Manston, Kent
XV865 Imperial War Museum, Duxford Airfield, Cambridgeshire
XW530 Ian Aitkenhead, Buccaneer Service Station, Elgin, Grampian
XW544 Rob Goldstone, Bruntingthorpe, Leicestershire
XW547 ('Pauline, Guinness Girl') RAF Museum, Hendon, London
XX885 (G-HHAA, 'Caroline, Hello Sailor') Hawker Hunter Aviation Ltd, RAF Scampton, Lincolnshire. Permit to fly granted.
XX889 Gary Spoors & Dave Price, Jet Age Museum, Gloucestershire
XX894 Guy Hulme, Bruntingthorpe Aerodrome, Leicestershire
XX895 Privately owned, near Bicester, Oxfordshire
XX897 Quicksilver, Bournemouth Aviation Museum, Hurn, Dorset
XX900 British Aviation Heritage, Bruntingthorpe, Leicestershire
XX901 ('Kathryn, The Flying Mermaid') Yorkshire Air Museum, Elvington, North Yorkshire

XK488 is currently in store awaiting refurbishment. For many years it graced the entrance to the Fleet Air Arm Museum at Yeovilton in a suitably dramatic pose, as this view shows. BBA Collection

At the conclusion of its service as a trials and test vehicle XV350 was preserved at the East Midlands Air Museum. Trevor Smith Collection

XN967 was on display at the Flambards Theme Park in Cornwall before being scrapped due to excess corrosion. The nose is currently preserved at Coltishall. Trevor Smith Collection

XW986 Classic Jets, Cape Town, South Africa as ZU-NIP (flyable)
XW987 Classic Jets, Cape Town, South Africa as ZU-BCR (flyable)
XW988 Classic Jets, Cape Town, South Africa as ZU-AVI (flyable)

Buccaneer S.2C

XV344 ('Nightbird' test bed) DERA, Farnborough Airfield, Hampshire

Noses and Other Major Sections

Buccaneer S.1

XK533 National Museum of Flight, East Fortune, Lothian
XN928 Gary Trigg, Kent
XN967 Mick Jennings, RAF Coltishall, Norfolk
'XN972' (really XN962) RAF Museum, Hendon, London
XN979 David Burke, Aeroventure, Lakeside and Leisure Complex, Doncaster, South Yorkshire

Buccaneer S.2

XT277 Sue & Roy Jerman, Welshpool, Powys
XT284 Glenn Cattermole, Felixstowe, Suffolk
XV163 Action Events, Heemstede, Netherlands

Buccaneer S.2B

XN981 (Fuselage) Privately owned, Errol, Perthshire
XN983 Fenland and West Norfolk Aviation Museum, Wisbech, Cambridgeshire
XT280 Dumfries & Galloway Aviation Museum, Dumfries
XV165 Farnborough Air Sciences Trust, Farnborough, Hampshire
XV352 RAF Manston History Museum, London–Manston Airport, Kent
XV867 Highland Aircraft Museum, Inverness
XW527 Albino Panigari, Italy
XW528 (Rear fuselage only) Stored, Thirsk, Yorkshire
XW541 Dave Thomas, Welshpool
XW550 Buccaneer Preservation Society, West Horndon, Essex
XX888 Tim Jones, Barnstaple, Devon
XX892 Privately owned, Perth
XX893 Eoin McDonald & John Morgan, Portmoak Airfield, Fife
XX899 Robin Phipps, Midlands Air Museum, Coventry Airport, Warwickshire
XZ431 Phoenix Aviation, Bruntingthorpe Aerodrome, Leicestershire

Buccaneer S.2C

XV337 Joe Goy, Diseworth, Leicestershire

Buccaneer S.2D

XK527 Privately owned, North Wales

Technical Details

Model:	Prototype NA.39	Pre-production NA.39	S.1	S.2	Pre-1973 S.2A	Post-1973 S.2A and S.2C	S.2B and S.2D	Gulf War S2B
DIMENSIONS								
Span:	42ft 4in (12.9m)	42ft 4in (12.9m)	42ft 4in (12.9m)	44ft (13.41m)	44ft (13.41m)	44ft (13.41m)	44ft (13.41m)	42ft 4in (12.9m))
Span folded:	N/A	19ft 11in (6.07m)	19ft 11in (6.07m)	19ft 11in (6.07m)	19ft 11in (6.07m)	19ft 11in (6.07m)	19ft 11in (6.07m)	19ft 11in (6.07m)
Length:	62ft 4in (19m)	63ft 5in (19.33m)	63ft 5in (19.33m)	63ft 5in (19.33m)	63ft 5in (19.33m)	63ft 5in (19.33m)	63ft 5in (19.33m)	63ft 5in (19.33m)
Length folded:	N/A	51ft 10in (15.8m)	51ft 10in (15.8m)	51ft 10in (15.8m)	51ft 10in (15.8m)	51ft 10in (15.8m)	51ft 10in (15.8m)	51ft 10in (15.8m)
Undercarriage track:	11ft 10.5in (3.62m)	11ft 10.5in (3.62m)	11ft 10.5in (3.62m)	11ft 10.5in (3.62m)	11ft 10.5in (3.62m)	11ft 10.5in (3.62m)	11ft 10.5in (3.62m)	11ft 10.5in (3.62m)
UNDERCARRIAGE								
Wheelbase:	20ft 7.5in (6.29m)	20ft 7.5in (6.29m)	20ft 8in (6.3m)	20ft 8in (6.3m)	20ft 8in (6.3m)	20ft 8in (6.3m)	20ft 8in (6.3m)	20ft 8in (6.3m)
Height:	16ft 6in (5.03m)	16ft 6in (5.03m)	16ft 3in (4.95m)	16ft 3in (4.95m)	16ft 3in (4.95m)	16ft 3in (4.95m)	16ft 3in (4.95m)	16ft 3in (4.95m)
Height folded:	N/A	16ft 8in (5.08m)	16ft 8in (5.08m)	16ft 8in (5.08m)	16ft 8in (5.08m)	16ft 8in (5.08m)	16ft 8in (5.08m)	16ft 8in (5.08m)
Tailplane span:	14ft 3in (4.34m)	14ft 3in (4.34m)	14ft 3in (4.34m)	14ft 3in (4.34m)	14ft 3in (4.34m)	14ft 3in (4.34m)	14ft 3in (4.34m)	14ft 3in (4.34m)
Inboard pylons (from centreline):	N/A	8ft 9in (2.67m)	8ft 9in (2.67m)	8ft 9in (2.67m)	8ft 9in (2.67m)	8ft 9in (2.67m)	8ft 9in (2.67m)	8ft 9in (2.67m)
Outboard pylons (from centreline):	N/A	11ft 7.5in (3.54m)	11ft 7.5in (3.54m)	11ft 7.5in (3.54m)	13ft 6.5in (4.13m)	11ft 7.5in (3.54m)	13ft 6.5in (4.13m)	13ft 6.5in (4.13m)
Slipper tank (from centreline):	N/A	8ft 9in (2.67m)	8ft 9in (2.67m)	8ft 9in (2.67m)	8ft 9in (2.67m)	8ft 9in (2.67m)	8ft 9in (2.67m)	8ft 9in (2.67m)
AREAS								
Wings:	508.5sq ft (47.24sq m)	508.5sq ft (47.24sq m)	508.5sq ft (47.24sq m)	514.7sq ft (47.82sq m)	514.7sq ft (47.82sq m)	514.7sq ft (47.82sq m)	514.7sq ft (47.82sq m)	508.5sq ft (47.82sq m)
Ailerons:	N/K	54.8sq ft (5.09sq m)	54.8sq ft (5.09sq m)	54.8sq ft (5.09sq m)	54.8sq (5.09sq m)	54.8sq ft (5.09sq m)	54.8sq ft (5.09sq m)	54.8sq ft (5.09sq m)
Fin:	68.6sq ft (6.37sq m)	68.6sq ft (6.37sq m)	68.6sq ft (6.37sq m)	68.6sq ft (6.37sq m)	68.6sq ft (6.37sq m)	68.6sq ft (6.37sq m)	68.6sq ft (6.37sq m)	68.6sq ft (6.37sq m)
Rudder:	10.74sq ft (1sq m)	10.74sq ft (1sq m)	10.74sq ft (1sq m)	10.74sq ft (1sq m)	10.74sq ft (1sq m)	10.74sq ft (1sq m)	10.74sq ft (1sq m)	10.74sq ft (1sq m)
Tailplane:	75.52sq ft (7.02sq m)	75.52sq ft (7.02sq m)	75.52sq ft (7.02sq m)	75.52sq ft (7.02sq m)	75.52sq ft (7.02sq m)	75.52sq ft (7.02sq m)	75.52sq ft (7.02sq m)	75.52sq ft (7.02sq m)

Model:	Prototype NA.39	Pre-production NA.39	S.1	S.2	Pre-1973 S.2A	Post-1973 S.2A and S.2C	S.2B and S.2D	Gulf War S2B
WEIGHTS								
Take-off:	N/K	42,000lb (19,000kg)	42,000lb (19,000kg)	46,000lb (21,000kg)	46,000lb (21,000kg)	46,000lb (21,000kg)	46,000lb (21,000kg)	46,000lb (21,000kg)
Take-off max:	N/K	45,000lb (20,400kg)	45,000lb (20,400kg)	62,000lb (28,000kg)	62,000lb (28,000kg)	62,000lb (28,000kg)	62,000lb (28,000kg)	62,000lb (28,000kg)
Landing:	N/K	31,000lb (14,000kg)	31,000lb (14,000kg)	35,000lb (16,000kg)	35,000lb (16,000kg)	35,000lb (16,000kg)	35,000lb (16,000kg)	35,000lb (16,000kg)
Weapon load:	N/A	8,000lb (3,600kg)	8,000lb (3,600kg)	16,000lb (7,200kg)	16,000lb (7,200kg)	16,000lb (7,200kg)	16,000lb (7,200kg)	16,000lb (7,200kg)
PERFORMANCE								
Design speed:	645mph (1,040km/h)	645mph (1,040km/h)	645mph (1,040km/h)	645mph (1,040km/h)	645mph (1,040km/h)	645mph (1,040km/h)	645mph (1,040km/h)	645mph (1,040km/h)
Take-off run 46,000lb (21,000kg):	N/K	N/K	N/K	2,360ft (720m)	2,360ft (720m)	2,360ft (720m)	2,360ft (720m)	2,360ft (720m)
Take-off run 56,000lb (25,500kg):	N/K	N/K	N/K	3,800ft (1,160m)	3,800ft (1,160m)	3,800ft (1,160m)	3,800ft (1,160m)	3,800ft (1,160m)
Landing run 35,000lb (16,000kg):	N/K	N/K	N/K	3,150ft (960m)	3,150ft (960m)	3,150ft (960m)	3,150ft (960m)	3,150ft (960m)
Range:	N/K	1,730 miles (2,800km)	1,730 miles (2,800km)	2,300 miles (3,700km)	2,300 miles (3,700km)	2,300 miles (3,700km)	2,300 miles (3,700km)	2,300 miles (3,700km)
ENGINES								
Type:	De Havilland Gyron Junior				Rolls-Royce Spey RB 168-1A Mk101			
Static thrust:	7,100lb (31.58kN)				11,030lb (49.07kN)			

Bibliography

Books

Allward, Maurice, *Buccaneer MCA-7* (Ian Allan, 1982)

Boot, Roy, *From Spitfire to Eurofighter* (Airlife, 1990)

Chesneau, Roger, *Aircraft Carriers of the World, 1914 to the present* (Arms and Armour Press, 1992)

Hobbes, Cdr David MBE RN, *Aircraft Carriers of the Royal and Commonwealth Navies* (Greenhill Books, 1996)

Laming, Tim, *Buccaneer – the story of the last British bomber* (PSL, 1998)

Sturtivant, Ray, *The Squadrons of the Fleet Air Arm* (Air Britain, 1984)

Sturtivant, Ray, Burrow, Mick and Howard, Lee, *Fleet Air Arm Fixed Wing Aircraft since 1946* (Air Britain, 2004)

Websites

www.thunder-and-lightnings.co.uk

www.blackburn-buccaneer.co.uk

Index